United States and French Security

United States and

A Study in American Diplomatic History

French Security

1917-1921

by Louis A. R. Yates

TWAYNE PUBLISHERS, INC.
New York

MANUFACTURED IN THE UNITED STATES OF AMERICA

UNITED PRINTING SERVICES, INC.

NEW HAVEN, CONN.

To Hazel
without whose help and encouragement this work
could not have been achieved

Preface

Three things have been attempted in this study: First, to show why the French attitude on security in general and against Germany in particular was inconsistent with many of the ideas of President Wilson and Lloyd George as they expressed them at Versailles; second, to show the extreme importance of the Guarantee Treaties in resolving the deadlock in point one; third, to show briefly the reactions of the British and the French to the Aid Pacts, and also those of the United States because of the revolutionary import which the Pacts held in American foreign policy.

While it is true that many detailed analyses have been made of the Versailles Treaty and the League of Nations Covenant, yet heretofore there has been little study devoted to the Treaties of Guarantee. Although the aid treaties were supplemental ones, nevertheless they were one of the most important agreements made at the conference. By means of them the French, British, and Americans were able to compromise their disagreements and thus enable the Peace of 1919 to be formally defined in treaty form.

In the preparation of this study the author has made use of many documents, histories, memoirs, reports, official papers, diaries, and letters. In order to study many official French reports and documents, the author was permitted to use the excellent facilities of the Hoover Library on War, Revolution and Peace. A partial list of the French records includes: *Journal Officiel de la République Française*, Chambre des Députés, *Débats Parlementaires*, 1919, 1920, 1921; *Journal Officiel de la*

7

République Française, Chambre des Députés, *Débats Parlementaires,* 1919, Tome LXXXXIII, 1919, Session Ordinaire, *Documents Parlementaires; Journal Officiel de la République Française,* Chambre des Députés, *Documents Parlementaires,* 1919; *Journal Official de la République Française,* Chambre des Députés, *Documents Parlementaires,* 1919, Session Ordinaire; *Annales du Sénat, Débats Parlementaires, Documents Parlementaires,* Session Ordinaire de 1919, Paris, 1920; *Journal Officiel de la République Française,* Sénat, *Débats Parlementaires,* 1918, 1919, 1920, 1921; *Journal Officiel de la République Française,* Sénat, *Documents Parlementaires,* Paris, 1919, 1920, 1921; *Journal Official de la République Française,* Sénat, *Documents Parlementaires,* Paris, 1919, Session Ordinaire, Annexe No. 562; *Journal Officiel de la République Française,* Sénat, *Documents Parlementaires,* 1920, Session Ordinaire; *État des Projets et Propositions de Loi Soumis a L'Examen Du Sénat* . . . . 1920-1922; Comité d'Études, *Travaux du Comité d'Études,* and several of the leading French newspapers. Likewise at the Hoover Library, the author had access to the *British and Foreign State Papers,* the *Parliamentary Debates* of the House of Lords and of the House of Commons as well as complete files of the *Parliamentary (Command) Papers* for the period under study, and a complete set of the privately printed limited edition of Hunter Miller's *My Diary at the Conference of Paris,* which was found to contain invaluable materials.

Furthermore, many documents and records of the American government were available there. For all the kindnesses and the unusual courtesy extended to me by the staff of the Hoover Library at Leland Stanford Jr. University, I am extremely grateful. Generous appreciation is also due to the staff members of the Doheny Memorial Library of the University of Southern California for their assistance in making available the official documents of the United States in the field of the Paris Peace Conference, the *Papers Relating to the Foreign Relations of the United States, Senate Documents,* and the *Congressional Record.* The extensive documentary collections and related works on the Versailles Treaty and the Paris Peace Conference which were provided by the Library of International Affairs at the University of Southern California were very helpful. The Los Angeles Public Library and the Library at George Pepperdine College gave valuable assistance. Finally, the materials made available at the University of California, Los Angeles branch, Bradley University, and the Library of Congress have been greatly appreciated.

The author wishes also to express his deep appreciation to the many professors at the University of Southern California who helped and encouraged him in this work with special thanks to Professor Richard W. Van Alstyne.

There has been no intention other than showing the basic relationship between the Guarantee Pacts and the manner in which they enabled the greater peace treaty to be written. Implicit in this is the meaning of the pacts to the United States and to France in the field of foreign relations. No attempt was made to analyze the many other difficult problems confronting the Conference in 1919. Some attention is devoted to the League of Nations because of its direct bearing on the question under investigation.

It is the desire of the author that this study may dispel much of the relative obscurity which has shrouded the Guarantee Pacts and in perspective give the pacts greater importance than they have enjoyed thus far.

Louis A. R. Yates

Bradley University
Peoria, Illinois
July 1956.

Acknowledgments

For permission to quote from copyrighted materials the author of this book extends his grateful thanks to the following:

Yale University Press, David Lloyd George, MEMOIRS OF THE PEACE CONFERENCE, New Haven, 1939, vols., I and II; Dexter Perkins, AMERICA AND TWO WARS, Boston, 1944; Robert Hale, Ltd., Robert Dell, THE GENEVA RACKET 1920-1939, London, 1941; Victor Gollancz, Ltd., David Lloyd George, THE TRUTH ABOUT THE PEACE TREATIES, London, 1938, vols., I and II; the Royal Institute of International Affairs, H.W.V. Temperley (ed.), A HISTORY OF THE PEACE CONFERENCE OF PARIS, London, 1920-1924, 6 vols.; Routledge and Kegan Paul, Ltd., Alcide Ebray, A FRENCHMAN LOOKS AT THE PEACE (translated by E.W. Dickes), London, 1927; Houghton Mifflin Company, Charles Seymour (ed.), THE INTIMATE PAPERS OF COLONEL HOUSE, Boston, 1926-28, 4 vols.; Harper and Brothers, Allen Nevins, HENRY WHITE, THIRTY YEARS OF AMERICAN DIPLOMACY, New York, 1930; Frances M. Foley for Hamilton Foley (comp.), WOODROW WILSON'S CASE FOR THE LEAGUE OF NATIONS, Princeton, 1923; Henry Cabot Lodge, Jr., for Henry C. Lodge, THE SENATE AND THE LEAGUE OF NATIONS, New York, 1925; to Mrs. Woodrow Wilson for these three: Ray S. Baker and W. Dodd (eds.), THE PUBLIC PAPERS OF WOODROW WILSON, WAR AND PEACE, New York, 1925-1927, Vol. I; James B. Scott (ed.), PRESIDENT WILSON'S FOREIGN POLICY, MESSAGES, ADDRESSES, PAPERS, New York, 1918; and Woodrow Wilson, CONSTITUTIONAL GOVERNMENT IN THE UNITED STATES, New York, Columbia Univ. Press, 1908; David Hunter Miller, MY DIARY AT THE CONFERENCE OF PARIS, New York, 1924-1926, 20 vols.; the editors of NEW REPUBLIC for use of materials from the issue of July 16, 1919; the MacMillan Company, George B. Noble, POLICIES AND OPINIONS AT PARIS, New York, 1935, and Thomas A. Bailey, WOODROW WILSON AND THE LOST PEACE, New York, 1944; the Bobbs-Merrill Company, Andre Tardieu, THE TRUTH ABOUT THE TREATY, (American Edition), Indianapolis, 1921; Charles Scribner's Sons, E.M. House and C. Seymour (eds.), WHAT REALLY HAPPENED AT PARIS, New York, 1921; the Council on Foreign Relations, Philip C. Jessup, INTERNATIONAL SECURITY, New York, 1935; Harcourt, Brace and Company, Arnold Wolfers, BRITAIN AND FRANCE BETWEEN TWO WARS, New York, 1940, and Georges Clemenceau, GRANDEUR AND MISERY OF VICTORY, (American edition), New York, 1930; the Stanford University Press, R.W. Van Alstyne, AMERICAN DIPLOMACY IN ACTION, revised edition, Stanford, California, 1947; and to Doubleday and Company, Incorporated, for materials from HOW EUROPE MADE PEACE WITHOUT AMERICA, F.H. Simonds, copyright 1927 by Doubleday and Company, Inc.; WOODROW WILSON AND WORLD SETTLEMENT, Ray S. Baker, copyright 1922 by Doubleday and Company, Inc., and from UNFINISHED BUSINESS, Stephen Bonsal, copyright 1944 by Stephen Bonsal, reprinted by permission of Doubleday and Company, Inc.

LOUIS A. R. YATES

Contents

Contents

Introduction

National security played perhaps the dominant role at the 1919 Versailles Conference. French fears of future attacks by Germany dictated a proposal to reduce to impotence the enemy across the Rhine. British apprehensions lest Germany be too severely imposed upon gave rise to many objections to the French plans. In the case of the United States Woodrow Wilson was torn between giving a relatively free hand to the French, erecting a new structure of international peace machinery, and providing for "self-determination" of peoples as widely as possible. That conflict would soon result from these three approaches to a peace settlement, was not unexpected.

Believing that force was the greatest detriment to aggressor nations or peoples, France vainly sought to have the League of Nations endowed with an international staff and an armed force sufficient to compel obedience to the dictates of the League Council. Furthermore, most French leaders were in agreement as to the course of action necessary for peace in the Rhenish area. At first there was to be an autonomous Rhenish Republic which would serve as a buffer between France and Germany. Nominally independent, though actually under French tutelage, the buffer would be economically very close to France. The main strategic Rhine crossings were to be occupied militarily for a long time as an additional means of enforcing good behavior upon the Germans. A large reparation settlement was expected to reduce German industry to a minor position competitively speaking. Above all else the "grande alliance" of the war between France, Britain, and the United States was to be preserved so

15

that overwhelming force would be available instantly to discourage an attack by a resurgent Germany. Such were the carefully thought out plans for French *sécurité*.

The United States and Great Britain were in agreement that separation of the Rhenish provinces from the rest of Germany would create more problems than it would solve. Wilson was anxious to secure French adherence to his plan for a League of Nations in which a general guarantee of each member's security would be embodied. He was resolutely opposed to making the League a means of enforcing its collective will upon recalcitrant members except in clearly evident cases of aggression. Furthermore, the American Chief Executive favored the principle of "self-determination" in working out the problems of nationalities. As for Great Britain, that government was fairly consistent in opposing the claims of France to a Rhenish buffer state and a long military occupation of the Rhineland crossings. In addition there was at least a modicum of resistance to requiring more reparations than reasonably could be expected to be paid. Much of the time, however, Lloyd George vacillated from one position to another so that it was difficult to tell from a long range view what was his real position. In general the British were favorably disposed toward a league of nations. Canada, Australia, the Union of South Africa, and New Zealand were inclined to look askance at any efforts of the Mother Country to bind future actions with conditions seeking to stabilize continental Europe. Much of the time at the Peace Conference the aspirations of Britain and America coincided to an extent which made collaborative action possible.

In the discussions among France, Great Britain, and the United States — with Italy also participating at times — on the concrete proposals for settling the questions confronting the Conference, a deadlock developed over French security and how to attain it. There never was any question as to *whether* France should be made secure against another German attack. The differences arose from disagreement over the *methods* of achieving the objective. In any case there was an overlapping of ideas and proposed solutions. Fortunately for those concerned with stabilizing world conditions, a compromise eventually was reached. The original suggestion by Lloyd George to Clemenceau that Britain would be willing to sign a pledge of assistance against future German aggression later was expanded into a joint undertaking by Britain and the United States to assist France. In return for their promises of aid the French agreed to demilitarization of the east and the west banks of the Rhine, a much shorter allied military occupation of some of the strategic crossings of the Rhine River, and a League of Nations which did not provide for a general staff and an international force to compel world-wide compliance with League directives. Wilson was also able to obtain French approval, as well as that of Lloyd George, for a provision in the covenant giving recognition to the Monroe Doctrine.

For their part of the compromise the British and the American leaders pledged themselves to recommend to their respective national legislatures a treaty providing for giving immediate assistance to France in case she was the victim of an unprovoked attack by Germany. In order to reconcile the differences between the League and the Aid Pacts, a provision was included which required favorable action toward the treaty by the Council of the League. When the League had become sufficiently strong to provide adequate security to all of its members, the Aid Pacts could be cancelled by a majority vote of the League Council. It was intended to make the interval of effective aid between the time of attack and the furnishing of the pledged assistance as short as possible. France had criticized the Covenant because of the disparity between the time when an attack could occur and that time when effective aid would be forthcoming from the League. The Aid Treaties were designed to remedy that shortcoming.

In reality the Treaties of Guarantee proposals acted as a catalyst in resolving the different points of view at Versailles. As such they were of extreme importance and served as the key factor in making possible the Versailles Treaty, including the Covenant of the League of Nations. Though supplemental to the larger treaty there was never any doubt as to the close integration between the two documents: the aid treaties and the Versailles treaty. In several instances the provisions of the former were contingent upon the fulfillment of the stipulations of the latter. Having for its object the stabilization of world peace by contributing to French security against Germany, the aims of the pacts were high and the motives praiseworthy.

Perhaps one of the most unusual features of the compromise was the implied change in the traditional aloofness from European affairs which had characterized the foreign policy of the United States for more than a century. By the terms of the Guarantee Pacts the United States was pledged to a much narrower range of action and to a much more decisive role in European events. The commitments were much more precise than those in the Covenant to which it was assumed the United States would give its approval.

Woodrow Wilson as well as Lloyd George made a radical departure from traditional foreign policy when he gave his approval to the Guarantee Treaties. As later events were to show, the United States refused to approve the actions taken by Wilson at Paris. Thus the acceptance of a portion of responsibility for the preservation of world peace and stability by the United States upon which the Versailles Settlement had been predicated, was not consummated. Directly and indirectly the results of the lack of affirmative action by the United States against potential aggressors was reflected in world unrest, uncertainty, instability. Wilson had had high hopes that adherence by the United States to the League of Nations would provide the great stabilizing influence of a powerful impartial arbiter for world peace. So great had been this idea that the President believed no occasion would arise in which the lesser pacts guaranteeing aid to France would have to be used. They would attain their object merely by their existence. The United States would never be called upon to act. However, the senators who declaimed in 1919 and 1920 against the Versailles Treaty and the Guarantee Treaties did not share that view. They were obsessed with the idea that more relative advantages would accrue to the rest of the world from the two treaties than would come to the United States. They gave little evidence of being aware that the United States had participated in nine world wars since 1689, and that an active part had been played in the world community whether as a colonial unit or as an independent nation. Not only did Wilson pledge the tremendous power and resources to collective action by the league members, but the implications to foreign policy were not lost sight of, either by him or by the Senate.

The French and the British reactions to the Guarantee idea were generally favorable. Parliamentary approval was obtained in both nations. There was considerable resentment in many French circles over the failure to implement the Guarantee Treaty by senatorial action. When the lesser agreement was swamped in the squabble over the larger settlement, a chance was given to the British to withdraw their pledge of assistance in accordance with a treaty provision which had been inserted by Lloyd George. The British Prime Minister was aware of the exigencies and the uncertainties which the pledge given by Wilson to the French might face before a critical and almost a hostile Senate.

By failing to approve either the Versailles Treaty or the Guarantee Treaties the Senate placed insurmountable obstacles in the rough and uncertain path to world peace and long-range stability.

"We have been attacked; we want security . . ."
    Stephen Pichon, French Foreign Minister in a
    speech at The Versailles Meeting

"Scratch the surface of any problem at the Conference . . . and you get French security."
    Professor Thomas A. Bailey in *Woodrow Wil-
    son and the Lost Peace*

"There has occurred in the course of centuries . . .
a conflict moving back and forth across the Rhine
and it would be to the higher interests of civilization that these conflicts cease . . . . However, that
will be possible only when there shall come a victor
who can rise above his victory, and a conqueror
who will be a hero in moderation . . ."
    Georges Clemenceau in a speech in the French
    Parliament in 1912

CHAPTER ONE

The Past Is Prologue

The years 1917-1921 mark some of the most tremendous changes in the foreign policy of the United States from the standpoint of French security, and in a general way, world security. From 1917, when the United States entered the struggle then in progress, until 1921, when the separate treaty of peace ending the war with Germany was signed, security in relation to foreign policy was a paramount issue in both the United States and France.

The strength of the United States provided the assistance so sorely needed by the Allies. When the necessary measure of cooperation in economic, financial, and military affairs had been completed, the signing of the Armistice was not far distant.

When the war ended, France was dangerously close to exhaustion. There was a strong feeling of deliverance from the overwhelming and hated force of German arms. Perhaps no other Allied or Associated Power[1] had received such grievous wounds, the results of which had proved almost fatal. Though for the moment France and her allies were the unchallenged victors, yet waves of fear and of doubt for the future swept over the land. A resurgent Germany in the future suddenly destroying France was the basis of the fear uppermost in French thinking.

Cold statistical figures do not tell the complete story of French losses. Billions of francs in damage to property were lost; a fourth of the productive capital was blotted out in the invaded industrial districts of the northern and the eastern sectors of France by the systematic destruction of the Germans; ninety per cent of the iron ore supplies and eighty-six per cent of the pig iron production had been taken over by Germany in the invaded areas. The flower of French manhood was lost;[2] this was the worst blow of all. The homes and factories could be rebuilt, but the expended human resources were not retrievable. Hardly a home in France had escaped the hand of war. Sick at heart, men totalled up the long lists of casualties. Placing the blame for these losses was an easy matter, for in the minds of most Frenchmen there could be only one nation responsible: that nation was Germany.

Furthermore, the bitter memories of the defeat of 1870-71 still rankled in the minds of many of the fathers and the grandfathers of the youth of 1914-18. Not without cause did Clemenceau, the Premier, and Poincaré, the President of the Republic, resolve to make France secure against another German assault. Both men had undergone the humiliating and hated experiences of the Franco-Prussian War. Both had seen Alsace-Lorraine torn from their beloved country.[3] And both men typified quite well the attitude of their countrymen toward *Allemagne*.

Since 1871 when a position of relative inferiority had been forced upon France,[4] there had been considerable ill will and rivalry between the Germans and the French. Whether this resentment was indirect or direct, covert or overt, its very continuance boded no good for the rest of the world. Of particular concern to the French leaders was the fact that the position of importance in Europe formerly occupied by France had been taken over largely by Germany. Consequently, it was logical for France to make a determined effort to reassert her influence after the German Empire collapsed in 1918.[5] To that end, therefore, all efforts were to be bent.[6] The invasions of France by Germany in 1870-71, 1914, served as additional reasons why German power was so feared in 1918. If not sufficiently curbed, the story of 1914-18 might be repeated.[7]

The emphasis upon the Rhine River came out of the realization by the Frenchmen of 1918 that natural barriers must be utilized in the struggle to try to place France in a position of relative security against a future German aggression.[8] The development of this attitude that France, not Germany,[9] should control the river as a means of defense was tacitly accepted by Great Britain[10] and the United States[11] as well as by French officialdom.[12] As early in the war as 1916-17,[13] there were indications that France was giving some thought to using the Rhine as a possible barrier in case of Allied victory. The defection of Russia in 1917 from the coalition against Germany imparted new direction to previously made French plans for the Rhineland and the river which gave its name to the region. Never was there any thought of retreat from the essential policy — the reduction of their German neighbor to a position of comparative harmlessness.

The outlines of the coming events were beginning to take shape at this time (1918-19). Hints of what might be the French outlook on security were discernible in the following statement by Georges Clemenceau: "I am not content to sign an invitation to Germany to prepare for another attack by land after an interval of three, ten, or even forty years."[14] And with practically all of France uttering a chorus of approval for that policy, it was not difficult to understand that the past was indeed playing the prologue to the future. Sometimes fancied, sometimes real, were the incidents since 1870-71 which had caused so much tension in Franco-German relations. Undue sensitivity resulting in large part from the strains of war served to accentuate and to sharpen the hatreds and the bitterness of the French populace. They believed, as with one accord, that their sacrifices must not have been in vain. In almost the same vein of fervor they were united in desiring security.

Professor Arnold Wolfers of Yale University made a statement that is so revealing it is deserving of closer scrutiny. He was attempting to put into one paragraph all of these events that had occurred since 1870 (and probably before that) which had impinged upon France and had resulted in what may be termed "the security phobia of 1918-19." The pertinent parts are as follows:

> The specific meaning of the term (sécurité) becomes more apparent when the French speak of their desire for "garanties de sécurité contre une agression de l'Allemagne" . . . *This*

psychological background has to be remembered in order to understand a policy of security such as France came to pursue . . .[15]

What stands forth so clearly from the statement above is the injunction against underrating the results of the past which have assuredly produced deep and lasting impressions. Thus the French demands formulated and presented in the guise of peace proposals at the Conference of 1919 become easier to understand and to defend.

> "We live upon the traditions of the past which force themselves upon our notice in the glitter of words that engender hopes dissipated all too soon. It allows us to adorn mediocre thoughts . . . To sum up, peace is a disposition of forces supposed to be in equilibrium, in which the moral force of organized justice is surrounded by strategical precautions against all possible disturbances."
>
> Georges Clemenceau in *Grandeur and Misery of Victory*

NOTES

1. The term *Allied* will be used in this study instead of the longer expression, *Allied and Associated* powers.

2. Ministère des Affaires Étrangères, *Documents Diplomatiques; Documents Relatifs aux négociations concernant Les Garanties de Sécurité contre une Agression de L'Allemagne,* (*10 janvier 1919-7 décembre 1923*), (Paris, 1924), 26-27. Hereafter cited as M. des A.E., *Documents Diplomatiques.* There were officially: 1,364,000 killed; 790,000 crippled; 3,000,000 otherwise wounded; 438,000 prisoners of war.

3. The important part which has been played by Alsace and Lorraine in French history is presented in this brief chronology of the attempts to control the areas adjacent to the Rhine River from about 1559 to 1806:

1559 — Henry II, successor of Francis I of France, gained the important bishoprics of Toul, Verdun, and Metz, in his attempt to extend the French frontiers toward the Rhine.

1648 — With the exception of the city of Strasbourg, Alsace was given to France as one of the results of the Thirty Years' War.

1678 — Spain ceded Franche-Comte to France by the terms of the Treaty of Nymegen. Charlemont was also annexed and Louis XIV claimed ten other districts including such cities as Luxembourg and Strasbourg.

1688 — France annexed the city of Saarlouis. The inheritance of the Spanish Throne by the grandson of Louis XIV, Philip, provoked the War of the Spanish Succession. Also this was the beginning of the War of the League of Augsburg (1688-1697).

1697 — The Treaty of Ryswick permitted France to retain the city of Strasbourg and other small towns, but forced the relinquishment of the Duchy of Lorraine. All fortresses within the duchy had to be dismantled by Leopold to whom it (the duchy) was restored. Also he had to disband his army, being allowed only a guard.

1733-1738—The War of the Polish Succession. After Leopold's death (March 27, 1729) his heir Francis III was betrothed to the daughter and heiress of the emperor Charles VI, Maria Theresa of Austria. The possibility of a union between the Empire and the duchy of Lorraine could not be admitted by France. To forestall such an event Louis XV in 1735 in Vienna, negotiated an arrangement by which the duchy of Tuscany (left vacant by the death of the last Medici) would go to Francis in exchange for the duchy of Lorraine. In addition the dethroned king of Poland and father-in-law of Louis XV, Stanislaus Leszczynski, was given Lorraine with the proviso that it was to go to his daughter after his death. The Treaty of Vienna of November 18, 1738 confirmed these arrangements. However, in 1736, Stanislaus had by secret agreement turned over to Louis XV the administration of his estates (financial supervision was the main point involved) in return for an annual subsidy.

1766 — The duchies of Lorraine and Bar were formally incorporated in the French kingdom.

1792 — The War of the First Coalition. France overran and occupied the Austrian Netherlands and the lands west of the Rhine River.

1795 — Prussia relinquished to France, by the Treaty of Basel, all of her territory on the west side of the Rhine. The French promised not to annex Prussian lands on the right bank of the Rhine.

1806 — France annexed ninety-seven small German states west of the Rhine. Napoleon dissolved the Holy Roman Empire by decree. A Confederacy of the Rhine was formed to aid Napoleon in his attempts to conquer Europe.

From then on to 1871, France retained control of Alsace and Lorraine. By the Frankfort treaty of that year the two provinces were placed in the newly founded German Empire where they remained until the Treaty of Versailles formally restored them to France in 1919. (*The Encyclopedia Britannica,* eleventh edition [New York, 1911], XVII, 9-12). Permission of the editor of *Encyclopedia Britannica* was granted to use the above material.

4. Paul Birdsall, "The Second Decade of Peace Conference History," *Journal of Modern History,* XI, No. 3, September 19-39, 362-370. Also, see André Tardieu, "The Policy of France," *Foreign Affairs,* I, September, 1922, 23.

5. E. M. House and Charles Seymour (eds.), *What Really Happened at Paris* (New York, 1921) 38.

6. Ray Stannard Baker, *Woodrow Wilson and World Settlement* (Garden City, N. Y., 1923), I, 379. Hereafter cited as Baker, *World Settlement*.

7. *Journal Officiel, Documents Parlementaires*, Sénat, 1920, Session Ordinaire, Annexe No. 266, p. 257. (M. Imbart de la Tour, rapporteur). Hereafter cited as Sénat, *Documents Parlementaires*.

8. *Journal Officiel de la République Française*, Chambre des Députés, *Documents Parlementaires*, Session Ordinaire, Annexe No. 6657, 1919 (Paris, 1920), 305-322. Hereafter cited as Chambre, *Documents Parlementaires*.

9. *Annales du Sénat, Débats Parlementaires, Documents Parlementaires*, Session Ordinaire de 1919 (Paris, 1920), 1819 *et seq.* Hereafter cited as *Sénat, Annales du débats.* Also, *Journal Officiel de la République Française*, Sénat, *Débats Parlementaires*, June, 1920, 1064. Hereafter cited as Sénat, *Débats*.

10. David Lloyd George, *The Truth about the Peace Treaties* (London, 1938), I, 385. Hereafter cited as Lloyd George, *The Peace Treaties*.

11. *Congressional Record*, 66th Congress, 2nd sess., vol. 59, part 4, 3612.

12. André Tardieu, *La Paix* (Paris, 1921), 366.

13. A secret treaty was made in 1916-17 between Russia and France. The text was released to the world by the Bolshevists after their accession to power. F. Seymour Cocks (ed.), *The Secret Treaties* (London, 1918, 2nd edition), has the complete text in English on pp. 69-73.

14. United States Department of State, *Papers Relating to the Foreign Relations of the United States. The Paris Peace Conference 1919* (Washington, D. C., 1942-47), IV, 189. Hereafter cited as State Dept., *Papers of the Paris Peace Conference.*

15. Arnold Wolfers, *Britain and France between Two Wars* (New York, 1940), 11. Hereafter cited as Wolfers, *Between Two Wars*. Italics added. It should be pointed out that it is impossible to discover every one of the many intricate and underlying motives for national action. In some instances the imputed motives are real and not superficial. In other cases they may be hidden and devious. It seems logical to assume that France was reasonably direct and above suspicion in her motives for security against Germany in 1918-19. This statement is made with the full remembrance that hardly a century before, France had been the aggressor instead of the victim.

CHAPTER TWO

The Versailles Conference—
A Quest for Peace and Security

From December, 1918, to January 10, 1919, Paris[1] was a mecca for the numerous delegates, advisers, military leaders, territorial experts, and others who were to participate in the Versailles Peace Conference.[2] It was the largest conference of its kind in history. While it is true that the detailed work of the conference was done by various commissions and committees, most of the responsibility resided in the persons of the chief delegates from France, Great Britain, the United States, Italy (for a limited time), and Japan.[3] In the case of France, the delegation was headed officially by Premier Clemenceau who was ably assisted by his foreign minister Stephen Pichon, André Tardieu, an aide, and M. Bourgeois. Great Britain sent Prime Minister Lloyd George. In addition there was the Secretary of State for Foreign Affairs, Arthur J. Balfour, as well as others. President Wilson, Secretary of State Robert Lansing, Colonel E. M. House, Henry White, and General Tasker Bliss, along with others, comprised the delegation from the United States. Italy's Premier, Orlando, came as that nation's chief delegate, and, as has been mentioned, Japan sent delegates. In addition many smaller nations were represented by a delegate or an observer, who at times participated in the deliberations. However, most of the important questions were decided by the Supreme Council.[4]

In view of the fact that suggestions, plans, and proposals for settling the many vexing problems left in the war's aftermath, in the main were presented by France, the United States, and Great Britain, it will be in that order that they will be considered. Many of the plans dealt with attempts to obtain greater security. Reparations, boundary disputes, the disposition of colonial possessions, economic welfare, and many other questions had to be considered.

Perhaps more than any other participant in the Peace Conference France had a clearly enunciated and articulated plan for presentation at the peace meetings. In Clemenceau France had one of the most determined and remarkable men at Versailles. The "tiger" was well-schooled in the obvious as well as the devious ways of diplomacy. Shrewdness and practicality were two of his salient points. He feared *no one* and *no thing*. He was steeped in an intense hatred of Germany which was reflected in his determination to impose upon her the status of a second-rate power.[5] The fruits of a victory so dearly won must not be thrown away at the conference.[6] Clemenceau thought Wilson was too opinionated,[7] but he admired Colonel House and consulted with him frequently.[8] He once referred to Wilson's plan for an association of nations as ". . . a bridge leading to the New Jerusalem."[9] Obstinate, and tireless (despite his burden of seventy odd years), Clemenceau nevertheless presided over the conference in a manner generally approved.

In brief, the plans for security which France wanted approved included the weakening of Germany by: separating the Rhineland from the rest of the nation, requiring the payment of large sums for reparations, and contracting where possible strong alliances against Germany. Clemenceau asserted that no superstate without a strong force to enforce its decisions made much of an appeal to them.[10] Under the pressure of circumstances variations were made in the above plans but always there was a constant objective in mind: security against Germany. Always that theme was there — whether hidden or apparent.

There was little doubt on the part of most observers that the Peace Conference had a most difficult problem in the delineation of the Franco-German frontier.[11] France wanted a buffer state or a politically independent body set up in the Rhineland which would in effect advance the French frontier to the Rhine River.[12] Inherent in that plan was the practical idea that with the gateway for a *westward expansion* or movement blocked for Germany there would be available to the French forces in the area, a channel of communication with potential allies east of Germany. Furthermore, the German west flank would be unprotected and open to invasion. This plan was especially appealing to the military leaders in France. The potentialities of the plan were not lost on others such as Tardieu, Pichon, and Poincaré. The details rather than the principle of Marshal Foch were questioned. Foch was insistent that

> . . . le Rhin devra etre la frontière militaire occidentale des peuple Allemands. . . . C'est la, pour le present et l'avenir proche, une garantie indispensable du maintien de la paix . . . .[13]

The indispensable guarantee, (for France) said Foch, must be the Rhine because of the material and moral situation of Germany in conjunction with her numerical superiority over the democratic nations (France and Belgium). In addition there must be a cooperative military occupation by the Allies, of the strategic crossings on the Rhine and the deprivation of all German territorial sovereignty on the left bank of the Rhine.[14] The necessity for an Inter-Allied occupation of the Rhineland crossings was re-iterated in February, 1919, in a memorandum by Tardieu.[15] The arguments for an independent Rhenish state were amplified and sharpened. If the German power for aggressive action was to be abolished, the territory on the left bank of the Rhine, as well as the bridges, must be removed from German control.[16] No territory would be annexed by France. The chief objective in the French program was: the movement of France's eastern border to the Rhine.

Subordinate to but still an adjunct to the above idea was the controlled disarmament of Germany.[17] Inasmuch as the French considered themselves to be in an inferior position as regards manpower,[18] they wanted to reduce that disadvantage as much as possible. A close link between the Rhineland and the disarmament questions was the demand by France that all fortifications and military establishments be prohibited on the left bank and also on the right bank for a prescribed distance. When the terms of disarmament had been determined, some means would be required for the supervision of their execution, reasoned the French.[19] Whenever disarmament was seriously discussed, France usually assumed that the grand coalition of the war would be continued in effect, if not in name. The value of such a move had been so amply demonstrated as to obviate further argument in the matter. The last article in the "Fourteen Points"[20] set forth Wilson's idea of the need for an association of nations under specific agreement to maintain stability and peace as far as possible. In the combined strength of the three democracies (Britain, France, and the United States) could be found the bulwark of peace and security.

In reparations, France saw an opportunity not only to obtain the means with which to repair and restore the damages sustained during the war, but also to weaken Germany economically for a long period of time. There was no doubt of French needs for huge sums of capital for the restoration of the invaders' destruction.[21] These sums were far in excess of what France could raise. On this as on many other points the French could cite historical precedent in support of their demands. By the Treaty of Frankfort whereby the Franco-Prussian War was ended, the newly formed German Empire demanded (and received) from France an indemnity of a billion dollars. Perhaps there was another reason why huge reparations were desired. Marshal Foch on December 6, 1918, echoed the attitude of Tardieu, Pichon, Klotz, Clemenceau, Bourgeois, and Poincaré — to name several of the leaders — *that France would demand a huge indemnity in order to continue the Rhineland occupation until it was paid.*[22] Another time (January 1919) during a discussion of the plans for a league of nations and the question of French annexation of the left bank of the Rhine, Marshal Joffre voiced his opinion that there should be such an occupation by the Allied armies to insure the fulfillment of the terms of the Armistice and of the final peace settlement *including reparation payments.*[23] Recognition by France came tardily that modern wars are often won as much in the modern factory and mine as on the battlefield. There would be a corresponding relative increase in the security of France to the extent that German industrial potential was reduced by the imposition of high reparation payments. To recover its strength the crippled French economy planned to use German assistance. Besides, the average Frenchman believed Germany had caused the war and should pay for it. In this view there was not enough difference from that of Britain to merit special comment. As originally planned by the French (ably seconded by the Belgians and the British), the amount of reparations was to be set at an extremely high figure.[24] In fact the demands could be placed so high that it would be impossible to meet them. A result might be the prolonging of the Rhineland occupation. But the problem of reparations proved to be so very complicated that finally a special commission was created to deal with it and to make recommendations on possible amounts to be paid. Consequently, in the Versailles Treaty there was no specified sum to be paid as reparations. The basis for imposing and collecting reparations was that German aggression in 1914 had begun the war. This was a relatively weak manner of placing the "war guilt" at Germany's door. While it is true that Senator Henry Cabot Lodge was agreeable in principle to much of the French program for weakening Germany, his viewpoint was not completely shared by Wilson.[25]

The last point in the French plan for security was concerned with alliances. This reaffirmation of the traditional concept of "balance of power" played an important part in the continuous questioning as to the details of the new scheme for a league of nations. While not opposed to such a plan, at least in principle, France did insist (unsuccessfully, however) that plans be included for a General Staff and an international force of such size that it could discharge successfully any task entrusted to it.[26] Other provisions calling for sanctions and economic boycotts should be used to give strength and purpose to such a group.[27] In one sense an association of nations would be an alliance. However, there would not be the definite terms of commitment and integration of military forces which nearly always accompanied a traditional formal military alliance. Power groupings could be

re-arranged and the balance shifted by new alliances. The new
Poland which was called for in the *Fourteen Points* could be
allied with France alongside any other countries created out of
the old German Empire. Inasmuch as these cooperating nations
would be liberally endowed with former German territory there
would be compelling reasons for an alliance with France to help
preserve the *status quo*.[28] At the same time it was indicated by
M. Larnaude and M. Bourgeois, two of the French delegates,
that if a choice had to be made between alliances and a weak
and ineffectual league of nations which did not permit "special
accords," the French Government unhesitatingly would choose
the alliances.[29] It has been pointed out by Professor Arnold
Wolfers that

> Once it was conceded that there was need for "special ac-
> cords," the Covenant became merely a general treaty supple-
> menting, as far as this group of countries was concerned,
> the far more solid foundation of security which these coun-
> tries (France and Poland, Yugoslavia, and Czechoslovakia)
> were laying down for themselves by stringent and reliable
> special agreements. Why the French were so eager to assure
> themselves of the right to enter upon special agreements is
> not hard to discover. General treaties, such as the Covenant
> were expected to furnish security of no more than a "doubt-
> ful" and "indeterminate" nature. Even at best the assistance
> in case of war . . . would be "progressive" instead of "auto-
> matic," "conditional" instead of "instantaneous," and of
> "limited" instead of "total" efficiency. In these words the
> French described . . . the two different types of assistance
> which they could expect from other countries in case of a
> new war with Germany.[30]

In trying to analyze the aims and plans of the United States
at Versailles in 1919, one is baffled to a great extent by a lack of
clarity in the aims that were presented. In strange contrast to
the vivid enunciation by the French of their aims was the vagueness and inconsistency and contradiction so often apparent in the
proposals of the United States. While France was trying to use

the conference in 1919 as an anvil for shaping and effectuating her demands, the concepts for which President Wilson was groping would have revolutionized the foreign policy of the United States. Inevitably, and perhaps not unexpectedly, there were clashes between France and the United States as to what should be done to settle the world's weighty problems.

From the time when it became known that Wilson would head the United States' delegation to Paris, there was much opposition to the idea. London and Paris reacted against the President's coming.[31] Professor Harley Notter believed that the decision to attend constituted a reversal of the foreign policies of the United States because it was unprecedented for the head of a state to take a direct part in framing a treaty.[32] But the very determination of Wilson to participate and to present personally the idea of collective cooperation to insure stability and peace shows the importance which he attached to the idea, even though it was in the outline stages. Because of the great power and prestige of the United States in 1918-1919, Wilson's vague and incomplete views on security were suddenly clothed with the mantle of international concern. The world was willing to accord the President's views a position commensurate with the moral, military, and political resources of the United States.[33]

Lloyd George states that Wilson's principal interest was in the formation of a league of nations. All else was subordinate to that aim.[34] He states also that the greatest truth learned at the conference by Wilson was:

> . . . that our greatest difficulties come not so much from deciding whether we should follow the dictates of a clear principle or not, but in choosing the particular principle which is most applicable to the facts or in ascertaining accurately the particular facts upon which the principle is to be shaped. Thus President Wilson discovered that the chronic troubles of Europe could not be settled by hanging round its neck the phylacteries of abstract justice . . . . He found that he could not measure accurately with his rigid yard-stick timber gnarled and twisted by the storms of centuries.[35]

If the President did learn that lesson the secret was well kept. Clemenceau believed that Wilson had too much confidence in the ability of his proposed association of nations. Too much "talky-talky and super talky-talky in a league without executive power" could lead only to disappointments engendered by a faith in the words spoken.[36] But Wilson was of the firm belief that some type of organization (international in scope) would have to be used to provide the collective strength necessary for future peace, stability, and security. As a matter of course, the strength of the United States would be one of the great factors for peace. In reality this was equivalent to adding an almost preponderant weight on the side of peace in the world's balance of power. And much as the idealistic Wilson chose to ignore power policies and power politics in his ideas and utterances, power in the form of naked force hovered in the background of all plans for an enforced peace.[37] It was essential, according to Wilson, that the potential forces for peaceful progress always be greater than the forces available to potential aggressors. In-so-far as humanly possible, there should be a rising above selfish national and local interest in making the new peace. If peace was to have a reasonable chance to survive it must be founded on the security of *all* nations. The President stated ". . . the key to . . . peace was the guarantee of the peace, not the items of it . . . ."[38] The United States would be among those who would guarantee the peace. Recent events had shown only too well the interdependence of the United States and of Europe. Unless guarantees which would make amends for the sorrows and mistakes of yesteryears[39] were introduced into the peace terms, there would be a situation that was worse than hopeless for the future. So intense was Wilson's feeling in this matter that he referred to it as a fight against events which had just brought civilization to the brink of disaster.[40] And as the President emphasized with great logic, his contemplated organization for world peace would minimize the danger of war from the disputed Rhine area[41] and would make relatively safe from attack those new states to be erected from former nations according to the principle of self-determination.[42]

Several indications had been given by Wilson as to his attitude on the blueprints for peace and the future policies of

the United States concerning foreign relations.[43] Even as the
preparations went forward in November, 1918 for the departure
of the Presidential Party to Paris,[44] Wilson was emphasizing his
belief that strong collective action on an international scale must
supersede the individual actions of states.[45] He also had demonstrated that the United States must ensure its own security by
departing from some of its traditions in diplomacy.[46] The President offered the *Fourteen Points* not only as an indication of his
policies at Paris, but also as a possible basis for coming to an
agreement with the still undefeated enemy at the time the
famous points were enunciated. Wilson wanted a peace negotiated on the ". . . prescription of open, just, and honorable relations . . ."[47] He had a clear realization of what a victorious
Germany would have meant in 1918 to the principles of the
United States. While the President did not actually declare his
views in the words used here, yet he was aware of the necessity
of preventing any power with hostile intentions toward the
United States from coming into the Atlantic Area. If possible,
nations akin in customs, language, legal principles and general
heritage should control the western part of Europe. Thus would
be formed an indispensable link in securing the New World
against external aggression.[48] There had been a great statement of
principles in the request of the Chief Executive for a declaration
of war on Germany in 1917. Many believed the shell of safety
provided by comparative isolation from the events of the rest of
the world had been cracked by the threat of a German victory.
Safety for democratic institutions must be assured. Otherwise the
danger of militarism would be so great that free nations would
have to engage in an armaments race entailing unheard of burdens.[49] These seem to be indications that a decided change was
taking place in the foreign policy of the United States from 1917
through 1919. There was also the possibility, as one author stated,
that in all of this the President was viewing the security of the
United States from the long-range standpoint rather than from
that of the immediate future.[50] By his announcement that "The
United States have not the distinction of being masters of the
world, but the distinction of carrying certain lights for the world
that the world has never so distinctly seen before . . .,"[51] Wilson

seemed to imply that moral force and good example if supplied by this nation might lead to its adoption elsewhere. But it should be noted that such utterances fell unheeded for the most part in the places of power and authority in Europe. Again, this may be indicative that Wilson was considering the idea of setting up a new arrangement of world power, balanced in such way that the United States could tip the scales.

There was never any close relationship nor confidence between the President and the members of the American Commission to Negotiate Peace. Such aims and objectives as were agreed upon, for that reason as well as because of Wilson's inability to delegate responsibility, to accept opinions opposed to his own, and to divorce himself from personal spites and prejudices, did not receive the support necessary to save many of them from mutilation by other nations' delegates.

Furthermore, one other item of great import should be explained at this point. This is the question of whether Wilson was aware of the major plans for peace, compiled and indeed written by the French, before the Peace Conference was officially opened on January 10, 1919. Inasmuch as this involves the interpretation of several points which are discussed in Chapter III, the answer to the above question does have meaning beyond that of passing interest. Did Wilson go to the conference with information on the French desire for large reparations, the *Rhenish frontier*, military occupation of the Rhine crossings, disarmament of Germany, in addition to many other items (return of Alsace-Lorraine, etc.)? If he did, nothing could conceal from him the fact that several of these proposals violated some of the *Fourteen Points* and were contrary to the purposes of an association of nations. If territories were to be handed around from country to country without too much regard for the wishes of the inhabitants of them, self-determination as a principle of action was dead.

It seems quite possible that word had been given to Wilson that France wanted to base the peace of Europe upon principles of military and strategic consideration. Shortly before sailing for France, the President was informed as to the contents of a note that had been received on November 29, 1918, at the State

Department, from M. Jusserand, the French Ambassador to the
United States, in which the policies and proposals of terms for
the peace conference had been stated.[52] In December, 1918,
Wilson was favorably impressed by the arguments of M. Jusserand who amplified the peace plans contemplated by M.
Clemenceau.[53] Nor can we assume that the President was not
informed of the contents of the following note received at the
State Department, especially when Wilson many times practically
ignored the Secretary of State and did that officer's work himself:

763.72118/3276   The Chargé in Great Britain (Laughlin) to
the Acting Sec. of State. London, December 10, 1918. Received Jan. 4, 1919. No. 10334.
          (in part, the note was this.)
Sir: . . . I . . . enclose . . . copies and translations of a paper
recently left at the Foreign Office by the French Ambassador, entitled "Projet de Preliminaires de Paix avec l'Allemagne," and copies of a memorandum prepared by Mr.
Gunther of my Staff, telling how he obtained this document,
and giving a report of the conversation held with him on
the 7th instant by the Counsellor of the French Embassy,
M. de Fleuriau . . . I have reason to believe that the French
Ambassador has not yet been formally authorized to communicate this document to us and our possession of it, therefore, should for the present be kept secret . . . . Irwin
Laughlin. (Gunther) Enclosure 1. London, December 7,
1918. (This tells how the document was obtained.) Enclosure 2. Proposed Basis for the Preliminaries of Peace with
Germany. There are three essential problems to be solved
in order to reconcile the necessary guarantees and international Law: I. Guarantees on the Left Bank of the Rhine
(military neutralization, without political intervention). II.
Complete restoration of Poland (for she is irreconcilable
with the Kingdom of Prussia). III. Future administration of
Germany (in conformity with the rights of peoples to self-
determination). 1. Territorial clauses . . . . 2. Reparations,
Restitutions and Guarantee. (a) as safeguard for the carrying out of the Preliminaries of Peace. (b) Special military
administration of the German territories on the left bank of
the Rhine.[54]

There *in* (*b*) was the heart of the French program for security on the Rhine. There was the germ (and much more can be said of it) of the idea which was opposed so strenuously by Wilson as well as by Lloyd George.

While the role played by Great Britain and the Dominions was very important and should not be minimized, only those items having immediate relationship with the question under study will be presented. This is not to imply that such contributions were not as valuable to the making of peace as were those of France and of the United States. In some cases there was tremendous significance. As early as the latter part of December, 1918, at a meeting of the British Imperial War Cabinet in London, Lloyd George made the observation that he did not think the war aims of France in regard to the west [left] bank of the Rhine would be tolerated by Wilson or by the British. He was of the opinion that the President might accept the idea of annexation of the Saar Valley by France.[55] At the same meeting Prime Minister Hughes of Australia said that the British and the Dominions would find themselves being dragged unnecessarily behind the chariot of Wilson unless they were very careful. While readily acknowledging the part played by the United States, Hughes was not prepared to admit that Wilson was entitled to be "the god in the machine." To him, Wilson's proposals would not bear the weight of experience and as for the scheme for a league of nations, that was a toy to Wilson and he would not be satisfied with anything else.[56]

Colonel House had made preparations for a conference of Wilson and the British Premier soon after the arrival in Paris of the Presidential party. Political problems in Great Britain required the postponement of such a conference until a later date. During this interval, Wilson talked privately with Clemenceau and Orlando. The President also gave many public addresses.[57] Soon after Christmas in 1918, Wilson went to London and held private conferences with Lloyd George. There was at least one bond of common interest between the two leaders — a league of nations.

Wilson was informed by the British Premier that he ". . . placed the establishment of a strong League of Nations and

disarmament in the forefront of ... [his] programme of peace."[58]
Lloyd George maintained that a league was absolutely essential
to permanent peace. He was going to attend the Peace Conference with that in mind, and would fight for a guarantee of its
establishment. Of course there would have to be an efficient
army to police the Empire even though a League were formed.[59]
Disarmament, as the British saw it, would consist largely of the
destruction of the German Fleet and the reduction of some land
armaments. Only in the field of reparations was there considerable agreement with the French views. It was the considered
judgment of Britain's statesmen that Germany was responsible
for the war and its resulting damages.[60] In the first Interallied
Conference held in December, 1918 (shortly after the visit of
Marshal Foch to London), the first thing discussed was the
question of reparations. There was no disagreement over *whether*
Germany *should* pay but only as to *how much* and *her ability
to pay*.[61] None of the other important points which would be
faced at Paris by the conferees came up for an exchange of
views. Too much stress cannot be placed on the fact that Lloyd
George cooperated well with Wilson in many of the questions
coming before the "Big Three" for settlement. In this connection
Lloyd George's comment about Wilson is timely and revealing;
in part it is:

> President Wilson, in the main favored the proposals which I
> had put forward. Considerable pressure was brought to bear
> upon him through Colonel House to modify his attitude,
> but he remained firm in his determination *to resist the
> French proposals as to the Rhineland* ....[62]

Thus there was collaboration between the two great English-
speaking nations almost from the beginning of the Versailles
meeting in 1919.

With the formal opening of the conference and the necessity
for committee work and actual consideration of the carefully and
not so carefully worked out plans, conflict and deadlock were
brought nearer.

The manner in which an actual deadlock in the work of peacemaking was reached, the steps taken to resolve it, and the final agreements which were reached not only make a very detailed story but one that is interesting and timely. The interplay of personalities, of economic forces, of fear, of traditions — some of the many factors entering the question — had a vital part in the final outcome.

> "The Guarantee Pact thus assumed the position of the keystone of European peace, far above all theories."
>> Georges Clemenceau in *Grandeur and Misery of Victory*

NOTES

1. In this study of the Peace Settlement of 1919 the terms *Paris* and *Versailles* will be used interchangeably.

2. State Dept., *Papers of the Paris Peace Conference*, XIII, 1-5. The reference just cited lists ninety pages of the names of the personnel who were involved in the work of the conference. Although the meeting was scheduled to convene in December, it was not until January 10, 1919, that the first formal session was held.

3. Much of the time Japan did not participate in the discussions held by the other four great powers. It should be noted, too, that Russia and Germany were conspicuous by their absence from the conference, but they were often in the minds and in the speeches of many of the delegates.

4. This name was used to designate the heads of the delegations from France, Italy, Britain, Japan, and the United States, together with their respective ministers of foreign affairs. Another popular term for them was the Council of Ten. Later this was changed to the Council of Five, then to Council of Four, and later to Council of Three (when Italy temporarily left the conference).

5. James T. Shotwell, *At the Paris Peace Conference* (New York, 1937), 47.

6. Robert C. Binkley, "Ten Years of Peace Conference History," *Journal of Modern History*, I, (1929), 618.

7. Georges Clemenceau, *Grandeur and Misery of Victory* New York, 1930) (translation by F. M. Atkinson), 199. In another place (p. 148) Wilson is referred to as coming on the scene ". . . armoured in his Fourteen Points, symbolized in as many pointed wisdom teeth that never let themselves be turned aside from their duty."

8. Charles Seymour (ed.), *The Intimate Papers of Colonel House* (New York, 1926-28), IV, 252. Hereafter cited as Seymour, *House Papers*. The comment made on the Colonel by the French premier is so enlightening that it is here given in full: "Edward House, 'Colonel House,' a super-civilized person escaped from the wilds of Texas, who sees everything, who understands everything, and while never doing anything but what he thinks fit, knows how to gain the ear and the respect of everybody. A good American, very nearly a good Frenchman, a sifting, pondering mind — above all, the traditional gentleman. I should be most ungrateful if I could forget the eminent services that this man, one of the best types of the true Americans, rendered the cause of civilized peace. Were it only for picking out this good auxiliary, Mr. Wilson would deserve the gratitude of the friends of humanity." (*Grandeur and Misery of Victory*, p. 148).

9. Stephen Bonsal, *Unfinished Business* (New York, 1944), 69.

10. Chambre, *Documents Parlementaires*, session ordinaire de 1918, 3733-3734. Also, see Seymour (ed.), *op. cit.*, IV, 267 ff.

11. John H. Latané and David W. Wainhouse, *A History of American Foreign Policy* (New York, 1940), 2nd revision, 626.

12. See Appendix B, pp. 159-168, for text of the French memorandum by Marshal Foch on the Rhineland.

13. M. des A. E., *Documents Diplomatiques*, 12.

14. *Ibid.*, 9-12. Also, see David Hunter Miller, *My Diary at the Conference of Paris* (New York, 1924; privately printed in 42 sets), IV, Document 246, 212-214. Hereafter cited as Miller, *Diary*.

15. See Appendix E, pp. 177-198 for the full text of the memorandum.

16. M. des A. E., *op. cit.*, pp. 19-21.

17. See Appendix A, p. 154. An excellent study of the question of disarmament is that made by Major-General J. H. Marshall-Cornwall in *Geographic Disarmament: a Study of Regional Demilitarization* (London, 1935).

18. M. des A. E., *op. cit.*, 22. At one of the meetings of the Supreme Council of the Allies (Feb. 15, 1919), Winston Churchill is said to have remarked that "There are twice as many Germans as French and by reason of the high birth rate, Germany has annually three times as many young men of military age as France."

19. Miller, *Diary*, V, Document 316, 30-32.

20. See pp. 174-177 for Appendix D, "The Fourteen Points." Article XIV, the point in reference, will be found on pp. 176-177. As a matter of fact, under the terms of the Versailles Treaty as finally approved, not only was the provision for the Covenant of a League of Nations included, but an Interallied Council was set up under the League to supervise the enforcement of German disarmament and to provide a continuing inspection body charged with ferreting out any treaty violations.

21. One of the best works on the question of reparations is Philip M. Burnett's, *Reparation at the Paris Peace Conference from the Standpoint of the American Delegation* (New York, 1940).

22. Miller, *op. cit.*, I, 36-37.

23. State Dept., *op. cit.*, I, 380-385.

24. David Lloyd George, *Memoirs of the Peace Conference* (New Haven, Ct., 1939), I, 320 and 337-338.

25. See Chapter III (II), p. 95, footnote 13, and footnote 68, p. 143 for additional details of Lodge's views on this subject.

26. Seymour (ed.), *op. cit.*, IV, 38. For the official French plan for a League of Nations, see Baker, *World Settlement*, III, Document 17 (Annex 2, to Minutes of the First Meeting of the League of Nations Commission), 152-162. The parts dealing with military affairs, international forces, a general staff, and similar matters are on pp. 157-159.

27. William Harold V. Temperley (ed.), *A History of the Peace Conference of Paris* (London, 1920-1924), II, 30. Hereafter cited as Temperley (ed.), *History of Peace Conference.*

28. Miller, *Diary*, V, Document 409, 428-429.

29. *Ibid.*, VII, Document 565, 55.

30. Wolfers, *Between Two Wars*, 169.

31. State Dept., *op. cit.*, I, 130-135.

32. Harley Notter, *The Origins of the Foreign Policy of Woodrow Wilson* (Baltimore, Md., 1937), 625. Hereafter cited as Notter, *Wilson's Foreign Policy.*

33. David Hunter Miller, *The Drafting of the Covenant* (New York and London, 1928), II, 181.

34. Lloyd George, *op. cit.*, I, 185.

35. *Ibid.*, I, 152-153. Lloyd George relates that "When the conference was drawing to a close, Clemenceau asked me in his abrupt manner: 'How do you like Wilson?' I replied 'I like him, and I like him very much better than I did at the beginning.' 'So do I,' said the Tiger." (p. 145 of *Memoirs of the Peace Conference, I*).

36. Clemenceau, *op. cit.*, 149.

37. *Ibid.*, 167. Among other things, Clemenceau thought that Wilson was the inspired prophet of a noble ideological venture ". . . to which he was unfortunately destined to become a slave . . who by the Monroe Doctrine kept America apart from the clash of European affairs and at the same time intervened in Europe in the name of the historical solidarity of civilized peoples. He acted to the very best of his abilities in circumstances the origins of which had escaped him and whose ulterior developments lay beyond his ken."

38. Ray Stannard Baker and William E. Dodd (eds.), *The Public Papers of Woodrow Wilson, War and Peace* (New York, 1927), I, 348. Hereafter cited as Baker and Dodd (eds.), *Wilson Papers.*

39. State Dept., *op. cit.*, I, 144-146.

40. Charles T. Thompson, *The Peace Conference Day by Day* (New York, 1920), 198. This is a diary account telling of the events on a day by day basis. For additional material on Wilson's ideas on the League

of Nations see Baker, *World Settlement*, I, 280-286, and State Dept., *op. cit.*, III, 208-230.

41. George B. Noble, *Policies and Opinions at Paris, 1919* (New York, 1935), 176. Hereafter cited as Noble, *Opinions at Paris*.

42. Notter, *op. cit.*, 605.

43. *New York Times*, October 15, 1916, and November 18, 1917.

44. State Dept., *op. cit.*, I, 136-138. Besides the President and his wife, there was Mrs. Wilson's secretary, the President's physician, Rear-Admiral Cary T. Grayson, Gilbert F. Close, George Creel, and many others. They left the United States early in December, 1918, on the liner *George Washington*.

45. Miller, *op. cit.*, XX, 124-125.

46. Notter, *op. cit.*, 651.

47. Miller, *op. cit.*, IV, 181.

48. Dexter Perkins, *America and Two Wars* (Boston, 1944), 56-57. Professor Perkins posed this provocative question: "But *is it* very hard to believe today that a German victory a quarter of a century ago would have been the prelude to new acts of ambition and power on the part of the victorious Reich?" In part, he answered, ". . . No one, of course, can say with certainty, what would have happened if events had not been what they were," but he left the impression that such might very well have happened.

49. *Ibid.*, 55.

50. Temperley (ed.), *op. cit.* I, 176.

51. Quoted, *Ibid.*, I, 177.

52. State Dept., *op. cit.*, I, 365-371.

53. Miller, *op. cit.*, II, Document 48, 206.

54. State Dept., *op. cit.*, I, 371-378.

55. Lloyd George, *op. cit.*, I, 119.

56. *Ibid.*, 121.

57. Seymour (ed.), *op. cit.*, IV, 251.

58. Lloyd George, *The Peace Treaties*, I, 162.

59. *Ibid.*, I, 163.

60. Lloyd George, *op. cit.*, I, 310.

61. *Ibid.*, I, 320.

62. *Ibid.*, I, 277. [Italics added.] While it is true that Wilson had demanded acceptance of "freedom of the seas" in his "fourteen points," there was little disagreement between the United States and Great Britain over that question at Versailles. Both nations seemed to sense the necessity for a semblance of unity on that point even though there was some disparity in actual points of view. Therefore the question was kept in the background.

CHAPTER THREE

The Guarantee Treaties

PART I. ORIGIN AND HISTORY

The complex factors in the different plans presented at Versailles for peace and security played an important part in causing a deadlock which finally was resolved by the treaties of guarantee.[1] Two vital reasons for the stalemate were: first, the Rhineland, and second, the insistence by Wilson that a league of nations patterned after his ideas should be made an integral part of the final peace settlement.

Of course other influences were discernible. More than an ordinary effect was produced by the nearly parallel views held by both Britain and the United States on the Rhineland questions. Personalities, national pride, social and economic differences — these and many other influences — entered the background to the question of what should be done to settle the disparity between the French conception of insuring their own security and the view generally thought of as being a good representation of the combined attitude of the United States and of Great Britain.

Overshadowing everything else was the question of the Rhineland. Included in this was where should be the location of the border between France and Germany. The problem was referred to as: ". . . one of the fundamental and one of the most troublesome problems of the peace conference . . . ."[2]; and as the French program's center or core.[3] Therefore, almost the entire efforts of the participants in the conclave to write a new peace treaty were affected to a greater or lesser degree by Wilson's and Lloyd George's opposition to the plans of France.

The American Chief Executive's refusal to accept a French frontier on the Rhine stemmed from the following: (1) the part of the Fourteen Points dealing with self-determination of peoples would be violated.[4] (2) Such a frontier would provide a source of chronic irritation between the two nations concerned. (3) It was not feasible to cut off one of the main economic units of a nation and join it to another. (4) It offended Wilson's sense of justice and concern for the consent of the governed. From the British standpoint there was no justification for "making a new Alsace-Lorraine";[5] Germany's power and influence must not be destroyed totally by placing her completely at the mercy of France; and only an uneasy peace or armistice would result if Germany were treated vindictively.

Both leaders frankly admitted the validity of French claims for security. Both leaders were adamant in their stand against the proposed manner to secure it. Many factors pressed for an early peace. The world needed forceful and dynamic measures. The danger of revolution was ever-present. Austria, Germany, Bulgaria, and Hungary were threatened by Bolshevism. People were weary of war. Some constructive action had to be taken as quickly as possible. But France clung to the position she had taken in the Foch Memorandum of January 10, 1919,[6] the substance of which has already been given.

Much of the time from January 10, 1919, to February 14, was used in private discussions and in producing a rough draft for a league of nations. Approval of the idea of making the Covenant an integral part of the treaty was reached on the 14th of February at a plenary session. The next day Wilson left for the United States leaving Colonel House and Secretary Lansing to carry on the work of the delegation from the United States. General Tasker H. Bliss, Henry White,[7] and the lesser personnel were engaged in committee work of various kinds. An agreement should be reached with the French and the British if at all possible. On February 23, 1919, Wilson received a cablegram from Colonel House, who was in Paris, to the effect that there was no lessening of the efforts of the French to obtain the creation of a Rhenish Republic. Then in another cablegram sent the next day the Colonel said, in part:

> Our territorial experts are in substantial agreement with the British and the French respecting boundaries of Germany. Tardieu, who since the attack on Clemenceau has become more prominent, said to me yesterday that France would be willing to have the Rhenish Republic set up only for a limited period of years . . . . In this way a breathing space would be given us and France would secure protection until she re-covered from the present war.[8]

It should be noted that before his departure, Wilson had given House strict warning against being inveigled into any approval of the "schemes for the Rhineland."[9] The President may have been moved to impart such advice because the Colonel had told the British Minister for Foreign Affairs, Arthur J. Balfour, on February 9, that he had profound sympathy for France and he hoped that the League of Nations would provide the necessary protection against Germany.[10] Presumably Wilson did not know of the meeting of House with Balfour on February 19, in which the latter had said he thought perhaps a way out of the Rhineland problem could be found by letting the bridgeheads be occupied by the French until after Germany had fulfilled the obligations placed upon her by the treaty of peace.[11] It is quite likely that House was aware of the tenacity with which his chief (as well as Lloyd George) was wedded to the idea of erecting a new system of states in Europe which would be based upon the principle of ethnic nationality.

During Wilson's absence (he returned to Paris on March 14), the conferees soon came to an agreement on the need for demilitarization of the east bank of the Rhine. As proposed by France, the zone of demilitarization would be limited to one fifty kilometers in width in which no fortifications or military installations could be constructed. Those presently in existence would be razed. No German armed forces could be sent into the area without permission from the League of Nations.[12]

On February 21, 1919, British and American territorial experts agreed that:

> The terms of peace should include a full guarantee to France that her frontier would be protected by the removal of all military establishments, fortifications, and strategic railroads from the Left Bank of the Rhine.[13]

Clemenceau and his aides received this news with enthusiasm. Then the suggestion was made by André Tardieu that power be given to a commission composed of French, British, and American officers to make on-the-spot checks of compliance with those terms. To this, in principle, House and Lloyd George agreed.[14] Colonel House then instructed his son-in-law Gordon Auchincloss, who also acted as secretary for his father-in-law, to draft some tentative plans for the permanent disarmament of that area of Germany under discussion.[15] Included in the draft was to be a statement of the reasons for the disarmament.[16] Nothing definite, however, was done in the matter until Wilson returned.

On February 25, Stephen Pichon, Minister of Foreign Affairs for France, held a conference with Balfour in the *Quai d'Orsay*. At this meeting Balfour intimated that the question relating to the left bank of the Rhine could hardly be settled until Wilson returned, but that no doubt other questions "connected with the future frontiers of Germany"[17] practically could be settled in his absence. To reinforce their argument in the case, the French sent a Memorandum to the delegations on February 26, 1919.[18] In reality this was only a refined statement of many of the instructions given on January 21, 1919, to the French conferees to advocate acceptance on the part of the other nations' delegates.[19] But March 7 found the negotiators as far apart as ever and the idea was developing that all efforts to write a treaty of peace might be futile. Clemenceau sensed the implications of such a deadlock and also of the possibility of a total collapse of the conference. At a Paris meeting of the Supreme War Council early in March the "Tiger" stated that he would not sign a peace that did not disarm Germany permanently and give to France the needed security.[20]

On March 10, 1919, just four days before Wilson's return to
Paris, Lloyd George admitted in principle that basically France
was justified in requesting security against Germany. Historically,
the facts in the case seemed to require some affirmative action.
However, he was not ready to accede to the French plans for
the Rhineland. Balfour made the point that perhaps Germany
should be guaranteed against aggression. To this there was a firm
but polite declination by Clemenceau who observed that possibly
the solution of protection for Germany (admitting that she might
possibly need it) would come from the league of nations *if one
were established*.[21] The impasse was fast approaching.

Meanwhile, a meeting of more than usual importance was
held in Paris on March 12, 1919. Colonel House and Lloyd George
engaged in a long and serious discussion of the entire situation.
Both men were aware of the tremendous import of an agreement
as well as what an insurmountable obstacle would do too. The
fiery Welshman was afraid another war would soon ensue if he
agreed to the French terms. Also, he was not in favor of occupying the Rhineland bridgeheads for an indefinite time. He was
sure there would be a league but he also believed that it would
take time for it to grow into a strong organization. Therefore
there was validity in the argument of House to give France
security in the meantime.

At this point Lloyd George declared he would be willing
to pledge Britain's support to France in case of an invasion by
Germany.[22] The offer of aid would be *in lieu* of occupation of
the bridgeheads and of the setting up of an independent republic
in the Rhineland (or its alternative, the military occupation of
the left bank of the territory for an unspecified period). The
Prime Minister inquired of House if the United States would
join in such a pledge. House did not know. It was then that
Lloyd George conceived the idea of offering France a joint military guarantee by the United States and Britain.[23] Clemenceau
is very emphatic in stating that it was Lloyd George who fathered
the idea, when he says:

Do not forget that it was Mr. Lloyd George who had made
the original proposal, offering to do all he could to induce

the American President to agree to it. Mr. Wilson merely came in in the second line as the defender of interests less immediately concerned with us.[24]

Moreover, the French leader gave further confirmation to the quotation above when, in part, he stated that:

> In a conversation . . . Mr. Lloyd George stated that, in exchange for the occupation and for the independence of the left bank of the Rhine, he would offer a military guarantee on the part of Great Britain against unprovoked German aggression. He even stated that he would use all his influence with Mr. Wilson to obtain the same agreement from the American Government . . . .[25]

Additional evidence supporting the view that Lloyd George originated *the idea* of a pact to assist France is found in the Minutes of the meeting of the Supreme War Council held at the *Quai d'Orsay* on March 10 and 11. Captain André Tardieu, one of the most active French participants in the peace negotiations (as well as a close confidant of Clemenceau) makes an unqualified statement that Lloyd George first made the offer of a guarantee to France against German invasion.[26] Tardieu's explanation for the "unprecedented offer" emphasizes the point that it was essentially an acceptance by Britain of the great lessons of the war.[27] Professor Paul Birdsall in his study of the Versailles Treaty,[28] maintains that Lloyd George's offer of assistance to France — which he suggested on March 12, 1919, to Colonel House — was the first mention of the idea. Much of the credit for converting the idea into an acceptable form for presentation in a draft pledge should be given to Colonel House.

With the return of President Wilson on March 14, 1919, the discussions took a decisive turn. During a secret meeting on that date Lloyd George explained to Wilson just how serious was the situation with France. Furthermore, in an attempt to avoid a breakdown in the conference, Lloyd George said that he was going to make the offer to Clemenceau which had been discussed with House two days before. The President agreed with the general tenor of these proposals and admitted things were grave.[29] House was instructed to devote his attention to working out a presentable idea for a joint guarantee. The same afternoon the French Premier spent more than two hours with Wilson and Lloyd George. During that time the three men presented their views of the situation. No secretary was present to record what took place at this memorable meeting.[30] The offer of a joint guarantee made a deep impression on Clemenceau.[31] He was somewhat taken aback and asked for more time to consider such an unusual offer. Well might the French have been surprised as the offer was a radical departure in the traditional policies of both nations. Although the offer was no doubt totally unexpected,[32] it seems unlikely that it was too surprising.[33]

Several factors of major importance may have prompted Wilson to agree to Lloyd George's general proposal for breaking the deadlock between France and her two allies, Britain and the United States. It was one thing to secure acceptance of the idea of making *a* league of nations a part of the treaty. It was another thing to induce the major nations to accept those concepts for a league which Wilson now regarded as vital for any world peace organization.[34] Furthermore, the President knew that his position in March was far weaker than it had been in December and in January (1918-19). Instead of consolidating the views of the majority of the Senate in favor of his proposals at Paris, Wilson had discovered much opposition. Undoubtedly there would be no approval of a treaty including a league covenant unless there were clarifying amendments and possibly some changes. Of particular moment was the necessity for Wilson to ask the Peace Conference for approval of clauses of peculiar interest to the United States (such as the Monroe Doctrine). And the President had not forgotten the insistent efforts of the French to change the nature of the League into a formal recognition of the *Big Three* wartime coalition with a general staff and an army. A policy of *quid pro quo* would be necessary to achieve Wilson's version of a league of nations.

Instead of adjusting himself to compromises which he knew must inevitably be made, Wilson landed at Brest in a mood of hostility toward making any concessions at the meeting with the European premiers.[35] When one considers that a dilemma of an unusual nature confronted the President, his concern with the Rhenish question is understandable. Wilson had to devise a plan which would assure genuine support by the United States for the league, while at the same time he dared not violate too patently an American tradition against participating in foreign alliances. That he did consent to offer such an unprecedented guarantee with its change in the foreign policy of the United States was indicative of Wilson's changing personal outlook.

The movement of events from March 14, the date of the first suggestion of an aid pact, through April 15, when the compromise was practically accepted by all parties concerned, forms one of the most interesting features of this study. While there is a close integration of all the factors involved, they will be dealt with from these three aspects: (1) the French moves in the crisis; (2) the moves of the British, and (3) the moves of the United States.

After Wilson's dramatic announcement to Clemenceau that France would get neither an independent Rhineland Republic nor an occupation of the Rhine but would get instead a pledge by Britain and the United States against a German attack, time was needed by the French for consultation and deliberation. Clemenceau would not take the responsibility of deciding such a grave matter. The offer was so important it required nearly three days for the French to reach a decision. Pichon, Tardieu, Loucheur (a delegate to the peace conference), and Clemenceau met in the offices of the Minister of War to plan what should be done.

The Premier told the group that he threatened not to sign any treaty of peace which failed to give security to France. The offer of assistance was studied from every angle before a decision was reached that it might be used as the basis for an acceptable compromise of differences providing changes were made which would allow France to retain most of her original demands.[36] It was generally agreed at the three-day meeting that *tangible guarantees must not and could not be exchanged for an intangible guarantee.*[37] Therefore, a Memorandum was composed and sent to the heads of the two delegations, British and American.[38] In their reply the French again presented their sharply drawn arguments for depriving Germany of the Rhine as a base for aggressive operations in the future. Point after point was stated, the British-American objections enumerated, and the counter evidence adduced. In the minds of the French leaders there was no doubt as to the sincerity of the offer of assistance, but there would have to be further considerations affecting the *time to receive the needed aid* before France could consent to such an arrangement as was proposed.

The great value of the offer was fully appreciated, of course, but it really was not fair or possible to expect France to give up what appeared to be a certain safeguard for the sake of "uncertain expectations." However, as France did not want to be put in the position of refusing such an unprecedented offer, perhaps some possible basis of agreement might be suggested.

The French wanted it to be distinctly understood that they did not want territorial annexation of the Rhineland, but they did want instead, if the offer was to be revised so as to be acceptable, for Britain and the United States to agree that any violation of the conditions of peace which should be imposed upon Germany was to be considered as an aggressive action not only against France, but also against those two nations as well. In addition there should be a provision for the evacuation of the occupying forces of the Allies from the bridgeheads on the right bank and from the territories on the left bank of the Rhine. No German military forces or fortifications of any kind were to be permitted on the left bank nor on the right bank for a distance of fifty kilometers. No German maneuvers were to be allowed in the designated regions. The three occupying nations were to set up a permanent commission by means of which they could satisfy themselves that Germany was complying faithfully with all of the terms of the treaty in regard to the Rhenish area. Finally, any entry or attempted entry of German military forces into the demilitarized area was to be considered as an act of aggression against France, Britain, and the United States. In case of a *threat* of war, France must be allowed to occupy all the bridgeheads on the Rhine. Assent must be given to French reannexation of the lands which had constituted her frontier in

1814. A few other detailed items were included, none, however, was of a major character. That, in brief, was the basis on which an acceptance of the offer of assistance would be given by France.[39]

Clemenceau, in an effort to secure the advantage of the influence of his close friend, Colonel House, in persuading at least one leader, Wilson, to agree to these counter proposals, sent House a special confidential copy of the memorandum which has just been described.[40] House and Clemenceau were often in conference. The Premier was very careful to inform his friend that a more explicit guarantee was needed by France. The response of House was favorable and immediate. He was sure that some means could be found to bridge the gap between the divergent views. He would personally intensify his own efforts to reach a solution of the problem.[41]

At this point it should be noted that President Wilson apparently had not conferred with any of the other members of his delegation (except House) before making the joint offer with Lloyd George on March 14, 1919. All of this secrecy on the part of Wilson disappeared when the French memorandum of March 17 was received and studied. Henry White, one of the Commissioners, stated that he most sharply condemned the tendency of House to make improper compromises.[42] This may have been a reference to the frequent conversations between the Colonel and the Premier as well as to the known sympathy of the former for the French.[43] Hunter Miller has related, in part, the report made by House to the rest of the American Commissioners to Negotiate Peace:

> Clemenceau had said that the British were not treating them right . . . and that he wanted some protection from the United States, upon which the French would give up their claims to a buffer state on the left bank of the Rhine. Colonel House asked us all, including myself, to think of what could be drawn along these lines. I said to Mr. Lansing, in answer to his inquiry, that in view of the sentiment in the United States, it looked like trying to make two and two into five.[44]

Furthermore, the Colonel added, there was an impasse in the attempt to reach a compromise with the French. Clemenceau was not satisfied with the League of Nations as it stood. He desired a more explicit guarantee that both England and the United States would come to the assistance of France in case of an invasion by Germany at any time in the future.[45] House was thus trying to incorporate into the Covenant a proposal which would give to France the British and the American guarantees of assistance.

As another indication of the widespread interest in this matter among the advisers and members of the United States delegation at Paris was this letter from Thomas W. Lamont, one of the financial experts attached to the group. It was sent by Lamont to his friend Hunter Miller on March 19, 1919. In substance Lamont pointed out the intense feeling in France on the closeness of her security interests with those of the United States. Such an interest must be expressed in very clear and definite terms in the Covenant. Unless this were done, or if there was any attempt to limit responsibility for the future, then France would believe it to be to her advantage to make a different kind of peace with Germany and not to have a league. If there were no league, the United States could hardly deny France the right to make as secure a peace as possible. However, such a thing would be against everything America had fought for. It seemed impossible to devise a formula for the Covenant which would give France the necessary security to which she felt entitled and yet not at the same time, technically, give the same guarantee to any and all other member nations. Of course, an alliance to that effect could be made with France but one should not be as it would be contradictory to the idea of the league.[46]

In brief, Lamont's position was much the same as that held by Hunter Miller. The latter was never very optimistic about guarantees unless they were worked out very carefully and provided definitely for specific commitments of the type and the quantities of assistance to be furnished in given situations.[47]

As late as March 20, 1919, apparently there had been no effort by Wilson to take the rest of the United States peace delegates into his confidence concerning the proposed aid to the

French. Henry White says that he learned of the matter through Colonel House and that Lansing, General Bliss, and Hunter Miller (together with a Colonel Olds and a Mr. Herter, technical advisers) seriously questioned the wisdom of making a specific pledge of a guarantee to France in the body of the Covenant and they opposed more strenuously the idea of an alliance with France. *The Commissioners* (including House) *felt that it was most essential that the entire matter be discussed freely with the President in the near future.* Inasmuch as Wilson did not confide in any of his advisers other than House, such a lack of knowledge on their part of his offers to France should occasion, the President believed, but little concern. White told House that all the Commissioners[48] absolutely were opposed to Wilson's giving an alliance guarantee to France and he asked the Colonel to so inform the President as soon as possible. Colonel House had told White that the Chief Executive *appeared* to be in favor of giving France a guarantee in a triple treaty of alliance, and that Britain would give such a guarantee regardless of favorable or unfavorable action on the part of the United States. It was this information of strong opposition which prompted House to go to Wilson with the messages of disapproval.[49]

In the meantime, House had shown Clemenceau, presumably at Wilson's request or at least with his knowledge, the rough draft to which reference has been made.[50] There was a moment of hesitation before the Premier made his comment that a more formal commitment of the pledged aid should be made. To this House replied that his proposed draft was only a recommendation and that it might be necessary to make a "Treaty on the Outside" even though the pledge was merely a repetition of the obligations assumed by the United States under Article X of the Covenant. It was very clear in the President's mind, said House, that France must be accorded adequate security against another onslaught from Germany.[51] Lloyd George and Wilson were opposed to the occupation features of the plan submitted by the French in their memorandum of March 17. As Lloyd George expressed it, "I stubbornly refused to agree to the plan. President Wilson adopted the same attitude and appeared to me to be equally irreconcilable."[52]

From March 21 to the 24th there were conferences between the British and the American delegations. Nothing of a definite nature resulted. However, House was assigned the specific task of drafting a formula to meet French security demands without giving them the Left Bank territory. This was on March 24. The draft of March 20 which House had shown to Clemenceau had been changed in one place by the French leader — *attack* being substituted for *invasion*.[53] But the suggested changes in Article X of the Covenant had been disapproved by Wilson. The result was another draft along another line. This draft, as changed by Wilson in the manner just described, then was submitted to Lloyd George and Balfour for their approval. The two men acceded to it in principle.

On March 27 the French, the British, and the Americans recognized that any compromise which might be reached should have as an essential part the giving of assistance to France by Britain and by the United States.[54] A note giving the substance of Wilson's decision to offer an assistance treaty to France was sent to Clemenceau on March 28, 1919. From that time on, the President morally was committed to signing some form of assistance treaty with France. Despite the denunciations of such a move by every member of the official delegation from the United States, the President stood by his announced purpose. The day before the March 28 Note was dispatched, House, in another of his reversals of position on the question of aid to France, was convinced by his colleagues that an aid treaty was the worst thing possible for the League of Nations. He resolved to inform the President of this conclusion.[55] But Wilson was not moved by the Colonel's arguments and conjectures. Some progress had been achieved. A new element, however, had been introduced into the discussions by the Memorandum sent by Lloyd George on March 25, 1919, to Premier Clemenceau.[56] Lloyd George made so many pertinent observations in the carefully prepared — so he said — statement that some space should be devoted to what he wrote.

The peace should be one of justice and fair play declared Lloyd George. Nothing unnecessary should be done to arouse German resentment which might culminate in a future explosive

situation (war); instead of irritating Germany by onerous restrictions and huge, unpayable reparations, which might conceivably
drive her into Bolshevism, a policy of restraint and help should
be adopted as the policy for peacemaking. There should be no
reparations payable by a generation which had not been personally involved in the struggle of 1914-18. Arrogance and a
spirit of vindictive triumph would do more to create world instability than moderation and fair play. The conferees at Versailles
should act as impartial arbiters rather than as victors. Only such
terms should be offered as a responsible German government
could reasonably accept and put into effect. Furthermore, the
Premier maintained, if the menacing shadows of Bolshevism
were to be dispelled, the League of Nations must be constructed
in such a way that it offered to the nations of Europe a safeguard
for fair dealings and stability, while at the same time it posed
as a menace to those nations with aggressive designs upon their
neighbors. The league must be made into an effective guardian
of international right and liberty with Germany as an active
member as soon as a stable government had been established.

Finally, until the prestige and the authority of the League
of Nations had been sufficiently established and demonstrated,
Great Britain and the United States should give to France a guarantee that would safeguard that nation against the possibility of
future German aggression. Lloyd George admitted there was a
justifiable reason for the French to ask for such a guarantee.
Germany had attacked France twice in the last half century.
Therefore, it was only right that the two great democracies
(Great Britain and the United States) should enter into an
arrangement for aligning themselves with France in case there
was danger from German aggression. Such an agreement should
be effective until such time as the League of Nations could supply
such a guarantee. Then, in a paragraph which today seems pre-
scient, Lloyd George warned the conference that a secure peace,
a lasting peace, could be won only by dealing with the Russian
situation which threatened all of Asia, Europe, and America.[57]

The last part of the memorandum was devoted to an outline
of the terms of peace which should be incorporated into the final
settlement. Of interest was the observation that no attempt

should be made to cede any German territory in the Rhineland. Also, the Prime Minister believed that a section of the treaty should bind Britain and the United States to come to the assistance of France if Germany should move any troops across the Rhine without the specific authorization of the Executive Council of the League of Nations. Also, there was a clause on reparations which did not place the onus of war guilt on Germany.[58]

As no acceptable compromise had been reached by the 28th of March, Clemenceau drafted a reply to the memorandum of the Prime Minister of Britain. The French leader was aware of Wilson's failure to placate the Senatorial opposition in its demand that something be done to obtain recognition of the Monroe Doctrine in the Covenant. There had been some progress in the attempts at disarming Germany, of providing for the disarmament of the Right Bank, for aerial terms, and for some new means of control over all of these by an International Commission appointed by the League of Nations with power of inspection and report.[59] But on France's basic demand for control of the Left Bank of the Rhine there was nothing but a hardening of opposition.[60] Then at a meeting of the Council of Four[61] on March 28, a formal request was presented by Clemenceau asking for the restoration of the Rhenish border as it had existed on May 30, 1814.

In the ensuing debate, which at times became so acrimonious that Wilson was accused by Clemenceau of being pro-German, the rift instead of being diminished was widened. Clemenceau maintained that to ask France to give up her plans for a Rhenish occupation would be equivalent to asking Britain and the United States to sink their fleets.[62] It was unthinkable for such a request to be made. To the statements by Wilson and Lloyd George that the League would provide adequate security in conjunction with the offer by the two nations to speed to the aid of France when needed, always there was the standard reply that this did not meet France's security requirements. The meeting was deadlocked.[63] The hopes of reaching some kind of compromise agreement now seemed to be dimmer than ever. And it should be added that the French reply to his memorandum of March 25 had an infuriating effect upon Lloyd George.

Most of the period from March 31 through April 10, 1919, was only an intensification of differences between France and her two main allies, Britain and the United States. Marshal Foch appeared before the three leaders and in an impassioned plea which stressed the points he had presented in his memorandum of January 10, asked for the permanent occupation of the Rhine.[64] The report was circulated in the *Quai d'Orsay* that American territorial experts at last had been convinced of France's need for the Rhine as a barrier against Germany.[65] It was stated also that the British were refusing to accede to the arguments, but whether this was because they were harder to convince or slower to admit the point was not stated.[66] The Marshal again emphasized that compensatory factors such as the Rhine should be allowed France.[67] The guarantees as they then stood were not enough and would have to be supplemented. Clemenceau added that an intact Germany was a danger to all of Europe.[68]

Evidently biding his time and not daring to push matters to a climax, the French leader reiterated his logical but unaccepted arguments day after day. Wilson was showing signs of the strain under which he worked. He and Lloyd George answered in the negative a demand that any treaty of assistance which might be given must remain in force until *all three* of the nations concerned agreed that sufficient protection was offered to France by the League.[69] Fears of what might result from a collapse of the conference added to Wilson's anxiety (and perhaps, possibly, to those of the British Premier). Such tension and worry proved too much for the frail, nervous man, and Wilson collapsed early in April.[70] At one time it was doubtful if Wilson would recover. Conference work from April 3 to 18 was conducted from the President's bedside, and from an adjoining room House did as much of the work as he was permitted to do. At last on the 7th of April, illness and the apparently hopeless situation induced the bedridden man to order the Navy Department to send instructions for the *George Washington* to leave New York for Brest.[71] President Wilson was going home. Henry White's advice of more than a week before apparently was to be fulfilled. Such a portent was not lost upon the French leaders. If the United States left the conference there might be chaos

in Europe. France would be accused of having wrecked the
chance for world stability and peace. Moreover, though Clemenceau often had pretended to regard the offers of assistance as
minor matters, actually he regarded them as his principal gain
and the most important object to be achieved at the conference.[72]

As he had done many times previously, House had sided
strongly on April 5 with the French on most of their demands,
but in the case of reparations he had yielded entirely. Privately
he was urging a bedfast Wilson to accept the French proposals
on the Saar Valley and in the Rhineland dispute. Lloyd George
had returned to London for parleys with some leaders in Parliament. Clemenceau decided to visit Wilson as soon as he could
be admitted to his presence.[73]

From April 10 through the 14th,[74] personal meetings between the French and the American leaders were unusually
successful in enlarging the areas of agreement between the two
men. Clemenceau gave his pledge to support the inclusion in the
Covenant of a clause on the Monroe Doctrine. Wilson stated
that he would support the French claims to the Saar Valley provided there was no annexation and that the administration was
performed under a directive from the League of Nations. In addition, there was an agreement to reach an accord on the Rhineland, to put into treaty form the pledge of assistance to France,
and finally, orders for the return to Brest of the *George Washington* were cancelled.

On April 14, 1919 Clemenceau informed the President of a
decision to accept fifteen years rather than the thirty years
formerly demanded as the period of military occupation of strategic Rhine crossings. Withdrawal might be arranged to be made
at five-year intervals for different segments of the area included
in the strategic zones. Some concessions had to be made to the
French military authorities in order to keep them from interfering
too much in the final peace settlement. On the 16th of April,
House took the news to Clemenceau that Wilson had agreed to
all the suggestions.[75] Even though one thing remained to be
done — secure Lloyd George's approval of the agreement — the
deadlock had been broken. The nucleus of the compromises was
the Guarantee of Assistance to France. No longer was there any

likelihood of a major split in the three dominant nations at the peace Conference.

Several major tasks still faced the weary conferees, Clemenceau, Wilson, and the recently returned British Prime Minister. The latter two were again in conferences at which it was agreed to include in the final peace terms the demilitarization of the Left Bank and a similar action for a zone on the Right Bank. As there had been substantial agreement on these points for more than two weeks, the only new element introduced was to include both of them in the final terms.[76] Likewise, both men agreed there was justice in the French demand for a temporary guarantee by their respective nations. There was a cautious endorsement of the principle of using an Inter-Allied force to garrison strategic bridgeheads along the Rhine, but this was not under any circumstances to be interpreted to mean approval of political separation of any of the Left Bank territory. Formal approval of the proposed terms of agreement which Wilson and Clemenceau had achieved during his absence was not given until April 22, 1919, by Lloyd George.[77]

This notable meeting of April 22 was held at Wilson's house in Paris. Present, besides the host, were Clemenceau, Lloyd George, a secretary, and an interpreter. The French leader brought up the question of a draft agreement on the demilitarization of the Left Bank of the Rhine. All were agreed it was comprehensive enough but then Lloyd George interposed a query as to the period of maximum occupation of the bridgeheads — if it would be conditioned by the extension of the aid treaty. Clemenceau believed the aid treaty would not be affected. The next item to be considered was the study of a document entitled "Treaty between France and the United States." It was an outline or rough draft of an agreement made by Wilson to give United States' aid to France. Approval in principle already had been given to it on April 20. In part, the draft was as follows:

. . . Between the Government of the United States of America and the Republic of France it is agreed:

(1) Any violation by Germany of the engagements taken by her according to articles ...., ..., and ...., of the

present treaty to be regarded as an hostile act against the
signatories to the treaty and as calculated to disturb the
peace of the world

(2) A pledge to be taken by the President of the
United States of America to come immediately to the assistance of France as soon as any unprovoked movement of
aggression against her is made by Germany.

(3) This pledge to be subject to the approval of the
Executive Council of the League of Nations and to continue
until it is agreed by the Contracting Powers that the League
itself affords sufficient protection.[78]

When asked why there was not a treaty pledging each of the
three nations to assist the other signers, Wilson replied that he
did not think it wise under the circumstances to have a single
treaty,[79] but that a treaty between France and the United States
and another one between France and Great Britain would be
tripartite in effect but not in form. Apparently there would be
more flexibility in separate treaties than in one tripartite treaty.
Furthermore, Wilson may have doubted the wisdom of allying
the United States by treaty with Great Britain in view of the
attacks on him in some sections as being pro-British. Historically,
there was a precedent for an alliance with France, however, and
much sympathy in the United States for the French attitude in
the dispute over security against German aggression. The Prime
Minister finally answered that he thought it would do for Great
Britain. Sir Maurice Hankey, the secretary, was instructed to
show the draft to Mr. Balfour, and, subject to his approval, the
matter was dismissed. After the meeting Balfour's assent was
obtained and made a matter of record by Hankey.[80] Hankey
had been instructed to send the draft of the demilitarization provisions to the final drafting committee.[81]

The outline agreement of an assistance pact, from the French
viewpoint, lacked two very important clauses. France immediately started negotiations to obtain them. One of the omitted
points dealt with the lack of a means of inspection to ascertain if
Germany were complying with the terms of disarmament and
demilitarization; the other was to provide for possible non-ap-

proval of the treaty by Britain or by the United States. Article 429 of the Versailles Treaty had a proviso that German refusal to observe all or part of her obligations as to reparations could be used as a pretext to delay the evacuation of the occupation troops from the Rhine crossings. Inasmuch as the amounts of reparation had not been determined, some means had to be found to give France a legal right to continue the occupation even after the reparation obligations had been met in case of non-ratification of the Guarantee Treaty. Wilson admitted the question was a perfectly logical one and agreed to try to find a solution to it. The debate lasted more than a week with at least five different draft suggestions passing from Clemenceau to Wilson and *vice versa*. On April 29, an acceptable solution was reached which added a final paragraph to Article 429 of the Versailles Treaty. The new section stated:

> If at that date (the end of fifteen years), the guarantees against an unprovoked aggression by Germany are not considered sufficient by the Allied and Associated Governments, the evacuation of the occupying troops may be delayed to the extent necessary for the purpose of obtaining the required guarantees.[82]

Thus did the French Premier try to anticipate the future and provide for it.

Although at all the previous meetings on drafting a covenant for a League of Nations there had been dilatory and obstructionist tactics by the French delegates,[83] the Plenary Session convened by Clemenceau on April 28, 1919, was uneventful. Without permitting any changes to be suggested to the draft which had been presented by the Committee under Wilson's chairmanship, Clemenceau steered the entire group to an approval — without the changing of a word in the document. His bold action in refusing to entertain motions was responsible for the inclusion by the Plenary Session of Wilson's resolution pertaining to the recognition of the Monroe Doctrine.[84] It would seem, thus, that part of the earlier compromise was redeemed.

Having hurdled his latest obstacle, Clemenceau had yet another and possibly a more difficult one in the opposition of the military leaders of France led by Marshal Foch, who was aided and abetted by the President of the nation, Raymond Poincaré. Foch, in a passionate appeal to the two premiers and the American President, on May 6, begged them to reconsider their decision not to give the Rhine as a border to France. Lacking faith in any League of Nations, and as a soldier of the old school which believed in the doctrine that force and force alone could provide security, Foch represented the point of view of those who rejected the idea of *moral suasion* as a substitute for overwhelming force. The differences between the two attitudes has been expressed, in the following manner, by a noted British historian, who said, in part:

> The real difference lay between the adherents of the rigid, the definite, the logical; in other words, the juridical point of view, and those who preferred the indefinite, the experimental, the diplomatic; between those who feared human nature and wished to bind the future, and those who believed in human nature and were content to trust the future; between those who desired written guarantees and those who desired moral obligations only; to be cynical, between those who expected to receive under the Covenant, and those who expected to give . . .[85]

Foch would have accepted such a League as that contemplated by the official delegates of his country who served on the commission to draft the covenant, but he disliked the document as it was accepted by the Plenary Session of April 28.

May 6, 1919, holds a two-fold significance in the development of the idea of giving, by treaty, a pledge of aid to France. The first point deals with a meeting which was held in Paris and at which additional refinements were made in the phraseology and textual outline of the Assistance Pact; the second deals with the plenary session at which there was a public announcement of the decision to write the guarantees in treaty form.[86]

At the earlier meeting Clemenceau, who was being hard pressed by Foch and President Poincaré to overcome all opposition to occupation of the Rhineland, inquired if it could be possible for him to announce officially to the afternoon session the guarantees as *fait accompli*. M. Tardieu stated that he had discussed the announcement time with a member of the American Embassy[87] and both had agreed that it would be better to disclose the treaty to the press simultaneously with the signing of the main treaty, but that the aid treaty should not form a part of the larger document. Then Tardieu read this proposed draft for the Franco-American agreement:

> As these conditions may not at first provide adequate security [the reference is to Article X, occupation of the strategic bridgeheads, and disarmament of Germany] and protection to your Country, I (Wilson) agree to submit to the Senate for its advice and consent a treaty with France by which the United States of America shall be bound to come immediately to her assistance in the event of any unprovoked movement of aggression against her being made by Germany.[88]

Then the draft prepared by Balfour was read by Tardieu as soon as he had received it from Lloyd George who had been perusing it. Its proposed form was slightly different from the other draft just read as this text shows:

> As these conditions may not at first provide adequate security [the conditions referred to are the same as in the above citation] and protection to your Country, His Majesty's Government agree to ask Parliament to authorize a Treaty with France by which Great Britain shall be bound to come immediately to her assistance in the event of either [sic] unprovoked movement of aggression against her being made by Germany. The Treaty will be in similar terms to that entered into by the United States and will come into force when the latter is ratified. The obligations imposed under this Treaty shall not be binding on the Dominions.[89]

Wilson said he did not like the form used as it confused the question. He added that a treaty provision forbade Germany to

maintain facilities of a permanent nature for mobilization west
of the Rhine. If Tardieu's ideas were followed as to the form in
which he presented them, if Germany should send any troops
into the designated areas for any purpose — whether for a peaceful transit of the region or for moves aggressive in their intent —
Wilson maintained that such an action would mean that the
United States would have to send troops at once to assist France.
Such was not the intent of the proffered pledge. *It was to become
operative only in case there was a movement of German troops
into the areas for hostile purposes and with the intention of being
used aggressively against France.*

Because sometimes there is difficulty in detecting aggressive
intent in the movement of troops by another nation, Wilson's
interpretation was not entirely satisfactory. In general, however,
the draft of Mr. Balfour was clearer and more specific than that of
M. Tardieu. But there was an error in it. The word *either* should
be changed to *any* before the words *unprovoked movement,*
Wilson stated, and if this were done and provided the clause
on the Dominions was deleted, he would give his approval to
such a treaty. There was no objection by Clemenceau to these
suggestions. Then the British Prime Minister indicated his willingness to sign, also, but he could not act for the British Dominions. He added that news of the decision to give such a pledge
to France had been discussed with the Imperial War Cabinet.
After a short discussion Tardieu offered to incorporate the suggested changes. Then Wilson said he was satisfied with the Balfour draft but that he thought it eliminated the idea of a tripartite agreement. He agreed the treaty was tripartite *in effect* but
not *in form.* There might be objections in the United States if a
tripartite form were used.

Then Clemenceau raised the question of the form of the
announcement to be made that afternoon in the plenary session.
Tardieu suggested the use of this form:

So far as the question of the French frontier on the Rhine
is concerned, the United States Government and the British
Government are in agreement to submit to their respective
legislatures the text of a Treaty according to the terms of

which the Republic of the United States of America and
Great Britain will immediately bring their assistance in case
of an unprovoked German aggression.[90]

To this Wilson made objection as there was no mention of approval of the agreement by the League of Nations. Then Tardieu
suggested as a remedy the use of the words "with the approval
of the League of Nations" after the words "respective legislatures." Lloyd George observed that the inclusion of the words
"approval by the League of Nations" would assist him in getting
Parliament to accept the treaty. Wilson then suggested an alternative draft announcement:

> In addition to the securities afforded in the Treaty of Peace,
> the President of the United States of America has pledged
> himself to propose to the Senate of the United States, and
> the British Prime Minister of Great Britain has pledged him-
> self to propose to the Parliament of Great Britain an engage-
> ment subject to the approval of the Council of the League
> of Nations, to come immediately to the assistance of France
> in case of unprovoked attack by Germany.[91]

It was agreed that the form which Wilson had proposed for
the announcement should be used for the afternoon meeting and
that letters based on the Balfour draft which had been accepted
earlier[92] should be sent to Clemenceau by Wilson and Lloyd
George. Inasmuch as the two letters expressed such important
objectives, the greater part of each document is presented here
for comparison.[93] Wilson's letter is given first as it is somewhat
shorter than its British counterpart.[94]

The secret plenary session on May 6 was assembled to give
tentative approval to the final terms of peace before their presentation to the German delegation for study and for their acceptance or rejection of the treaty. Clemenceau presided. To the
French Premier's inquiry as to the question of responsibility
(war guilt), Wilson replied that he understood the final determination of the form in which such guilt should be stated had
been delayed at a recent plenary, owing to some objection by
the British Dominions (Premier Borden of Canada, W. M.

Hughes of Australia, and W. F. Massey of New Zealand). Lloyd
George said it was now too late to bring the question before the
present session. The President answered that he had always felt
this question of responsibility for the war was the weakest spot
in the treaty. Lloyd George thought that would depend on the
mentality of the Germans.[95] Then M. Tardieu of France, acting
as spokesman for the entire conference in order to present completed drafts of articles for the Versailles Treaty, presented, explained, and interpreted draft after draft of intricate articles.[96]
It should be remembered that this took place after the failure
of the previously mentioned plea to the conference, by Foch, to
give France more security.[97] Then Tardieu informed the group
that France had been given pledges of assistance by Britain and
by the United States in the event of an unprovoked attack by
Germany.[98] A few hours after the momentous plenary had ended,
the letters[99] of Wilson and of Lloyd George were received by
Clemenceau.[100]

Four days later, May 10, it was discovered that an error of
serious proportions had been made in Article 430 of the Versailles Treaty. The right to re-occupy all or any part of the areas
specified in Article 429 of the treaty draft had been omitted.
The mistake was rectified in this manner:

> In case either during the occupation or after the expiration
> of the fifteen years referred to above (in Article 429), the
> Reparations Commission finds that Germany refuses to ob-
> serve the whole or part of her obligations under Part VIII
> (Reparations) of the present Treaty, the whole or part of
> the areas specified in Article 429 will be re-occupied im-
> mediately by the Allied and Associated Forces.[101]

Thus did France secure not only the guarantees given to all the
League members, and the supplementary guarantee from Britain
and the United States, but also, if worst came to worst, the means
to prolong legally the occupation or the right to reoccupy the
strategic bridgeheads on the Rhine.

There is one more important development which should be
clarified because of its bearing on the settlement of the Rhineland

problem. Near the end of May an attempt was made to set up an autonomous Rhenish Republic. The effort had been extended into June before being effectively extinguished. There was a strong desire in February 1919, to establish some form of Rhenish State which would have strong ties with France.[102] As late as March 7, the French were "hoping" that such an independent state would materialize through a "spontaneous movement."[103] That able French leader, Tardieu, advocated such a policy of encouragement as one that was deserving of the approval of the Council of Four (March 8-13).[104] Flat refusal greeted such an official effort to separate the western Rhineland from Germany and make it into a governmental unit. In view of this there was little surprise in Paris at the end of April when reports began to circulate that separatist movements had begun again in the Rhineland.

On May 22, 1919, French General Mangin, had requested permission for fifty German deputies to enter the zone adminis-tered by American General Hunter Liggett. As the deputies had been engaged in promoting a separatist movement in the French zone of the Rhineland, the reason for the request was obvious. They were expected to continue their efforts in the American zone. General Liggett refused the request but he thought the matter of enough importance to refer it to General Pershing who studied the report and then sent it on to President Wilson. Wilson in turn asked Clemenceau to investigate the entire case. It is to the credit of the latter that he acted promptly and decisively. The general uprising which had been scheduled for May 24, 1919, was an ignominious failure. Similarly ineffective were the disorders on June 1, 1919, in the cities of Apire, Wiesbaden, Mayence, and Aix-la-Chapelle. The extent of most of these dis-orders was the posting of proclamations that an autonomous Rhenish Republic had been set up.[105]

But there were other and more serious effects of the entire incident. President Wilson hastened to discount the news when he heard of the proclamation of the "autonomous Republic." The whole scheme was an imposture according to Wilson. Then, an admission was made on June 9, 1919, by General Mangin to Colonel Repington, that the proclamation posters were issued at his (Mangin) behest.[106] Lloyd George was furious when told of the incident and of the French involvement in it. Clemenceau and Wilson were informed by the Welshman that he was deeply shocked that such underhanded actions had been taken to gain what he and Wilson had been unwilling to grant. Furthermore, his British colleagues had felt from the moment when the guarantee had been given to France that there should have been no question of any kind of occupation. It was doubly dangerous, said Lloyd George, to have a large French army quartered among a people toward whom there was so much hatred. An incident might be created which would involve Great Britain by virtue of the assistance pact. He had been too hasty in agreeing to both the occupation of the bridgeheads and to a treaty of guarantee. Britain could not support that conclusion. France must make a choice between the aid treaty and the occupation. Unless one was relinquished, he would return to London at once.

Clearly this was an attempt to re-open the Rhineland problem which had been so difficult to settle. Wilson agreed with Clemenceau's argument that an agreement had been made and should be kept. The Frenchman answered Lloyd George's threat to quit the conference by stating that he, too, would go to his Parliament and resign rather than consent to a re-opening of their compromise agreement. Finally, after many angry words, the Prime Minister of Britain was induced by Clemenceau, strongly supported by Wilson, to withdraw his objections.[107] The action was taken grudgingly. Thereafter, the way seemed to be clear for the signing of the Versailles Treaty on June 28, 1919.

On June 16, 1919, the Declaration on the Joint Occupation of the Rhine Provinces (the bridgeheads) was signed. This constituted almost the last step in preparing the final draft of the peace treaty.[108] The final date for making any changes in the text of the guarantee to France was set at June 27, 1919.[109] Consequently, on that day, Foreign Minister Pichon, Lloyd George, Sir Cecil J. B. Hurst, Wilson, Clemenceau, and several secretaries met in Paris at the house used by Wilson.

In the discussion which took place Lloyd George said that a text of the convention to give effect to the guarantee agreement with France had been made by Hurst on the basis of the United

States' draft. One important change had been made, however, which would require the approval of the treaty by the Council of the League acting by a majority if need be, rather than by a unanimous vote. This would eliminate the failure of approval because of the opposition by *one* nation. The change was approved readily by Wilson and by Clemenceau. Lloyd George explained that he could not bind the Dominions against their will. This too was understandable, according to Clemenceau. Then the final draft embodying such changes as had been approved was to be drawn by Hurst for the British version and by Dr. James S. Brown, an American, for the United States in anticipation of the ceremonial signing the next day.[110]

Shortly before eleven o'clock on June 28, 1919, President Wilson signed the Treaty of Guarantee. To the same document, a few minutes later, were affixed the signatures of Lansing, Pichon, and Clemenceau.[111] Signing the British version of the guarantee to France were: Balfour, Lloyd George, Clemenceau, and Pichon. With the signing of the Versailles Treaty that afternoon in the Hall of Mirrors of the Palace of Versailles, the first colorful phase of the peace conference passed into history although there were negotiations until August, 1920, regarding treaties with other enemy states.[112]

PART II. ANALYSIS AND IMPORTANCE

Before analyzing the guarantees to France, some attention should be devoted to the views on and the reactions toward that pledge which were held by Secretary of State Robert Lansing, Henry White, and Major-General Tasker H. Bliss, and other members of the American Commission to Negotiate Peace. President Wilson and Colonel E. M. House have had considerable space given to their respective parts in this treaty study. For that reason neither will receive further treatment in this chapter except as it may be necessary to point out a few more interesting and pertinent facts regarding House's role.

Generally speaking, all three of the Commissioners listed in the above paragraph were opposed to the treaty with France. The intensity of General Bliss's opposition was somewhat less

than that of his colleagues. As a group they believed that Wilson
had tried to achieve too much in an idealistic way. All of them
believed in the sincerity of the President in his plans for peace.
To them, the Guarantee Treaty constituted a revolution in foreign
policy for the United States.[1] The United States had never before
been willing to guarantee in advance the eastern border of
France. Britain, too, never had been willing (except in the case
of Belgium in 1839 and of Luxembourg in 1867) to guarantee
in advance the borders of a European nation. The Commissioners
agreed with Tardieu that such a pact was a break with the
American past.[2] It was as Clemenceau had said, "A thing unprecedented in history."[3] When Wilson referred to the special treaty
as a written pledge of the United States' moral obligation to
France and to herself for insurance against another German
attack, all the other delegates on the Commission except General
Bliss disagreed. They believed that it was expedient to do some
things for security but inexpedient to bind the nation in advance
of known circumstances.

Lansing's training and temperament colored his outlook on
many of the questions at Paris. He was obsessed with the legal
approach to a treaty and was also very isolationist in sentiment.
Wilson's custom of not conferring with his advisers unless circumstances compelled him to was criticized severely by Lansing.[4]
None of the Commissioners except House was ever informed of
decisions except when it was expedient for Wilson's plans (according to Lansing). The Secretary of State thought he was
looked upon by Wilson as a "glorified office boy" and this did
not make for cordial relations between the two men. Lansing
believed a more effective spirit of cooperation between the
President and his advisers would have resulted from a more
frequent exchange of views and plans. After all, as Lansing said,
there were good and compelling reasons for the treaty when one
gave some thought to the matter.[5] Lansing thought there were
two reasons for the negotiating of the aid pact. One was Wilson's
conviction that it was necessary to obtain French support for the
Covenant; the other, Wilson's belief that a tendency to make the
league into a military coalition under French domination had
to be checked.[6]

There seems little doubt that Wilson gave the final drafting of the aid pact to Lansing who turned the formal task over to Dr. James Scott Brown, as has been noted previously.[7] In some ways this was a strange action by the President. He was fully aware of Lansing's opposition to the idea,[8] and yet the task was not assigned to House, perhaps, because by this time (near the end of May, 1919) the close friendship of Wilson and House was beginning to move to its tragic ending.

Nevertheless, it was House who had been given the assignment in March of finding a formula for solving the French security puzzle. Regarding his relations with the President, Lansing stated that when the President held an occasional conference with all the Commissioners it was very obviously not for the purpose of obtaining their opinions and counsel. There was none of the frankness that was essential between the Chief Executive and his agents and advisers with the consequence that the American Commissioners, other than Colonel House, were in almost complete ignorance of most of the preliminary negotiations.[9]

When the Secretary of State asked the rest of the delegation how the aid proposal would be received in the United States, he was told that it would be preposterous to consider such a thing seriously.[10] It is well-known that Wilson paid little heed to the resentments and other reactions of Lansing.

Much has been written concerning Henry White, the only Republican member of the Commission. He dismissed as impossible the aid to France treaty and said that he did not believe that Wilson really had faith in it.[11] White was sure the Senate would never give its approval to such a pact. His whole outlook was one of hostility to that treaty. White believed that the whole idea was in complete defiance of the League of Nations' purpose. The period from April 7-14 he referred to as a week "spent in arriving at a series of compromises."[12] A great deal of writing passed from White to Senator Henry Cabot Lodge. In a letter dated May 20, 1919, Lodge wrote that he had no marked objection to the special treaty for American military aid to France in the event of a German attack.[13] In a like manner White agreed with Lansing that the treaty would cut the ground from under the reasons for having a league with an Article X. Furthermore, he said the United States would never depart from its traditional foreign policies to give approval to such a military guarantee. Besides, the treaty was not in accordance with constitutional principles. White fearlessly told Wilson what he believed to be right in their discussion on the advisability of giving an aid pact to France. Part of White's criticisms were softened by his belief that Wilson was overworked and needed assistance in his meetings with Clemenceau and the British leader, Lloyd George.

With the exception of House, whose vacillating stand on the question of the aid agreement needs more elucidation, Major-General Tasker H. Bliss was most nearly in agreement with Wilson, at least in principle. While he did not place too much faith in any guarantee, and did not believe that guarantees should be made the sole end of achievement,[14] Bliss did approve assisting France. He thought the force of an announcement in advance would act as a deterrent to war.[15] In his opinion Germany would not have started the war in 1914 unless there had been an expectation of complete victory in from six to eight weeks. As long as the world situation required preparation for war, it was better to use a little insurance against having a war than in trying to extinguish one after it began. Wilson respected the advice of this military man who was generally sympathetic to the disarmament of the Rhineland and who wanted to see the idea of disarmament applied to all the world. Bliss did not worry over a legal conflict between some articles in the Covenant and those in the suggested treaty of assistance. One was simply a reinforcement of the other. Besides there seemed to be only a slight chance of imperilling the league of nations.

Colonel House changed his ideas on the efficacy of the aid treaty to conform with those of the person or group with whom he had last conferred. Of broad international outlook, House was in complete sympathy with the French in their need for security against Germany. He approved the idea of an aid pact. When he was convinced by his colleagues that the Covenant would be violated by inserting in it a special guarantee for France, House disapproved the idea. When the President said *he would approve a separate treaty,* House tried to dissuade him. Then from his unsuccessful venture of dissuasion the Colonel

turned to one of praise for the stand taken by Wilson and intimated that perhaps there might be value in such an assistance
treaty.

So important was the influence of the Dominions in shaping
parts of the assistance treaty that some comment should be made
here at this point.

The Dominions were somewhat perturbed in 1918 by the
proposed inadequate representation accorded to them by the
French at the coming peace conclave.[16] Later there was a compromise in which the Dominions received separate representation
but on a scale which placed them lower than many other states
which had contributed much less to the final victory, "Hence the
indignation of the Dominion Premiers."[17] No feeling of jealousy
or of hostility was felt toward the Dominions by Wilson. In fact,
he had a very warm and close friendship for Canada.[18] At a
meeting of the Imperial War Cabinet in late December (1918)
Sir Robert Borden, the Premier of Canada, remarked that it
would be regrettable for the Empire to enter the peace meeting
with any feeling of antagonism toward either Wilson or the
United States. He added that he wished to make it clear that:

> If the future policy of the British Empire meant working in
> cooperation with some European nation as against the
> United States, that policy could not reckon on the approval
> of the support of Canada. Canada's view was that as an Em-
> pire we should keep clear, as far as possible, of European
> complications and alliances. This feeling had been immense-
> ly strengthened by the experience of the war . . . . He . . .
> admitted . . . the Dominions had not been committed to any
> treaty binding upon them without their knowledge.[19]

At a meeting of the American Commissioners on March 20,
1919, it was announced by David Hunter Miller that in a meeting
the previous night, during a discussion of Article X of the Covenant, both Canada and Australia had proposed weakening
amendments.[20] At the same meeting (the one at which Canada
and Australia were present) it was pointed out that Canadian
objections were based on the theory of a possible involvement

in a European war. Lord Cecil of Britain said that some amendment regarding that subject would be proposed by "that shrimp Hughes"[21] of Australia. The Canadian delegates showed some anxiety over whether their autonomy as a Dominion would be lessened by the principle of a League of Nations. The Canadian Minister of Justice, Mr. C. J. Doherty, and the Premier, Borden, made attacks on the value of Article X.[22] Doherty observed that opinion in Canada would not approve the taking of an obligation imposing direct and binding military action.[23] The Dominion delegates did not view with enthusiasm many of the territorial settlements made by the Great Powers. "It is significant that . . . a sentiment . . . had developed . . . that it was essential to resume the traditional British policy of holding aloof from entanglements in Europe."[24] There was enough of this feeling in 1919, moreover, to prevent any of the Dominions from desiring to join in the guarantee to France.

Of further importance is the fact that General Botha and General Smuts (both from the Union of South Africa) after a mission to Budapest in April, 1919, returned profoundly impressed with the danger of bringing the Empire too much into European problems.[25] A logical consequence of the voting status given to the Dominions was the decision that the treaties should be ratified by the Dominion Parliaments as well as by the Imperial Parliament. This action (to approve the suggestion) was taken on Sir Robert Borden's demand that no Dominion should be bound without its express consent. The Imperial Parliament wanted to dispense with the express approval of the Dominions, but it failed in that move.[26] The smaller nations such as Australia, Canada, New Zealand, and others, strongly opposed the separate treaty of guarantee with France. In view of the general guarantee in the Covenant, their objections were that the treaty of assistance was superfluous, or if it was considered necessary, then it discredited the value of Article X in the League of Nations. The argument was logical. Thus there were many worried delegates from the smaller countries which had to rely on the League for a guarantee to protect them from the aggressive designs of powerful neighbors. With good reason many delegates declared that if such a guarantee was sufficient for them, France also should consider herself to be sufficiently protected by the Covenant guarantee. The smaller nations would doubt the strength of Article X if France (a larger and more powerful country) doubted it. It was difficult for them to do otherwise.[27] Consequently the Dominions argued against the engagement with France and would have nothing to do with it.

Finally, there is the analysis of the Guarantee Treaty. The treaty, in reality, was a promise by Britain and the United States to intervene if the Franco-German border on the Rhineland should be violated by Germany. In effect this was a double assurance that the territorial integrity of France would be preserved — by the aid treaty as well as by the provisions of Article X of the League Covenant. The guarantee was also designed to remove the danger of a sudden invasion of French soil. This operated through the demilitarization of the Left Bank and of a zone on the Right Bank of the Rhine. The intention was to give to Britain and the United States an interval in which to send assistance to the French if Germany attacked despite the safeguards.

Moreover, the Guarantee Treaty was an agreement to guarantee by military force, if necessary, those provisions of the Versailles Treaty known as Articles 42, 43, and 44, all of which were assembled in the Aid Pact under Article 1.[28] What should be regarded as the heart of the guarantee was this recognition of Article 44 in the Versailles Treaty which stated:

In case Germany violated *in any manner whatsoever* the provisions of articles 42 and 43, she shall be regarded as committing a hostile act against the powers signatory of the present treaty and as calculated to disturb the peace of the world.[29]

Therefore, any German violation of Articles 42 *and* 43, or 42 *or* 43, as stated by Article 44 of the Versailles Treaty, was defined in Article 1 of both versions of the Guarantee Treaty as constituting a *movement of unprovoked aggression against France*. By virtue of a violation (it might consist of sending troops into the demilitarized zones, rebuilding forts, manufacturing munitions, taking ammunition through the zones, and many other things) Britain and the United States would be brought into the defense picture.

The terms of the Franco-American pact stated that the United States *shall be bound to come immediately* to her (France's) assistance. The terms of the Franco-British pact stated that Britain *agrees to come immediately* to her assistance. The latter is permissive, not absolute. The other binds the United States to come *at once, without delay, instantly,* to the aid of the French. Only conjecture may tell us why there was this difference. Perhaps some pressure may have been exerted on the British Prime Minister by the Premiers of the several Dominions not to rush headlong into an entangling situation on the Continent. Such an action — the sending of aid — should be taken after some deliberation and perhaps in consultation with the rest of the Empire. The geographical position of Britain in relation to France — when contrasted with that of the United States which was more than three thousand miles across an ocean with a consequent increase in the time needed to get aid across it — may have played an influential part. Likewise, there was much dissatisfaction with the possibility that French troops could create an incident in the occupied Zones (before the expiration of fifteen years) and thus bring Britain unwillingly and perhaps unwittingly into a quarrel unless some degree of permissive action against such a possibility were allowed. Also this would serve as a brake upon the French military leaders who might otherwise be too impetuous in their dealings with Germany, knowing in advance that assistance would be sent by both guarantors. It may have been none of these or it may have been other reasons not mentioned. However, this should be pointed out. Only the violations of these Articles (42 and 43) were contemplated as requiring that assistance be sent from Britain and from the United States.

Let us contrast the actions proposed under the League of Nations with those under the Guarantee Treaty. It was contemplated in the Covenant to set up measures to be taken for the relief of any power which should be threatened or attacked by another Covenant-breaking power. Such action for assistance would take a considerable amount of time and the nation so threatened or attacked would have to wait for help. In the meantime it might even be invaded and overrun. But while there was a long interval between effective action and the beginning of the trouble in the one case, in the case of the aid pact, assistance was to be given immediately to the attacked nation (France). The guarantee of Article X appears weak and very permissive when compared with that of the guarantee agreement. Although there was some leeway in the minds of some critics in the Senate of the United States as to what constituted a movement of unprovoked aggression, a detailed study of the treaty will disclose as the logical answer what has been shown. While a slight discrepancy does exist in the statements, "in the event of unprovoked aggression by Germany"[30] and "in the case of an unprovoked movement of aggression being made against France by Germany,"[31] both of which are found in the British version, and the words "an unprovoked movement of aggression by Germany against France . . .,"[32] the first two are so minor in their differences that only the word *movement* differentiates them. There is no essential point of distinction between the phrase in the United States' pact and its counterpart in the British pact. In both there is an emphasis upon an *unprovoked movement*. The first one listed above refers only to an unprovoked aggression. The other two instances in the British version contain the word which presumably was to unlock the gates for British action — *movement*. In every case it must be any kind of movement so long as it had not been provoked. There was a loop hole if a nation was looking for a way to evade its pledges. The British were placing undue emphasis upon repetition of certain words as the key part of their treaty. This, perhaps, was a symbol of the British attempt to point out in no uncertain terms that a close interpretation of the obligations which had been assumed would be made.

Another interesting difference between the two versions is the inclusion of a strong war guilt clause in the American version and its omission in the other. The Treaty of Versailles placed the responsibility for the war upon the Germans and their allies in Article 231.[33] In one of the first drafts of the treaty there is a clear-cut statement that Germany was responsible for the aggression (attack) against France in 1914. House thinks that Clemenceau was responsible for its inclusion. When the draft was given to Wilson, he eliminated the provision. Tardieu, who made the redraft placed it in again and nothing was done by the Americans to remove it before making a final draft. Inasmuch as Wilson favored a relatively strong statement of Germany's guilt for having started the war, there was little reason for their diluting or eliminating the reference.[34] Wilson may have thought there was some value in having the enemy named as the source of all evil. Such action might assist in persuading toward a more favorable attitude on the work being done at Paris those Senators who felt strongly about the war. It is true that the war guilt clause in the larger treaty was used as a legal reason for assessing reparation damages against Germany.

Lloyd George was in favor of having Germany pay as much reparations as possible, but he did not want that nation totally crushed. He was willing for the war guilt clause to appear in the larger treaty to which the smaller was supplemental but not for it to appear in the aid pact.[35] The British Premier advocated a policy of studied restraint and fair play in dealing with Germany. Essentially this was a plan whose strategy was the removal, as far as was possible, of the causes of friction and revolt. Thereby he would eliminate the chances of an explosion. There was an almost constant stream of opposition tactics by the British to the French plans for repressing the Germans still more. There was nothing to be gained, Lloyd George believed, by harshness.[36] The clause of the final draft was not as strong as the one drafted by Auchincloss.[37] In a meeting in early June 1919, the Imperial War Cabinet with all the Dominion Premiers present, discussed reparations and war guilt. Apparently it was assumed that Germany was now a repentant nation. Her soul had undergone a conversion. The discussion was turned into the form of an "earnest and . . . passionate plea for justice for a fallen enemy. There was no note of vengeance."[38] This was on June 1 and 2, before the final drafts were made.

Moreover, the British had determined to give France a guarantee against a German attack even if the United States did not. Perhaps the shrewd Welshman, of whom Henry White said, "he rarely remains of the same opinion during two consecutive days,"[39] would not have offered the guarantee. Perhaps he would. No one knows.

Lloyd George has related the scene of the presentation of the terms of the Versailles Treaty to the German delegates on May 7, 1919. Count Brockdorff-Rantzau remained seated while reading aloud his short speech. He pleaded for justice, for moderation in the penalties and for a lessening of the difficult parts of the document. The effect upon Wilson's mind was quite noticeable. The President turned to the British Prime Minister and in a cold tone snapped, "Isn't it just like them?"[40] Then his face became more rigid and his stare much more penetrating as the German continued to read his plea for an impartial commission to determine war guilt. It is not Germany's (guilt) alone although some part of it must be borne by her. The German people believed they were waging a defensive war. The effect of the speech on Wilson could be detected quite clearly.[41]

A strong war guilt clause was also favored by Clemenceau. As long as he had the guarantees, he was not too concerned about the point of uniformity of clauses. In fact one of the arguments for having the guarantee in a bilateral form was to insure allowances for minor distinctions between the two versions.

The treaty with the United States was more explicit in its statement of the reason for its existence, than was its British counterpart. It emphasized the *general* importance of the treaty rather than the *particular* bearing of a German aggression against France, and stressed the union of the United States and France which would be called forth by such a *movement* of aggression. Then came the reasons for the *general* solidarity of the two nations. Next came the manner of giving effect to the treaty with the *definition* in Articles 2 and 3. The second article makes it clear that what is involved is *not* an agreement between two powers for *particular ends* (having bearing only upon themselves), but rather that this is a *common* measure of protection which will become effective with ratification by the signatory powers.[42]

Some of the weaknesses of the treaty are: it lacked permanence as its duration was limited to the development of the guarantees by the League of Nations which could annul the aid pact by a majority vote in the League Council at any time. One point was open to interpretation. An attack must be limited to France and must be made by Germany without cause on the part of the former. What would happen if Germany attacked Poland, or Czechoslovakia, and France went to their aid and became involved in a war with Germany? Would this be deemed an act of provocation and bring the United States — alone or with Great Britain — to the side of France? Obviously as the years passed this would raise questions which would be difficult to answer. The two guarantors were democracies with all the incident delays in sending aid which this fact entailed. There might be a delay until the question of whether an attack was *provoked* or *unprovoked* had been decided. Who would decide it? England? France? The League Council? The United States? No one knew. Such delays could take a great deal of time and in the meantime, France could be laid waste by the invader. No one had anticipated all of these questions. Perhaps there were no suitable answers for all of the questions.

In the preamble to the British treaty was a formula that was to symbolize to the French their humiliation of having to accept a status of inferiority as a "nation protégée." This was the phrase, ". . . His Britannic Majesty is willing . . . . to undertake to support the French Government . . ."[43] This was probably a portent for the air of triumph which was evident in Lloyd George's tones when he spoke to the Parliament in London and pleaded for the adoption of the guarantee.

The decision to use the bilateral form of agreement rather than the single tripartite form was unmistakably the work of Wilson. At his insistence the two premiers accepted separate bilateral treaties instead of one tripartite document. As has been noted earlier in this study, Wilson said that he wished to use two separate agreements that in effect bound the nations together as one treaty. While the President did not disclose the basis for his request, it may have been that a separate treaty with France (with whom the United States had been cordial for more than a century) conceivably would raise much less opposition in the Senate. Furthermore, one should recall that it was Wilson who refused to permit the insertion in the Covenant of the guarantees given in the pacts. Instead, he insisted upon bilateral forms. His reasons for not placing the guarantees in the league are known, but his exact reasons for wanting a one-purpose integrated treaty to be in separate bilateral pacts are not known.

Professor Dexter Perkins has stated that, "In 1919 . . . the idea of an . . . alliance to keep the peace . . . was a long step away from traditional policy . . . ."[44] The French idea of an international army (force) to keep the peace which was presented at the Versailles Conference was just as revolutionary to the European mind as the Wilsonian idea of guaranteeing the border of a nation in Europe against an attack by Germany was to the average American's mind. At that time there was a tendency to believe that the more powerful the guarantees of peace, the smaller would be the chance of having to use them. This was Wilson's idea as to the special treaty. It would prevent by its existence what the guarantee was intended to remedy if the need for it arose. But this was not enough. Moral suasion and world opinion could serve as deterrents to an aggressor's action, but they would not be able to stop such actions unless backed by overwhelming force. Wilson called the guarantee treaty a written pledge of our moral obligation to France. He also said it was a way of protecting the security of America.[45]

"The French, not without bitterness and disappointment, bowed to this compromise (the guarantee treaty) rather than lose the friendship and future support of their great allies."[46] Therefore, the President said, the United States owes at least a pledge of temporary protection for a moral purpose. But whether moral or not, it was felt that the security of the United States would be strengthened by assuring France against an action which might conceivably involve the United States. Nothing, other than a moral obligation, existed to require the other signers of the Versailles Treaty to take action against "a hostile move" by Germany.

What was meant by a *hostile* move? Did the rejection of all attempts at arbitration constitute aggressive designs? If German troops were moved into the demilitarized zone of the Rhineland with no intention of moving against France, would such an action involve Britain and the United States to send aid to France? No one knows. No answer can be given with any degree of finality.

These are some of the other differences between the two versions: the United States' treaty provided for the submission of the pact to the French *Chamber* of Deputies for approval, whereas the British text required the treaty to be submitted to the French *Chambers* for approval. Also, the time for the Anglo-French pact to come into force was stated to be of even date with that of the Versailles Treaty. This provision was omitted from the United States version. There was, however, a compensating article — Article 4 — which required the simultaneous submission to the United States Senate of the Versailles Treaty and the Guarantee Treaty. This was intended to insure that both treaties would be approved at approximately the same time. Inasmuch as the two documents were inter-related in many instances, this was understandable. It would also give the Senate an opportunity to study and to compare simultaneously the two treaties.

It has been pointed out before that the Guarantee Treaty had to be approved by the Executive Council of the League of Nations. This provision was included in order that no interested nation (France, primarily) could block the termination of the guarantees. Thus considerable time in which to function was given to the treaty. From the French standpoint the treaty would be more advantageous to them if it was extended over an indefinite period. New institutions such as the League grow slowly. There was nothing to indicate a rapid or formidable growth during the first year or two. Time was needed for the world's attitudes and opinions to evolve and crystallize into a strong force for the preservation of peace. In the meantime the needs of the present would have been met by the guarantees.

Article 2 of the Franco-American pact and of the Franco-British pact declared:

> The present treaty, in similar terms with the treaty of even date for the same purpose concluded between [the French Republic and the United States of America] [the French

Republic and Great Britain], a copy of which is annexed hereto, will only come into force when the latter is ratified.[47]

Thus, neither could become operative without the other. When the United States failed to ratify the Versailles Treaty or the Guarantee Treaty, Article 2 was used by Great Britain as a legal means of disclaiming all responsibility for the guarantees which had been pledged to France.

However, this failure on the part of the United States to ratify or at least the possibility of Senatorial non-ratification should not have been entirely unexpected. Clemenceau knew that any treaty submitted to the Senate of the United States ran the risk of being changed or rejected — or both. As if in anticipation of that risk, France had obtained the inclusion of a very important article in Chapter XIV of the Versailles Treaty.[48] Originally, Article 429 had provided for the progressive evacuation of the occupied strategic bridgeheads on the Rhine to be accomplished in three five-year periods. The evacuation or non-evacuation of these areas was to be made contingent upon the fulfillment by Germany of all her obligations for reparations and war damages. No mention was made of the guarantees for France. The assistance pact altered the meaning of the old Article and, at the behest of France, a significant change was made.[49] This meant that now France legally could prolong beyond the stipulated time the occupation of the left bank of the Rhine. This was possible if there were no implementation of guarantees against a German attack. The door was thus opened to the possibility of an indefinite occupation should France so desire.[50]

In this manner concerted action to redress hostile moves was provided for in the high degree of correlation between the safeguards in the Versailles and Guarantee treaties. Should Germany fail to observe the treaty clauses on reparations, demilitarization, and disarmament, penalties could be invoked with France pledged to receive the assistance of the two great English-speaking powers. In addition France interpreted the guarantee of aid as a substitute for the strategic frontier on the Rhine which she had been denied. Clemenceau echoed the idea that change must come slowly and gradually when he remarked, "Neither an Englishman, nor I, nor anyone will cast off his historical way of seeing things because he has contracted a temporary alliance with a foreign country."[51]

As late as January 20, 1921, Premier Aristide Briand told the Chamber of Deputies that the collaboration of the United States, Britain, and France was necessary for, "C'est leur intime union qui assure la paix du monde . . . ."[52]

One can only conjecture what might have happened if the Versailles compromise had failed to break the deadlock.

"After the event, even the fool is wise."
Homeric saying

NOTES FOR PART ONE

1. In this study sometimes the term *guarantee treaty* is used in preference to guarantee *treaties* because the essential idea — though embodied in bi-lateral pacts — was *one* in purpose, in intent, and in meaning. As the part linking France and Great Britain was so closely integrated with that linking the United States and France in order to serve as *one guarantee*, the two pacts were often referred to as one pact.

2. House and Seymour (eds.), *What Really Happened at Paris*, 37.

3. Paul Birdsall, *Versailles Twenty Years After* (New York, 1941), 195.

4. Seymour (ed.), *House Papers*, III, 231.

5. House and Seymour (eds.), *op. cit.*, 53.

6. See Appendix B, pp. 159-168.

7. These two men were official members of the American Commission to Negotiate Peace.

8. State Dept., *Papers of the Paris Peace Conference*, XI, 513.

9. Seymour (ed.), *op. cit.*, IV, 335.

10. *Ibid.*, IV, 345.

11. *Ibid.*, IV, 346.

12. M. des A. E., *Documents Diplomatiques*, 20.

13. Miller, *Diary*, XIX, 57.

14. *Ibid.*, XIX, 58.

15. *Ibid.*, XIX, 56.

16. *Ibid.*, VII, Document 563, 50-51.

17. State Dept., *op. cit.*, IV, 123.

18. See Appendix E, pp. 177-198 for complete text of Note.

19. Miller, *op. cit.*, IV, 212-214.

20. State Dept., *op. cit.*, IV, 189.

21. *Ibid.*, IV, 297-298. This seems rather fantastic inasmuch as France was maintaining that such security would not come to her from such a league.

22. Seymour (ed.), *op. cit.*, IV, 360.

23. Lloyd George, *The Peace Treaties*, I, 398-399.

24. Clemenceau, *Grandeur and Misery of Victory*, 243.

25. *Ibid.*, 235.

26. André Tardieu, *The Truth about the Treaty* (Indianapolis, Ind., 1921), 202. Hereafter cited as Tardieu, *The Treaty.*

27. *Ibid.*, 204. This was in reference to the need for concerted action by the two nations.

28. Birdsall, *op. cit.*, 204-206.

29. Lloyd George, *Memoirs of the Peace Conference*, I, 277.

30. Lloyd George, *op. cit.*, I, 399-401.

31. *Ibid.*, I, 265-266.

32. *Ibid.*, I, 402, 422.

33. State Dept., *op. cit.*, I, 334-338. So important seems this evidence that part of a vital telegram is quoted here: "David Hunter Miller to Col. House. London, December 3, 1918 . . . Davis (Norman H. Davis) has talked freely with Monnet (Jean Monnet, French financial expert) who Davis says is very close to Clemenceau and represents his views and Monnet says *the French idea* regarding a League of Nations *has as basis the idea that the security of France against any attack should be guaranteed by Great Britain and the United States* . . . that Clemenceau's attitude in discussion with President Wilson will be one of acquiesence in general principles of a League of Nations, but of continuous questioning as to details. . ." And a similar idea comes from pp. 25-26 of Vol. I, Miller *Diary,* with the addition that Clemenceau will ask the President to formulate economic and financial proposals in which the French are particularly interested.

34. Seymour (ed.), *op. cit.*, IV, 410. In this connection also see volume IV, pp. 1-4 of the *House Papers*. It is perhaps true (as Professor Seymour, the editor, points out in his concise commenting in and editing of the papers left by Colonel House) that House was more inclined and ready to compromise than Wilson was before March 14, 1919. "To compromise with the Europeans on the Treaty and then fail to secure the Senate's endorsement of the League, meant not merely disaster for his (Wilson) whole policy, but the bankruptcy of the liberal movement in the United States of which he was the leader." (p. 410.)

35. *Ibid.*, IV, 383-386. Seymour believes that as late as March 4, Wilson was not in accord with the belief of House that broad concessions would have to be made to France. Neither did the President give any impression that he believed a speedy settlement was necessary. This

attitude prevailed until March 14, 1919, at which time he was apprised of the extremely serious situation.

36. Tardieu, *op. cit.*, 176-177.

37. Miller, *op. cit.*, I, 25-26.

38. See Appendix F, pp. 198-202, for the complete text of the French Memorandum of March 17, 1919, setting forth counter-proposals as a possible basis of agreement.

39. M. des A. E., *op. cit.*, Document No. 4, 32-35.

40. Seymour (ed.), *op. cit.*, IV, 393-394.

41. State Dept., *op. cit.*, XI, 124.

42. Allan Nevins, *Henry White, Thirty Years of American Diplomacy* (New York, 1930), 425. Cited hereafter as Nevins, *Henry White*.

43. "It was certainly true that House was convinced that no essential advantage would be gained by the Americans through another month of discussion. If compromise was necessary, it were best to compromise quickly. 'My main drive now . . . (March 14) is for peace with Germany at the earliest possible moment.'" (Seymour [ed.], *House Papers*, IV, 384).

44. Miller, *op. cit.*, I, 189-190.

45. *Ibid.*, VI, Document 476, 476. The text of the proposed draft made by House was this: "The signatory Powers agree that they will recommend to the Executive Council of the League of Nations, pursuant to Article X of the Covenant, (a) That so long as Germany is not a member of the League, danger of aggression against France by Germany may exist; (b) That the means of meeting said danger, should it become imminent, would properly be immediate military, financial, economic, and moral support of France by Great Britain and the United States." Also in this connection reference should be made to State Dept., *Papers of the Paris Peace Conference*, XI, 124, and to the material on pages 125, 126 (same reference) which is, in part: "Mr. White stated that he had had a conversation with Colonel House during which the latter had shown him a suggested text for an agreement between France, Great Britain, and the United States, which he thought would satisfy M. Clemenceau. The Commissioners discussed the drafting of this text, and felt that the wording could be much improved upon. They therefore drew up a substitute text . . . to submit . . . to Colonel House with the statement to the effect that *in their opinion the subject matter thereof was most prejudicial to the whole structure of the League of Nations, and to the ideal for which the United States entered the war . . .*" Italics added.

46. *Ibid.*, VI, Document 546, 481.

47. *Ibid.*, VII, Document 560, 30-31. Some of the drafts of proposals for an agreement with France were drawn by Hunter Miller and Gordon Auchincloss. One draft of more than usual significance, was, in part, as follows: "In order to provide the protection for France which she desires and which is an essential part of the purpose of an agreement with her, the following resolution should be passed by the Executive

Council at its first meeting: 'It is the opinion of the Executive Council, that among the essential means by which should be fulfilled the obligations of the States, members of the League, pursuant to Article X of the Covenant, to preserve as against external aggression the territorial integrity and political independence of France, as defined in the Treaty of Peace, would be, in any case of threat or danger of such aggression, immediate commercial, financial, economic, and military support of France by Great Britain, and the United States of America.'" Neither Wilson nor Lloyd George supported the proposal.

48. With the exception, of course, of Wilson and House.

49. State Dept., *op. cit.*, XI, 125-133. (Minutes of the Daily Meetings of the Commissioners Plenipotentiary).

50. Seymour (ed.), *op. cit.*, IV, 394.

51. Baker, *World Settlement*, I, 288. See also, Miller, *Diary*, VII, Document 627, 258.

52. Lloyd George, *op. cit.*, I, 425.

53. Seymour (ed.), *op. cit.*, IV, 395. In part the *new* text read, "Because of the havoc which Germany has brought upon the world by her *attacks* upon Belgium and France. . ." It is a significant comment that Wilson changed the draft to read, "In a separate treaty by the United States, subject to the approval of the Executive Council of the League of Nations, to come immediately to the assistance of France as soon as any unprovoked movement of aggression against her is made by Germany." Italics added. Reference is to the one cited at the beginning of the paragraph.

Here is an interesting point. Wilson deleted a war-guilt clause from the formula (because of the havoc which Germany has brought upon the world . . .) ostensibly drafted by House but which in reality, says House, was reworded by Wilson. In the final draft of a guarantee treaty between France and the United States, the idea reappears in a much stronger phrased sentence. It is omitted from the British-French version apparently because the British did not want to give the Germans any additional causes for irritation. Perhaps the real reason for the deletion in the British-French version was the feeling that a war-guilt clause was in the Versailles Treaty and there was no necessity for repeating it in the special accord. France did not insist upon its inclusion in the British draft. Perhaps the French did not take note of the absence of such a provision. Little surprise was registered at the inclusion or the exclusion of some of the clauses — a case in point being the inclusion by Lloyd George of a clause to allow Great Britain to withdraw her offer of aid if there was no approval of the Franco-American pact by the United States. In the case of the United States' draft, the war-guilt clause was restored by the French who were probably aided by the connivance of Lansing and of House who foresaw a difficult time for the Aid Treaty in the Senate of the United States. Just as Lloyd George asked for the insertion of a provision in the special treaty requiring its approval by the Council of the League in order to obtain additional support for the treaty in the British Parliament, so House and Lansing may have thought that putting the onus (on Germany) for the war might add to the sentiment in the Senate for approval of said treaty. Most of the foregoing is speculation, but in the absence of precise documentation to indicate *why* the changes were made in the two texts, some comment seemed to be in order. In the hope of clearing up this and another point as to whether there was any substantial disagreement among Wilson, Clemenceau, and Lloyd George over the meaning of "an unprovoked movement of aggression," the author sent a letter to David Hunter Miller in Canada with the request that he answer as soon as possible. Mr. Miller complied with the request (in the latter part of February, 1950) saying in effect that he did not remember anything to the contrary, that he did not trust anyone else's memory in the matter, and that the documents must provide what information there is in the matter. This seems to substantiate whatever inferences may be made from the paucity of information in the documents on some of these questions. Therefore, it seems the *real* answers may never be known.

Furthermore, here is the first hint that the aid would be given in bi-lateral agreements rather than in a triple agreement. Also, to Wilson must be attributed the origin of the phrase, "subject to the approval of the Executive Council of the League of Nations" thereby linking the treaty with the Covenant even though Wilson was opposed to the drastic alteration of Article X as proposed in a previous draft. Here, too, seems to be the origin of the binding of the United States to "come immediately to the assistance of France in case of unprovoked movement of aggression" by Germany. House undoubtedly provided some of the ideas but the essential phraseology — according to the available evidence — belongs to Wilson.

54. Seymour (ed.), *op. cit.*, IV, 394.

55. *Ibid.*, IV, 395.

56. *Parliamentary (Command) Papers*: Cmd. 1614, *Memorandum Circulated by the Prime Minister on 25th March 1919*, (1922), most of which is cited in Appendix C, pp. 168-174.

57. Just what the action was to be in "dealing with" the Russian situation is not made clear. The Prime Minister, in the opinion of the writer, was well endowed with a propensity for cleverly adapting his views and attitude to the exigencies of the moment and sometimes with an apparent disregard for consistency or for the truth.

58. From this time until the definitive treaty was signed on June 28, 1919, the attitude of the Prime Minister has the appearance of becoming less insistent on German war guilt.

59. Tardieu, *op. cit.*, 182.

60. Paul Birdsall called that date, March 28, one of great historic crisis. (*Versailles Twenty Years After*, 228).

61. At that time consisting of Orlando of Italy, Clemenceau of France, Wilson of the United States, and Lloyd George of Great Britain.

62. Tardieu, *op. cit.*, 171-172.

63. State Dept., *op. cit.*, V, 413-414. It is interesting to note at this time that Henry White sent a letter to Elihu Root (dated March 19, 1919) in which he stated that Lloyd George had told the French that Britain would give them a written guarantee to the effect that all possible assistance would be forthcoming to them in case of an attack by Germany. He (White) did not know how the United States could give such a pledge and have the Senate approve it. His added comment that the promises of Lloyd George did not inspire a great deal of confidence in the French for they wanted the United States to endorse the British guarantee, reveals an attitude of skepticism which may explain the persistence of Clemenceau to secure American support. (Nevins, *Henry White*, 411).

Nevins also quotes a letter of White to Representative John Jacob Rogers (Mass.) dated March 21, 1919, that Wilson's actions in the Rhineland affair should be firmer and that matters should be brought to a head with the French. Two or three days later White saw Wilson and gave him that advice. He advised him to tell Clemenceau just how far the United States would go and to present an ultimatum saying that unless an agreement were reached soon, the United States would withdraw and make a separate peace with Germany. He also told Wilson that it was inexpedient as well as unwise to guarantee the security of France by a special provision in the League of Nations or by a special treaty with her. Moreover, White let Wilson know that the rest of the Commissioners felt as keenly about the situation as he did, and with the same conclusions. There was nothing said about House, however, for White was never an admirer of the man. (*Henry White*, 415-416). It is not known how Wilson received the advice, but how well he disregarded most of it is a matter of record. One thing should be noted, however, and that is there was a stiffening of the President's attitude for a time.

After the middle of April there were signs of a lessening of opposition by Wilson. One cannot say how far in meeting the French demands Wilson would have gone in order to attain his points on the Monroe Doctrine, the idea of collective security, Article X, and the entire Covenant. Tardieu has implied that Wilson would have gone much further than the British and that generally he was more sympathetic to their ideas. This may have been due to the friendly spirit of comradeship existing between the Colonel and Clemenceau. At least that relationship did play an important part. Thomas A. Bailey, Paul Birdsall, Karl Nowak, Harold Nicolson, and Frank H. Simonds imply that Wilson made concessions to France in return for the assurance of Clemenceau's support of the League of Nations as well as to save the entire conference from the impasse it reached in March and which continued through part of April, 1919.

64. M. des A. E., *op. cit.*, Document 5, 37.

65. Miller, *op. cit.*, VII, Document 564, 54.

66. Tardieu, *op. cit.*, 204.

67. M. des A. E., *op. cit.*, Document 5, 38.

68. He was using an argument which had appeared in the January 16, 1919, issue of *Le Temps.*

69. Tardieu, *op. cit.,* 205-208.

70. This attack of influenza of a virulent form was intensified by intestinal disorders. From their effects, the President seems never to have fully recovered his health or strength. The paralyzing stroke which was suffered in September, 1919, may have been an aftermath of the attack in Paris which left a pronounced twitch in his face.

71. Birdsall, *op. cit.,* 212.

72. Karl F. Nowak, *Versailles,* (New York, 1929), 161.

73. Baker, *op. cit.,* II, 67. Baker calls the meetings from April 8-13, ". . . those crucial five days of the Peace Conference . . ."

74. Harold Nicolson, *Peacemaking 1919* (London, 1933) 307.

75. Seymour (ed.), *op. cit.,* IV, 406-409.

76. See p. 158 of Appendix A, pp. 154-158, for an outline sketch of the final terms of the Versailles Treaty.

77. State Department., *op. cit.,* V, 112-113.

78. *Ibid.,* V, 118.

79. Wilson may have been influenced in his desire to have the aid agreements in two separate treaties by the thought that *if* one of them did not come into force (regardless by what reason) the other one would still give a large measure of assurance and potential assistance to France. There was no intention then of making one treaty depend upon the approval of the other. THAT WAS INSERTED IN THE FINAL DRAFT BY LLOYD GEORGE.

80. State Dept., *op. cit.,* V, 114-115.

81. *Ibid.,* V, 115.

82. Quoted in Tardieu, *op. cit.,* 210-211.

83. Temperley (ed.), *op. cit.,* II, 30. For excellent accounts of the development of Article X see also, Miller, *Diary,* V, Document 409, 431-432; and Florence Wilson, *The Origins of the League Covenant* (London, 1928), 24, 49-50, 95-99.

84. Seymour (ed.), *op. cit.,* IV, 430-431.

85. Temperley (ed.), *op. cit.,* VI, 441. Considering the circumstances of the time (1919) it is not too difficult to understand the position of the old and practical Marshal who was devoted to giving his country the greatest degree of security he could obtain.

86. State Dept., *op. cit.,* III, 379.

87. Arthur Hugh Frazier, a Counselor at the American Embassy, also served as a member of the Secretariat of the peace conference.

88. State Dept., *op. cit.,* V, 494-495. (The note is in Appendix A).

89. *Ibid.,* V, 495. (The draft is in Appendix B).

90. *Ibid.,* V, 474-476. It seems fairly evident that Wilson's inclusion of the phrase "an unprovoked movement of aggression by Germany" in the rough draft which Colonel House had submitted to him was not only the first time such a phrase was used in connection with the pledge of assistance

to France, but it was also an expression upon which there was general agreement among the nations concerned as to the overall meaning. It is true, however, that some technical points could be raised in the practical application of the interpretation of the phrase. There was never any difficulty along that line because the pledges were never effectuated.

91. *Ibid.*, V, 476. This was the origin of article 3 of the final draft of the Guarantee Pact. The writer believes that many of the technical ideas behind the final drafting of the pledges of aid to France were formulated in the minds of House and Wilson.

92. *Ibid.*, V, 486.

93. *Ibid.*, V, 495. (The Wilson letter to Clemenceau): "The stipulations relating to the Left Bank of the Rhine contained in the Draft Treaty of Peace with Germany are as follows: (1) Germany is forbidden to maintain or construct any fortifications either on the left bank of the Rhine or on the right bank to the west of a line drawn fifty kilometers to the east of the Rhine. (2) In the area defined above, the maintenance and assembly of armed forces, either permanently or temporarily, and military manoeuvers [sic] of either kind, as well as the upkeep of all permanent works for mobilization are in the same way forbidden. (3) So long as the present treaty is in force Germany undertakes to cooperate in any enquiry which the Council of the League of Nations acting if need by a majority, may deem necessary. As these conditions may not at first provide adequate security and protection to your Country, *I agree to submit to the Senate for its advice and consent, a treaty with* France by which the *United States of America* shall be bound to come immediately to her assistance in the event of any unprovoked movement of aggression against her being made by Germany. The Treaty will be in similar terms to that entered by *Great Britain* and will come into force when the latter is ratified. The Treaty must be recognized by the Council of the League, and will continue in force until on the application of one of the parties to it, the Council of the League agrees that the League itself affords sufficient protection.

(signed) Woodrow Wilson.
Robert Lansing."

The italics have been added to show the differences in text in this letter and the British letter which follows.

94. *Ibid.*, V, 494-495. "To Monsieur Clemenceau . . . The stipulations relating to the left Bank of the Rhine contained in the Draft Treaty of Peace with Germany are as follows: (the materials are those in the letter just quoted above). As these conditions may not at first provide adequate security and protection to your Counry, *His Majesty's Government agree to ask Parliament to authorize* a treaty with France by which *Great Britain* shall be bound to come immediately to her assistance in the event of any unprovoked movement of aggression against her being made by Germany. The Treaty will be in similar terms to that entered into by *the United States* and will come into force when the latter is ratified. The Treaty must be recognized by the Council of the League of Nations as being consistent with the Covenant of the League, and will continue in force until on the application of one of the parties to it, the Council

of the League agrees that the League itself affords sufficient protection. *The obligations imposed under this Treaty shall not be binding on the Dominions of the British Empire until the Treaty shall be ratified by the Parliament of the Dominion concerned.*

(signed) David Lloyd George.

Arthur James Balfour."

Italics added.

95. *Ibid.*, V, 494-495.

96. *Ibid.*, III, 333-368.

97. Miller, *op. cit.*, XX, 176-181; II, Document 48, 206.

98. State Dept., *op. cit.*, III, 379.

99. The text of these letters has been given on pages 93-94.

100. State Dept., *op. cit.*, V, 491-494. Also, see Miller, *Diary*, IX, 293-295.

101. *Ibid.*, V, 541-542.

102. *Ibid.*, XI, 513.

103. Miller, *op. cit.*, VI, Document 463, 271-272.

104. *Ibid.*, VII, Document 566, 57-59.

105. *Le Matin* (Paris,) June 2, 3, 4, 1919. For the text and the explanations of an interview between the French General Desticker and a Dr. Heim, Bavarian deputy and member of the Peace Committee of the German Reichstag, at Luxembourg, May 19, 1919, relative to the proposed formation of an "Anti-Bolshevik Confederacy" in South Germany to work with the French authorities, see State Dept., *op. cit.*, V, 899, 906-909.

106. Tardieu, *op. cit.*, 120. The Colonel was a member of the British forces.

107. State Dept., *op. cit.*, VI, 138-146.

108. *Ibid.*, VI, 521-522.

109. Wilson authorized Dr. James Scott Brown to make the final draft for the United States.

110. State Dept., *op. cit.*, VI, 735. Tardieu states in *The Treaty*, 208-209, that the British Crown Officers felt by the use of the word "all" the signatory powers would leave the decision as to the *time* for abrogating the guarantee treaty, entirely at the discretion of France. This was not expedient and the change in the wording to permit abrogation by a majority was suggested.

111. *Ibid.*, VI, 740-743.

112. *Ibid.*, VI, 743.

NOTES FOR PART TWO

1. Noble, *Opinions at Paris,* 376.

2. Tardieu, *The Treaty,* 204.

3. Clemenceau, *Grandeur and Misery of Victory,* 195.

4. Robert Lansing, *The Peace Negotiations, a Personal Narrative* (Boston and New York, 1921) 215. Cited hereafter as Lansing, *Peace Negotiations.*

5. *Ibid.,* 183.

6. *Ibid.,* 185.

7. *Ibid.,* 181-182.

8. *Ibid.,* 185-186.

9. *Ibid.,* 216.

10. *Ibid.,* 179.

11. Nevins, *Henry White,* 441.

12. *Ibid.,* 450.

13. *Ibid.,* 438. Senator Lodge believed that France should crush Germany so thoroughly there would never be any danger from that quarter. But he failed again to support (in the Senate) any official action to protect France against Germany.

14. House and Seymour (eds.), *What Really Happened at Paris,* 376, (article written by Bliss).

15. *Ibid.,* 377. This appears to be one of the main ideas in the present foreign policy of the United States.

16. Lloyd George, *Memoirs of the Peace Conference,* I, 125.

17. *Ibid.,* I, 127.

18. *Ibid.,* I, 135.

19. *Ibid.,* I, 123.

20. State Dept., *Papers of the Paris Peace Conference,* XI, 121-122.

21. Miller, *Diary,* I, 177.

22. Temperley (ed.), *History of Peace Conference,* VI, 349.

23. *Ibid.,* VI, 350.

24. *Ibid.,* VI, 358.

25. *Ibid.,* VI, 358-359.

26. *Ibid.,* VI, 361.

27. Lansing, *op. cit.,* 185-186.

28. See pages 214-218 for text of Aid Treaty.

29. See page 217 of Appendix H. Italics added.

30. See page 217 of Appendix H.

31. *Ibid.,* Appendix H.

32. See page 217 of Appendix H.

33. The Article's important parts were these: "The Allied and Associated Governments affirm and Germany accepts the responsibility . . .

for causing all the loss and damage . . . of war imposed upon them by the aggression of Germany . . ."

34. Seymour (ed.), *House Papers*, IV, 394-395; 150-152.

35. State Dept., *op. cit.*, V, 165, 234, 354-355, 360, 49, 55, 387-388.

36. Lloyd George, *op. cit.*, I, 277.

37. Miller, *op. cit.*, VII, Document 563, 50-52. (Part of the suggested text for the introduction of the peace treaty was drafted by Auchincloss, the son-in-law of House, in this manner: ". . . The unprovoked and unwarranted invasion of France and Belgium in 1914 by Germany plunged the entire world into . . . disaster . . ."

38. Lloyd George, *op. cit.*, I, 469.

39. Nevins, *Henry White*, 450.

40. Lloyd George, *op. cit.*, I, 469.

41. *Ibid.*, I, 455-456.

42. See Appendix H for text of the Guarantees, pages 214-218.

43. See pages 215-216 for full text of phrase.

44. Perkins, *America and Two Wars*, 82.

45. *Senate Documents*, 66th Congress, 1st Sess., July 10-November 6, 1919, 50-51.

46. Wolfers, *Between Two Wars*, 16.

47. See text of Guarantees, Appendix H, pages 214-218.

48. This explanation of Chapter XIV of the Versailles Treaty was made by a brilliant member of the French Delegation, André Tardieu. The material is quoted from Miller, *Diary*, XX, 169: "Part XIV relates to the guarantees of the execution of the Treaty . . . For fifteen years after the signing of the Treaty, the left Bank of the Rhine and the bridgeheads on the right bank shall be occupied by the Allied and Associated forces. If Germany carries out faithfully the clauses of the Treaty, a progressive evacuation is provided for . . . At the same time the Allied and Associated Powers reserve the following right: If at the end of fifteen years the guarantees against an aggression by Germany were not complete, the evacuation would be retarded as long as necessary to obtain all the guarantees. If after fifteen years the Commission of Reparations judges that Germany has ceased to carry out faithfully her engagements, all or a part of the zones may be reoccupied by the Allied and Associated forces. On the other hand, it is admitted that if Germany carries out faithfully the totality of her engagements within the time fixed, the troops would be withdrawn."

49. In connection with the withdrawal of occupation forces from the Rhineland, all forces were withdrawn almost five (5) years before the last time period stated in the Versailles Treaty.

50. In conjunction with the provisions for the demilitarization of the Rhine, see the statement of Premier Millerand on April 13, 1920, to the

Chamber of Deputies (Chambre, *Débats*, 1920, 916). Militarily important as Rhine crossings were the cities of Cologne, Coblenz, Kehl, Dusseldorf, Mannheim, and Mayence.

51. Quoted in Lloyd George, *The Peace Treaties*, I, 433.

52. Chambre, *Débats*, 1921, 51.

CHAPTER FOUR

How the French
Reacted to the Security Pacts

The attitude of these two nations — the United States and Great Britain — toward the security pacts should be kept in mind when an attempt is made to show how the French reacted to the aid agreements.

The French announcement of the assistance pledges gave rise to a jubilation which soon was followed by a tempered and restrained feeling of anxiety. In some instances there were hostile criticisms in some French quarters because of the feeling that France had made too many concessions. But in general there was a tendency to accept in good faith the unprecedented offer by Great Britain and the United States.

Not without good reason did the feeling of anxiety inject a somber note into the rejoicings. There was a possibility that either Britain or the United States might fail to ratify the agreement. The ceremonial signing on June 28 was not enough. According to the terms of the treaty each nation's parliament or legislative body must give its approval to the measure. Such action was required before the Council of the League of Nations could give its approval to the pact. None of the three nations involved believed that more than a perfunctory step was implied in the required vote by the Council. But there were some doubts and misgivings in some quarters as to whether the United States would give its approval.

Premier Clemenceau lost no time, therefore, in formally placing the Versailles Treaty and the aid pacts before the French Chamber of Deputies for its consideration. This move occurred on June 30, 1919, and immediately thereafter began that lengthy discussion which finally ended in an overwhelming approval for the assistance pacts.

During the debates on the merits of the treaties, the entire question of French security came under review. André Tardieu furnished some effective arguments to the forces seeking the Chamber's approval of the treaties. Tardieu had taken a prominent and a very important part in the negotiations for the guarantees and consequently was well-qualified to explain and defend them upon the floor of the French Parliament.

Speaking to the members of the Chamber on September 2, Tardieu stated that, in his opinion, there were three main classes of general guarantees for France. They were: first, guarantees of security; second, an expectation of execution of the treaties under debate; and third, a "politique générale — que le traité assure á la France . . . ."[1] The speaker then proceeded to explain the meaning of the memoranda sent by Foch in the fight made by France for the Rhineland and for adequate guarantees for security. The safety of the future demanded such a special agreement.[2] He pointed out that, ". . . le 14 mars, le jour même de l'arrivèe á Paris du Président Wilson . . . pour la première fois, succéder une suggestion positive."[3] That was the day on which the offer was made to assist France in case of a future unprovoked German attack. So important was that move on the part of the United States and Great Britain that Tardieu termed it one ". . . sans precedent dans l'histoire de leurs deux Pays . . ."[4] Here was proof that France would not be without adequate assistance in the event of a future aggressive move by Germany.

Furthermore, the deputies were assured by Tardieu, ". . . le Traité [of Guarantee] nous donne . . . les garanties essentieles que nous demandions en faveur."[5] Many safeguards had been provided in the larger settlement to which this one was supplementary (meaning the Versailles Treaty). The entire structure for peace and safety, he continued, had been crowned and made more secure ". . . avec l'engagement d'aide militaire immediate

de la Grande-Bretagne et des États-Unis."[6] Could a more stable
or a more lasting guarantee than that be wanted? He believed
that it could not. The assurance that France would be given all
the military support needed would tend to serve as a deterrent
to hostile acts that might provoke another war.

In concluding his moving appeal for acceptance of the Guarantee Treaties, the rapporteur (Tardieu) declared, ". . . je de-
mande . . . la ratification des Traités . . . ; j'ai dit que contre ces
dangers le Traité á crée pour la France le maximum de sécurité
dont elle ait jamais bénéficié."[7]

In the question period that followed the conclusion of
Tardieu's report, it was evident that many of the deputies were
eager to learn how long the proposed guarantee pacts would
remain in force. Tardieu was not prepared to commit himself
or the French Cabinet to a definite time limit. He did, however,
point out that Wilson and Lloyd George had suggested a three-
year maximum, but that this had been rejected by Clemenceau.

The French Premier had justified his refusal on the grounds
that it was not within the next few months that Germany would
become dangerous again. On the contrary it was likely to be
several years later. If the pacts were arbitrarily limited to the
period suggested by the leaders of Britain and of the United
States, then France would lose the protection afforded by the
guarantees at the time when they would be most necessary.[8]
The impasse had been resolved by including in the text of the
aid agreements a provision which would permit an abrogation
of the pacts by the Council of the League of Nations. That action
could be taken only on the application of *one of the parties* to the
Guarantee Treaties, and if the Council itself were agreed (by
a majority vote) that sufficient protection was afforded to France
by the League of Nations.[9] In addition, Tardieu stated that Wilson had proposed a pledge to continue the guarantees until such
time as *all* three of the signatory powers considered the League's
protection to be sufficient. This view was rejected by the British
who maintained that under such an agreement, the *final decision*
on the time for abrogation would rest with France.[10] It was in
the best interests of each nation involved that no formal date
had been included when the treaties must be renounced. The

negotiations had produced a document suitable to the occasion, the French leaders believed, and no good would result from a rejection of the pacts. That, in substance, was the argument of Tardieu.

A report of more than usual importance was made on August 5, 1919, in the Chamber of Deputies. This report dealt with the amount and the type of aid to be accorded to France under the terms of the treaties under discussion. Deputy Louis Barthou made an able presentation of the material which had been prepared by the Commission on Treaties. This Commission, composed of specially appointed deputies, had been instructed by the Chamber to examine thoroughly the proposals for security embodied within the guarantee agreements. Should the Commission deem the projects feasible, it was to prepare a law to put the treaties into effect. Barthou made a very effective plea for the defense arrangements. He spoke of the dangers to France if the proffered assistance were rejected. Much stress was placed upon the willingness of the United States and Great Britain to align themselves with France for mutual security. This, the speaker insisted, would lessen the probabilities of a future war with Germany. In conclusion, the Commission recommended, ". . . l'adoption du projet de loi . . . concernant l'aide à donner à la France par les États-Unis d'Amérique et la Grande-Bretagne en cas d'agression allemande non provoquée."[11]

Meanwhile, considerable doubt had been expressed in the Chamber against the new aid agreements. Such arguments took the form of questions as to the substance of the aid to be given, of the poor prospects for the consummation of future commitments in military assistance, and whether there were not too many hurdles to be crossed before France could receive the aid promised. There was some feeling that perhaps it had been a mistake to relinquish such tangible evidences of security as that of a separate Rhenish Republic, a permanently occupied demilitarized zone along the east bank of the Rhine River, and an economic debasement of Germany that might weaken permanently her potential as an aggressor. These points were countered by the advocates of the alliance who stressed that the more powerful and certain were the guarantees of peace, the smaller would be the possibility of having to use them.

So threatening did the opposition to the guarantee pact become on August 6, 1919, that one of the rapporteurs, Victor Augagneur, was impelled to state it was unfortunate that party politics were lessening the chances of ratification. Not only did the deputy attack those of his countrymen who were thrusting their efforts in the pathway to security for France, but he also referred to the situation in the United States. The speaker noted with some concern that some members of the peace conference (obviously a reference to Wilson and Lansing) were undergoing critical attacks by newspapers and individuals for their work at Paris. The members of the Chamber were then reminded of Wilson's great work in helping to create a League of Nations which would be closely allied with the security framework of the guarantees. There was a final appeal for a swift approval of the matter under discussion.[12]

Also, on the same day (August 6), another deputy, Charles Benoist, delivered a report to the members of the Chamber. In general there was little new material in his arguments or facts. However, one item of information which he presented was significant because of the question it raised rather than for those it answered. At a time when most of the deputies were indulging in some careless or half-formed definitions of terms used in the pledges to aid France, M. Benoist raised a question of great import. After having praised the agreements for mutual aid between France and her guarantors, Benoist pointed out that assistance would be given *only* if Germany committed an *act of unprovoked aggression* against France. He raised these three questions: (1) how would an act of hostility be defined? (2) What was aggression? (3) What constituted an "unprovoked" act of aggression? As far as the rapporteur had been able to ascertain there was no clear cut definition of any one of the three. Then he continued by implying that this vagueness in definition, so apparent in the treaty text, was likely to interpose hindrances to the *sécurité* of his beloved France. Fatal results might ensue. The situation called for some clarification as well as for decisive action. To the minds of those who were opposing ratification of the supplemental treaty these questions of M. Benoist were welcome indeed. As the immediate objective was to secure approval by the Chamber as soon as possible, the supporters of the work done at Versailles gave little opportunity for enlargement of the breach created by the doubt-inspired queries. Thus scarcely any attention was given thereafter to these interrogations by Benoist.[13]

One of the highlights of the official debates on the proposed security treaties was the appearance in the Chamber of Deputies on September 24, 1919, of Premier Clemenceau. The French leader went to the Parliament in order to bring his personal influence to bear upon those deputies who might be wavering. Many of the members were in greater fear of the wrath of the fiery old leader than they were of their own constituents. Clemenceau told the Chamber that while France had given up many things necessary to security, the pledges under consideration would restore at least partially the bulwark of protection.[14] In words of eloquence, Clemenceau warned the legislators that the aid treaties were not perfect. Under the circumstances they were probably the best obtainable. The Premier expressed his satisfaction on the score of the guarantees offered, but said that he could not direct the future course of events. Clemenceau stated that in a conversation between himself and Wilson, he had told the American President that neither of them held the keys to the future. Furthermore, he added, "you have a Senate and I have a Parliament. We cannot be sure of what they will do ten years hence, or even of what they will do tomorrow . . ."[15]

Then speculating on the position which France would occupy if the aid pacts were not approved, Clemenceau posed the question of a possible alternative guarantee. He said, in part:

> . . . If the treaties (of guarantee) are not voted, they will not be, and that will end the matter. But there is an article (429 of the Versailles Treaty) of which I myself secured the adoption, which says that in this case, we shall make fresh arrangements as regards the Rhine; consequently, we are covered in this matter and everything has been provided for.[16]

The speaker stated that he did not anticipate an adverse action by the Chamber. In fact, he was sure that approval would be forthcoming. By a vote of 510-0 the Chamber of Deputies placed its stamp of acceptance upon the guarantees (and upon the Versailles Treaty which was necessary to give validity to the former) shortly after the Premier's request.[17]

In the French Senate, unanimous approval of the treaties came after only two days of consideration. There the principal speakers were Léon Bourgeois, a participant in the peace negotiations, and Clemenceau. On October 3, 1919, Bourgeois presented a well-organized report to the Senate giving an over-all review of the security needs of France and of the manner in which these requirements would be met.[18] Particular attention was devoted to the relationships between the security provided by Article X of the League Covenant and that set forth in the mutual aid agreements.[19] The Senators were told that America and Great Britain had acted to help preserve the peace of the world in signing "avec la France un traité de garantie."[20] Surely the security of France would not be imperilled by the Senate's failure to approve such an important agreement. Bourgeois gained much support by his lucid factual arguments.

The issue was decided, however, by the appearance of Premier Clemenceau before the entire group of Senators. He explained the meaning of the Treaty of Alliance to France, to the United States and to Great Britain respectively. Many of the difficulties of negotiating such a proposal were laid before the attentive listeners. One should be aware that it had not been easy to translate into an acceptable French equivalent the meaning of "a movement of unprovoked aggression." If the work done at Paris were rejected, the security of France would be endangered. Such action would also throw the world into chaos.[21] He concluded the speech with a fervent appeal for Senate approval. There were no dissenting votes in the roll call which was taken soon after Clemenceau had left the rostrum.[22] The President of France affixed his signature to the "projets de loi"[23] and on November 20, 1919, the French Government was prepared to exchange ratifications with the British and United States governments.[24]

In the meantime, as the official discussions were going on in the French Parliament, varied reactions were appearing in the press of France. There was some reticence about judging the new security agreement with the United States and Great Britain before official ratifications had been exchanged. One French paper, the *Petit Journal,* stated without qualification that the aid pact would be no less than a defensive alliance between the three nations.[25] Such papers as *Echo de Paris, Le Temps,* and *Le Matin,* were somewhat more cautious. There was little more than a bare mention of the treaties of assistance.

During the debates in the Chamber of Deputies, the tone of editorial reaction generally was favorable to French acceptance of the proffered guarantees. The *Journal de Rouen,* for example, which had been very skeptical on pledges by the United States to give future aid, now welcomed the proposals.[26]

A reasonable degree of skepticism was prevalent in some semi-official quarters. It was known in most of France that Marshal Foch and President Raymond Poincaré had opposed Clemenceau's acceptance of Wilson's and Lloyd George's offer of aid. The two men believed too much had been asked in exchange. Marshal Foch, aided and abetted by President Poincaré, had been so determined to forestall any action which might be inimical to France that he had asked for permission to appear at a special meeting of the French Cabinet. That was in April (25) 1919. At the meeting which was held, Foch lashed out against the proposed settlement of Franco-American differences. When he had finished, Clemenceau dominated the session with an eloquent speech in which he stressed the value of the Anglo-American treaty of guarantee. He placed great emphasis upon the right to military occupation of the Rhineland bridgeheads. He pleaded with Poincaré for his support. The Cabinet gave the Premier a standing ovation.[27]

A section of French public opinion looked upon the offer of the aid treaties as an unusual opportunity. Never before had the United States and Britain pledged themselves to guarantee the eastern borders of France. It was reasonable to believe then that such a triple alliance would be unassailable. What could an acceptance of the offer cost France?[28] Any additional security

against a future attack by Germany was worthy of serious consideration. Perhaps this pact would provide the needed military
aid to tip the scales in favor of French superiority. The chance
was worth taking, reasoned the man in the street. At any rate,
it would be better to have the guarantees and not use them than
it would be to need them and not have them.

Finally, when all things have been considered, it is not
strange that France gave official acceptance to the assistance
pacts. As was emphasized in Chapter I, a fear of Germany
was so deeply ingrained in the French nation that serious attention would have been accorded to almost any kind of project
for security. In the offer to provide France with military aid
against any unprovoked aggression by Germany, President Wilson and Lloyd George had gone far to reassure the anxious
French claims for some means to reduce the overwhelming disparity between France and Germany. In fact if sympathy, com-
passion for the underling, and agreement on general objectives
had been the controlling factor in working out a solution, the
puzzle of security would have been solved. With the knowledge
that a pledge — convertible later into a legal commitment —
might add that needed measure of assurance so desperately
sought for by France, Wilson and Lloyd George gave it. That
the reaction in France was favorable, until 1920 brought with it
the United States' repudiation, seems to be a logical deduction
from the evidence presented.

> "The Guarantee Pact gave us what was nothing less
> than the ultimate sanction of the Peace Treaty."
> Georges Clemenceau in *Grandeur and Misery
> of Victory*

NOTES

1. M. des A. E., *Documents Diplomatiques,* document No. 16, 61.

2. *Ibid.,* document No. 16, 62-64.

3. *Ibid.,* document No. 16, 65.

4. *Ibid.,* document No. 16, 66.

5. *Ibid.,* document No. 16, 72.

6. *Ibid.,* document No. 16, 73.

7. *Ibid.,* document No. 16, 89.

8. Tardieu, *The Treaty,* 207-208.

9. See text of the Guarantee Treaties, Appendix H, pages 214-218.

10. Tardieu, *op. cit.,* 209.

11. Chambre, *Documents Parlementaires,* 1919, Annexe No. 6658, 322. The Commission on Treaties made its recommendation for a "Projet de Loi" to implement the Guarantee Treaties in these words: ". . . Le Président de la République est autorise á ratifier et a faire exécuter, s'il y a lieu, les traités . . . entre la France et les États-Unis d'Amérique à donner à la France en cas d'agression allemande non provoquée . . .' (Chambre, *Documents Parlementaires,* 1919, Annexe No. 6658, 322-323.)

12. *Ibid.,* 1919, Annexe No. 6663, 387.

13. *Ibid.,* 1919, Annexe No. 6664, 392. In part, the statement of Benoist was as follows: ". . . des conventions complementaires ont ete conclues entre la France d'une part, les Etats-Unis d'Amérique et la Grande Bretagne d'autre part, une signification plus large, si ce n'est pas trop en solliciter le texte que de dire qu'il contient ou qu'il sous-entend la definition de 'l'acte hostile,' celle de 'L'agression non provoquée' . . ."

14. Temperley, (ed.), *History of Peace Conference,* III, 122.

15. Quoted by Tardieu in *The Treaty,* 210.

16. Quoted by Alcide Ebray in *A Frenchman Looks at the Peace* (London, 1927), 175-176. (The translation was made by E. W. Dickes). Article 429 stipulated that delay in the evacuation of the Rhineland would be countenanced by the League of Nations *if at that time,* the periods set for the expiration of the occupation of the cities at the bridgeheads over the Rhine River, *there were not sufficient guarantees against an unprovoked aggression from Germany.* This meant that France should be furnished with adequate security before completing the withdrawal of Rhineland occupation forces.

17. Tardieu, *op. cit.,* 216.

18. Sénat, *Annales du débats,* 1920, Tome LXV, Annexe No. 562, 569-586.

19. *Ibid.,* 1920, Tome LXV, Annexe No. 562, 592-595.

20. *Ibid.,* 1920, Tome LXV, Annexe No. 562, 587-588.

21. *Ibid.,* 1920, Tome LXV, Annexe No. 562, 589-591.

22. *Ibid.,* 1920, Tome LXV, Annexe No. 562, 592-595.

23. *Ibid.,* 1920, Tome LXV, Annexe No. 563, 600.

24. Sénat, *État des Projets et Propositions de Loi soumis à L'Examin Du Sénat* (Paris, Imprimerie du Sénat, 1920), 129-130.

25. Noble, *Opinions at Paris*, 258-259.

26. *Ibid.*, 260.

27. Mermeix (pseudonym for Gabriel Terrail), *Le Combat des Trois,* 226-231. In this connection the letter of President Poincaré to Premier Clemenceau on the necessity for additional security beyond that contained in the Guarantee Treaties, should be noted. It follows in part:

"Paris, de 28 avril 1919.
Mon cher Président, [of the Council of Ministers]
. . . (here follows a discussion of the French need for the Rhine boundary) Nul n'appreciet a un plus haut prix que moi les offres d'alliances que M. le Président des États-Unis et M. le Premier Ministre de Grande-Bretagne ont généreusement faites à la France. Ce sera une grande et belle chose que l'association durable de nos trois Nations dans la défense du Droit et de la Liberté. Mais la precieuse assistance que nos amis nous donneront en cas d'agression germanique ne pourra malheureusement jamais être instantanée. Elle ne portera pas, d'autre part, directement, sur la garantie de la créance. Elle ne remplacera donc pas o'occupation J'ai pleine confiance que les Gouvernements alliés et associés se rendront compte cette situation et qu'ils . . . donner à la France, qui à tant souffert, la seule sûreté qui, à mes yeux, puisse garantir efficacement le payment de notre créance . . . Raymond Poincaré." (Quoted from M. des A. E., *Documents Diplomatiques,* document No. 8, 45-47). To the end of his term the French President remained unaltered in his opposition to the plans of Clemenceau for guaranteeing the security of France against Germany.

28. Thomas A. Bailey, *Woodrow Wilson and the Lost Peace,* (New York, 1944), 235-236.

CHAPTER FIVE

The British Reaction
to the Guarantee Pacts

Although this work deals largely with the relations of France and the United States, attention should be devoted to Great Britain's reaction to the aid pact. This interest stems largely from the British origin of the idea of the pledge to France as well as from the fact that Britain was a party to the pact. In large part this chapter will deal with the official actions of the British Parliament. Some consideration, however, will be given to a small segment of comment on the pact in the British press.

For more than a century preceding the Versailles Settlement, Britain's position was perhaps the most decisive and important in the struggles on the European continent. To a great extent that power stemmed from a freedom to act in any given situation. Thus the British were able to redress the shifts in the balance of power. Consequently, prior to 1919, any move to place the future freedom of action of a British Ministry under definite commitments was viewed with caution and distrust by His Majesty's officials. Lloyd George took a momentous step toward a new diplomatic policy when he offered to place Britain alongside the United States in pledging aid under certain conditions to France.

Most of the editorial opinion in Britain was disposed in a favorable way to the commitments with France. Beginning in the first week in July, 1919, many items relating to the aid agreement appeared in the press.[1] One interesting comment which

appeared in *The Times* of London was the assertion that the
Guarantee Treaty required approval by the Senate of the United
States before the British Parliament would act.[2] The assumption
was based on insufficient information and an inaccurate reading
of the texts of the conventions.

There were indications in some articles that the proposed
aid pact was popularly regarded as the guarantee of a peaceful
future. Perhaps it might be the seed which would grow and
mature into a harvest of universal harmony. Statesmen with clear
and comprehensive vision would be essential to the growth of
such an idea of security. After all, an idea had to have time to
develop.[3]

The purpose of the guarantees as the Paris correspondent
of the staid *Times* informed that paper's editor, was to ensure
the fulfillment of Germany's obligations in the Versailles Treaty.[4]
There was an expression of opinion that the aid agreement was
a wise undertaking. It was the editor's belief that the compelling
reasons for the conventions would appeal to the British and the
American peoples. Furthermore, the same arguments should
sway the practical statesmen — a familiarity with history and with
human nature. There was much to be said for France's desire
to obtain the strongest guarantees which prudent foresight could
furnish against the danger of another German invasion. The
League of Nations, in the considered judgment of French leaders,
did not provide sufficient protection. The appeal for aid was
justified by an opposition to becoming the future prey of Germany.[5]

An item which dealt with the proposed assistance pact appeared in *The Times* on the same day that Lloyd George submitted a significant bill for consideration by the House of Commons. According to the newspaper, that bill dealt with the
Anglo-French Treaty. By the terms of the agreement the guarantee given to France was made subject to approval of the
Imperial Parliament. It was hinted that a large number of the
members of the House of Commons very probably would be
surprised by the contents of the treaty. That was because of the
close secrecy in which the Ministry had kept the measure. No
public disclosure had been made by any of the Ministers. The

article also had declared that an exceptionally interesting constitutional point of view was involved. For centuries, it had been accepted as approved practice under the British unwritten constitution that the Crown exclusively was vested with the treaty making powers. Results were achieved through the device of the Crown acting on the advice of its ministers. Ratification by Parliament was not required. That practice was being followed in the case of the Versailles Treaty, but the Anglo-French Treaty was to be laid before the Parliament for formal ratification by statute. Here was the first step in that open diplomacy between nations which had been so strongly urged during the past five years. The article went on to hazard the guess that both Houses of Parliament would approve the work of the Prime Minister and that the Royal Assent would be given to the Treaty of Guarantee.[6]

Professor Arnold Wolfers has commented that popular feeling being what it was in Britain, ". . . if politics obeyed the rules of simple logic, . . . France could at least count on British military protection against Germany without . . . any specific commitment."[7] Diplomacy does not always follow the line of popular will. A nation which attempted to maintain that kind of foreign policy would soon find itself accused of insincerity and instability. It should be noted, however, that Britain's geographical proximity to France tended to reduce the security problems of both nations to a common denominator.

On Thursday, July 3, 1919, Britain's Parliament met to hear an address by Prime Minister Lloyd George who had selected that day to ask permission of the House of Commons to introduce two bills. These bills were to enforce a document which was described as ". . . the most momentous . . . to which the British Empire has ever affixed its seal . . . ."[8] While the speaker admitted that ordinarily it was unnecessary to obtain the approval of Parliament for a treaty, there were certain parts (of the Guarantee Pact) which required an Act of Parliament for its enforcement. He asked for the members' support in these words:

. . . I propose . . . a Bill in the usual form to enable His Majesty's Government . . . to obtain the sanction of Parliament to the Convention between His Majesty and the President of the French Republic. That Convention already . . . has been laid on the Table of the House . . . ."[9]

The House was informed by the Premier that he had been quite despondent of a future that might entail another war. He had not been in favor of all the compromises made at Paris,[10] but the Anglo-French aid convention with its American counterpart, gave promise to the world that one disturbing factor would be eliminated. That was encouraging. Mankind had gone on from war to war until some doubts existed as to whether conflicts would ever be stopped.[11] Then the speaker made an eloquent plea for the guarantees offered to France. He did not suppose that any member would object to giving aid to the French in the event of an unjustified attack upon them. The pledge was to be entered into with the approval of the Council of the League of Nations. Perhaps some might ask why the protection of the League was not enough for France or for any other nation. His own opinion, which happened to be the same as that of most French leaders, was that the League was an untried experiment — an unknown element in a world of practical affairs where power and force were needed. Moreover, France, within living memory, had been invaded twice by Germany. There was legitimate reason, therefore, for the French feeling of nervous apprehension. What security would be left when the forces of Britain and the United States had departed? Lloyd George answered this question in concluding his speech:

> . . . France sees herself there with only the Rhine between her and this foe . . . France says, "We would like to know that you, Britain, that you America, who helped to emancipate our soil, are still behind us if there is any wanton aggression." *I invite the British Parliament to say "Yes."*[12]

Lloyd George gave to the House of Commons some information concerning the possibility of adherence to the guarantee pact by other members of the British Dominions. The Anglo-French Treaty had a proviso to that effect. That stipulation had been included as the result of a development at Paris during the peace negotiations. Prevalent sentiment among the Dominion representatives was that British policy of aloofness from European quarrels should be resumed. So strong was that belief that not one of the Dominions desired to be associated with the Imperial Government in the assistance compact. Unless a Dominion Parliament expressly approved the agreement, there were to be no obligations incumbent upon the Dominion as a result of Parliamentary action at London.[13] That point of view was emphasized by the statement that, "The territorial arrangements for Europe, which found favour in the eyes of the Great Powers (France, Britain, and the United States) were regarded without much enthusiasm by the Dominion representatives . . . ."[14]

The House of Commons gave its final approval to the assistance agreement on July 21, 1919. Only eighteen days had elapsed since the measure had been first considered. That time was to contrast sharply with the action of the French Chamber of Deputies and even more so with that of the Senate of the United States.[15]

The House of Lords began its consideration of the aid pact on July 3, 1919. In his opening speech the Earl of Curzon stressed the importance of the undertaking by telling the Lords, in part, that, "No Government would desire to ratify a Treaty of this tremendous importance unless they knew that it was approved by Parliament and . . . the general . . . public opinion . . . ."[16]

Lord Bryce's brief speech in favor of the guarantee proposals was well received. The speech was concise.[17] Some desultory debate ensued which shortly thereafter resulted in a prediction by Lord Curzon that the House of Lords would approve the commitments for aid to France against a future German aggression. His Lordship also declared that he regarded this aid treaty as, "one of the most important guarantees . . . of peace in the world, which it is possible to create."[18] A brief recess then followed, but when the House met on July 24, it was agreed that the guarantees to France should have precedence over all other matters for that day. With no opposition the way was then clear for the third and final reading.[19] Thus the bill approving the agreement was given final passage. It was then returned to the House of Commons.[20] A Royal Assent was given to the measure and on November 20, 1919, London exchanged ratifications of the treaty with Paris.

The supplementary treaty was in reality an alliance between the two great English-speaking powers and France. It was a continuation of the wartime coalition. France was guarded — in theory — by the pledges of military support by Britain and the United States against unprovoked German aggression. By swiftly approving the pact, Britain and France disclosed their evaluation of it. To them, "This double guarantee was the corner stone of the whole settlement from the point of view of both European countries."[21]

With the completion of official action on the part of the French and the British governments, all that remained to validate the treaty was a similar move of approval and ratification by the United States.

> "And yet I wish we had taken the other road . . . ."
> Colonel E. M. House in *The Intimate Papers of Colonel House*

NOTES

1. *The Times* (London), July 2, 1919.

2. July 2, 1919.

3. *The Times* (London), July 3, 1919.

4. July 1, 1919.

5. *The Times* (London), July 1, 1919.

6. *Ibid.*, July 4, 1919.

7. Wolfers, *Between Two Wars*, 231.

8. *Parliamentary Debates, Fifth Series*, House of Commons, *Official Report*, Vol. 117 (1919) 1211. Hereafter cited as H. of C., *Parl. Debs.*, 5th Series.

9. *Ibid.*, 5th Series, Vol. 117, 1211-1222.

10. Lloyd George, *The Peace Treaties*, I, 427.

11. H. of C., *op. cit.*, 5th Series, Vol. 117, 1227-1234.

12. *Ibid.*, 5th Series, Vol. 117, 1223-1224. [The italics have been added.] To a question that such an engagement as the pledge to aid France might involve England needlessly in every European war, the Prime Minister

answered, "No. It only engages us if there be wanton provocation on the part of Germany. That is clearly and distinctly stated in the document itself. If there be a wanton attack on the part of Germany, which I do not anticipate, because I think Germany has had enough, I cannot imagine anyone hesitating . . . to . . . aid . . . that gallant country which has suffered more than any other . . . from this wanton aggression . . ." (H. of C., *Parl. Debs.*, 5th Series, Vol. 117 (1919), 1224-1225).

13. Temperley (ed.), *History of Peace Conference*, VI, 359.

14. *Ibid.*, VI, 358.

15. Wolfers, *op. cit.*, 15.

16. *Parliamentary Debates, Fifth Series*, House of Lords, *Official Report*, Vol. 35, (1919), 155-158. Hereafter cited as H. of L., *Parl. Debs.*, 5th Series.

17. *Ibid.*, 5th Series, Vol. 35, (1919), 1007-1023.

18. *Ibid.*, Vol. 35, (1919), 158-181.

19. *Ibid.*, Vol. 35, (1919), 1024-1035.

20. *Ibid.*, Vol. 35, (1919), 1036-1037.

21. Frank H. Simonds, *How Europe Made Peace Without America* (New York, 1927), 46-47.

CHAPTER SIX

The Guarantee Treaty—
How the United States
Reacted to it

In the numerous books, monographs, and other studies of the struggle in the Senate of the United States over the question of accepting or rejecting the Versailles Settlement, there have been two salient factors which have appeared many times.[1] One was the part played by the personalities involved in the bitter fight (whose principal casualty was the cause of world peace); the other was the shattering blow which the United States' refusal of the settlement dealt to proposals for guaranteeing international security through an organization for collective action. Heretofore, although some recognition has been given to the existence of the aid pact, no attempts have been made to do much more than that. No study of the reaction of the United States to the pledge to France had been made before this one.

With the conclusion in 1921 of a separate peace with Germany, the United States specifically disclaimed official responsibility for assisting in the keeping of the "Versailles made peace."[2] All of the benefits accruing under that agreement were accepted, however, but none of the liabilities. This was a new pattern of diplomacy.

The Senate Committee on Foreign Relations was given the aid to France treaty in 1919. It made no formal report on the treaty. The following sentence needs no further clarification:

"Not considered by the Senate; returned to the Secretary of State by resolution of the Senate February 12, 1935; unperfected Treaties H-9."[3] Although the supplementary treaty was not *officially* an issue in the attempts to secure Senatorial "advice and consent to ratify" the Versailles peace terms, there was sufficient interest in the first-named document to provoke much controversy. However, the significance of the guarantee pact lay in its implication that the United States — acting through its Chief of State — was aware of the close correlation of the security needs of Western Europe with its own. Professor Richard W. Van Alstyne has stated that "This treaty [of guarantee] was subsequently swamped by the quarrel in the United States over the greater treaty of Versailles, but it was of historic importance none the less."[4]

It has been said, "There is no such thing as an 'American attitude.' It is a composite. A great welter of forces come into play to create what we call public opinion."[5]

This chapter has as part of its purpose the presentation and analysis of that opinion. The pronouncements by the President, the debates in the Senate, the accounts in the newspapers and magazines, and the personal expressions of private individuals have been combined to portray the official and the un-official views and reactions to the Guarantee Treaty. As such they have great significance in the composite result.

Before President Wilson left France to return to the United States on June 29, 1919, he held a press conference. Two days later he was questioned as to the nature of the undertaking of the United States and Great Britain to come to the help of France with military force. The word *undertaking* had been used deliberately because of Wilson's dislike for the word *alliance*. At first the President was in doubt as to what was meant. Then he stated this must mean the French agreement and that it really was an undertaking.[6] Wilson was reluctant to discuss the details of the supplementary treaty. That reluctance was evidenced in his speech on July 10, 1919, when the President personally placed the Versailles Treaty before the Senate for action. After having stated that the peace settlement was the hope of mankind, Wilson continued:

I shall presently have occasion to lay before you a special
treaty with France whose object is the temporary protection
of France from unprovoked aggression by the power with
whom this treaty has been negotiated. Its terms link it with
this treaty. *I take the liberty, however, of reserving it, because
of its importance, for special explication on another occasion
. . . .* We are no longer isolated and devoted to a policy
which has only our own interest and advantage for its object . . . .[7]

This decision to submit the Guarantee Treaty at a later time,
has never been satisfactorily explained by Wilson. By the terms
of the (Franco-American) treaty, it was to be submitted to the
Senate at the same time as the Versailles Treaty. The delay was
very unfortunate inasmuch as it produced a suspicious attitude
in the Senate toward the agreement.

Wilson had reason to believe that the Executive and the
Senate would be antagonistic to each other in matters of foreign
policy. He had so stated in one of his books some years before.[8]
Now, many of his pronouncements of the past were used with
telling effect against him. Such expressions as, ". . . I shall never
myself consent to an entangling alliance,"[9] and ". . . there should
be no leagues or alliances within the League of Nations"[10] were
taken from their context and used in that manner. The President's
belief that, "We are facing a decision now in which we cannot
afford to make a mistake,"[11] should have impelled him to be
more concerned about his leadership.[12]

When Senate clamor for the details of the French Aid Pact
had become so insistent that echoes were reaching the White
House in such volume that Wilson could ignore them no longer,
he sent a message formally placing the Guarantee Treaty before
that body.[13] This was on July 29, 1919. After informing the
Senate in a courteous way that an early approval would be most
welcome, the President gave his reasons (at least those which
he cared to recognize publicly) for signing the treaty. Chiefly
these were a special feeling of friendship for France and a deep
sense of obligation to repay a debt contracted long ago.[14] Wilson
was finding — just as had many of his predecessors — that *it was*

easier to end a war than to make a peace acceptable to the Senate.

There is a strange contrast between these weak and unconvincing arguments for delay in presenting the treaty and the words and actions of Wilson while in Paris. The pitiable excuses which were offered in July, 1919, may have been the result of some of the effects of the President's illness in April. Again, that may not be true. One is at a loss to account for the real reasons. Those which have been advanced are not consistent with Wilson's character, or his previously known attitudes and utterances.

Some wag has jokingly remarked, "The Lord had made the Earth in six days but he didn't have the Senate to contend with." The message transmitting the treaty to the Senate might well have been much stronger and a more logical case could have been made for the pledge. Fewer personal reasons and more arguments for national security might have impressed the wary Senators. There was a stern lesson in the words of Theodore Roosevelt that, "I wish every American felt that American policy is a world policy and that we are and shall be identified in the future with all great questions."[15] The President had assumed quite accurately that the American people were tired of war and bloodshed. He was not justified in proceeding from that assumption to the belief that an overwhelming majority would be willing to approve a protective alliance. In effect, that was what he was asking the Senate to do. Robert Lansing had raised a pointed question as to how the United States with its traditional policy of avoiding entangling alliances would receive such an idea. He believed it would be rejected.[16]

Events were to prove that the Secretary of State was on firm ground. There was no doubt in Lansing's mind that Wilson sincerely believed in the need for the guarantees to France.[17] Despite the fact that the Chairman of the Senate Foreign Relations Committee, Senator Henry Cabot Lodge of Massachusetts, had no quarrel with the special assistance treaty — in fact the idea of holding Germany in check met with his approval — it was consigned to oblivion by that group. Lodge had asked the Senate on July 29, 1919, to receive the message and the treaty in open executive session. He also made a request that the injunction of secrecy be removed from the treaty. When the senator from

California, James D. Phelan, inquired whether Lodge intended to consider and to act upon the treaty at that time, the reply was "I want to have the message read and then to have it take the usual course required by the rule."[18] As soon, therefore, as the reading was completed, Lodge asked that the treaty formally be referred to the committee of which he was chairman and that it also be printed for the use of the Senate.[19] This was done. There was no official consideration of the aid agreement, although it was much discussed and referred to in senatorial debates. Such questions as whether it was constitutional, whether it had merits, whether it could be interpreted intelligently enlivened many an otherwise dull hour in the Senate.

In considering the complex question of official as well as unofficial American reaction to the Guarantee Treaty with the implications which it held for American security and diplomacy there is perhaps no more *enlightening* feature than that which is provided by a study of senatorial opinion. As early as May 28, 1919,[20] Senator Joseph T. Robinson (Arkansas) in a speech made on that date, declared that he did not regard as necessary an agreement to go to the aid of France. He was certain that the League of Nations would afford enough security. The Senator from Arkansas stated that he had read press notices dated May 9, to the effect that Senator Lodge had withheld comment, but that Senator Borah (Idaho) opposed the assistance pact because he wanted the matter of participation in any future wars to be decided by the generation involved. Senator Lawrence Y. Sherman (Illinois) was against any proposal of that type, and Senator Charles Curtis (Kansas) had voiced his disapproval. Senator George H. Moses (New Hampshire) stated that he preferred the tripartite agreement to the League as then drawn.[21]

The preceding incidents took place *before* a treaty had been drawn up and approved in Paris. On June 2, 1919, Senator Hiram Johnson (California) launched a tirade against the pledge to aid France which, he said, had grave implications for the United States. It was just another example of the secret deals that were being made. He had read the cable which Wilson had sent to Tumulty (presidential secretary at the White House). The cable intimated that there was no mystery or privacy about the promise made to France. Johnson bitterly criticized the lack of information on the pledge, stated that apparently it was the first pledge of its kind in American history, and sarcastically hinted that it was only a forerunner of the evils which the League of Nations would bring. Then he asked the rhetorical question, "Do you realize the full meaning of the alliance with France?"[22] It meant, he went on, that the United States was pledging that American boys would police the world; that we would destroy the Monroe Doctrine, and finally, that this nation would be at the mercy of European diplomats. Therefore he wanted none of it.[23]

More than a month elapsed before the aid pact was mentioned again in the Senate. On July 15, 1919, Senator George W. Norris (Nebraska) told the Senate that he was opposed to engagements which would have the effect of entangling alliances.[24] But on that same day, the Senator from Alabama, Oscar W. Underwood, pleaded for some kind of organization or alliance which would make the world more secure. He believed that the efforts to stabilize peace — through the Covenant and the Guarantee Pact — could be effective. He did not wish to return to the days of barbarous national morals in which the strength of a nation determined what it was allowed to do in society.[25] This was after the President had submitted the Versailles Treaty to the Senate on July 10. Underwood was followed by Senator Atlee Pomerene (Ohio) on July 21, 1919, who made reference to the fact that science had so annihilated distances that the United States no longer could say that what happened in Europe was of no concern to anyone else. He pointed out that if Washington were alive he would view the events of the day and counsel accordingly. It was inconceivable that the Father of his Country would say, "Make no alliance with either Great Britain or France; let them stand between us and destruction; let them bear the brunt of the battle while we stand aloof." To assume he would make such a reply would be to insult the memory of Washington. The United States need have no fear of temporary alliances for extraordinary emergencies.[26]

In a similar vein was the substance of an address given on July 22, 1919, by Senator Edwin S. Johnson (South Dakota).

His plea was for a realistic approach to the problem of how to
avoid future wars. His words were impressively earnest and were
of a timeliness beyond the year in which they were spoken. He
said, in part:

> . . . if we are opposed to an alliance with other great nations
> to prevent war, if we have reached a time when we really
> believe that a war in Europe is no concern of ours, then we
> might as well at once prepare for another war for the actions
> logically to follow such a position will be the same as have
> always been taken in olden times . . . . The next war, should
> it come, will be fought almost entirely from the air and under
> the water . . . It will be so . . . destructive, so terrible in its
> consequences that the power of good government may cease
> to exist. We may help to destroy our own institutions . . . .
> It is time people became awakened to the situation as it exists
> today, and not allow themselves to be lulled to sleep in
> imaginary security.[27]

So true were these statements that more than a quarter of a
century later they could be repeated with little change to describe
a similar situation.

Furthermore, with each passing day the Senate became more
displeased in not having had the Guarantee Treaty formally submitted to it. On July 24, the discontent broke into the open when
Senator Frank B. Brandegee (Connecticut) asked for permission
to make an important statement.[28] When the request had been
obtained, Brandegee, a violent opponent of Wilson, recalled the
President's promise to lay before the Senate, later, a special
treaty with France. The inattentive Senate was told that a copy
of *Harvey's Weekly* (a magazine edited by George Harvey) had
arrived that morning. In it was a challenging suggestion that
Article 4 of the Franco-American Treaty had been violated by
Wilson because he had not submitted that pact to the Senate
simultaneously with the Versailles Treaty. The Connecticut Senator ventured the guess that such a provision to submit both
treaties to the Senate at the same time had been inserted at the
instigation of Clemenceau. The French leader, he said, knew
that Wilson was unreliable. The Senate had a right to know the

contents of both treaties when they were so closely linked. Perhaps the President feared the two treaties would work at cross purposes; perhaps he did not want them to be too closely contrasted, compared and analyzed. Or it might be that there were provisions in the aid pact which should not be revealed to the Senate. At any rate it was the constitutional right of that body to have before it an authentic copy of the alliance with France.[29]

One can hardly avoid making the observation that much of what the Senator said was true. Certainly Wilson's ineptness in handling the assistance treaty contributed mightily to the case against it. Unwittingly or not, much effective ammunition was passed by the President to his opponents in the Senate. The Chief Executive's lack of frankness and directness in his dealings with the Senators produced an uncooperative response to the treaty. By all means, it seems, Wilson should have at least adhered to the text of the Guarantee Treaty which required that it be submitted to the Senate simultaneously with the Versailles settlement. Nebraska Senator Gilbert Hitchcock inquired where the speaker had obtained his copy of the treaty as it did not seem to be in accord with the authentic copy which he had.[30] A spirited exchange of accusations of bad faith and misrepresentation closed the incident. The point was made that two weeks before, the American press had carried a full coverage of the aid treaty, yet Brandegee was posing as if he had just discovered the text in the magazine he had received that morning.[31]

After that Senator John S. Williams (Mississippi) interposed the legalistic observation that it was impossible to submit the two treaties at the *same time,* and that he did not believe President Wilson could "any more satisfy five or six senators in this body than that poor helpless lamb of Aesop's fable could have satisfied that other wolf."[32]

Senator Lodge then offered the following resolution (Senate Resolution 132) which, in part, stated:

. . . Whereas said proposed treaty with France has been submitted to the Chamber of Deputies of the French Republic; . . . therefore be it resolved that the President is hereby respectfully requested, if not incompatible with the public interest, to transmit to the Senate the said proposed treaty with France, to the end that the Senate may consider said treaty in connection with the treaty of peace with Germany.[33]

Senator Robinson's objection blocked the immediate consideration of the resolution, but the temper of the Republican majority had been revealed. If the treaty would not be submitted willingly and freely, there would be an official request for it. This was tantamount to telling the President that the Senate was irritated with his method of handling the matter. The Senate was not averse to so informing him. Before the proposed resolution had achieved its purpose (on July 29), other senators had added to the confusion of ideas on the purpose, intent, and value of the guarantees to France.

Senator Hitchcock took the position that such an agreement to go to the aid of France would serve as a warning to Germany which could prevent a war of aggression. An advance knowledge of the position of the United States would act as a deterrent of moves such as had been made in 1870 and in 1914. But Borah disagreed. His argument was that no alliance was necessary if the League of Nations would function as it had been planned. To give a supplemental treaty of guarantee was similar to signing a promissory note twice. Therefore nothing was added by the second signature since it was by the same party. Hitchcock commented that Borah was bringing in the aid agreement somewhat in advance.[34] But, he continued, although he, himself did not think such pledges were necessary,[35] the people of France did because of their fear of Germany. France knew that the League would not spring into existence overnight. Therefore, something was needed as a temporary bridge of security during that period. Borah expressed his opinion that Germany would not be powerful enough to attack any nation for the next twenty years. It was more likely the time would be thirty years. In the meantime, why was there need for an additional treaty to protect France?[36] Florida's Senator, Duncan U. Fletcher, succeeded in drawing an unqualified statement of opposition to the proposed aid treaty from Borah who stated, "yes, I am opposed to it."[37] He was against the treaty because it contemplated war — a war which he, Borah, was certain would come. But in case of such a conflict, the Idaho Senator was not sure that participation by the United States was necessary or that this nation would have to go to the rescue of France. The Nebraskan said he was not prepared to cope with such an involved "mental antic."

The day before the arrival of the President's message of transmittal formally placing the supplementary pact before the Senate, that august body was enlivened by additional references to said treaty. Senator Robert L. Owen (Oklahoma) disclaimed the assertion that had been made alleging that such an alliance as was contemplated in the treaty was an entangling one.[38] Also on this same day Senator Williams of Mississippi exposed the July 24 speech of Brandegee as a carefully planned trick. He said that Lodge, Borah, Brandegee, and Philander C. Knox (Pennsylvania) had met the evening before and that Brandegee was told to feign surprise the next day at the contents of the French Aid Treaty. This was to be done in such a way that the Senate would believe the entire document was unfamiliar to him. Brandegee was also to attack Wilson for failing to submit the treaty in accordance with the provision of article 4. Williams concluded that such tactics had only one purpose — that of belittling the President.[39]

When Senator Williams had completed his speech, Brandegee arose and gave some cogent reasons for Wilson's immediate submission of the French treaty to the Senate. He emphasized that the two treaties (Versailles and Assistance) had been laid simultaneously before the British Parliament. The same was true in regard to the French Chamber of Deputies. Brandegee then stated that:

> If I had my way I would not proceed one day further in the consideration of the Treaty of Versailles in view of what the President of the United States has told us and in view of the fact that France and England have both treaties before their parliaments. I would not proceed one day further with the consideration of this treaty until I had the other link. I would not take one link and have the other gentleman (Wil-

son) keep the other link. I want to know what the two links are for, and why they should not be kept together. I think we are entitled to it, and I think the country is entitled to it. . . .[40]

Regardless of the fact that the Connecticut Senator was very strongly prejudiced against Wilson and his work at Paris, it would be difficult to deny the logic of the arguments which he had presented. Whether or not this implied threat to delay further consideration of the Treaty of Versailles until the Guarantee Treaty was submitted to the Senate, was the final argument which induced Wilson to act, may never be known. At any rate the President yielded and sent the supplementary treaty to Capitol Hill the next day.

Senator Edward J. Gay (Louisiana) gave a vivid picture of what might occur if the United States did not participate in the world's efforts to keep peace. Speaking in the Senate on the 28th of July (1919) he declared, ". . . the special treaty into which we are asked to enter with France . . . specifically mentions certain acts preparatory or threatening in character . . . upon the occurrence of which our active assistance may be called for."[41] And he added, ". . . civilization must destroy war or war will destroy civilization . . . ."[42] No peace has ever outlasted the force which imposed it. It bound only so long as the enemy saw the gleaming point of your sword behind the parchment. France had asked for a defensive alliance with Great Britain and the United States against Germany. If those nations would be true to themselves and to the impulses of their common origin, they would league themselves for the harmony and the well-being of mankind.[43] The argument for the defensive assistance of France was based upon the contribution which such an action would make to the prospects for peace. From July 29 to August 5, 1919, there was little reference to the French aid pact.

On the latter date, Montana's Senator, Thomas J. Walsh, offered a resolution[44] to inquire into the constitutionality of the guarantee pledge. Two days later, the resolution was called up for action. The Senate was enlightened by Senator Frank B.

Kellogg's (Minnesota) long discourse on the source and scope of the treaty-making power. Senator Walsh asked for approval of the resolution. Some local newspaper reports, according to Walsh, had hinted that senatorial opposition to the defense pact with France was centered on two points. These were, first, that the pact was directly antagonistic to the tradition of no entangling alliances; and, second, that it subverted the constitutional right of Congress to determine the question of war or peace. Senator Borah had maintained that the treaty had all the force of an alliance, but Wilson had stated that it was not properly an alliance. For the purpose of removing any constitutional questions, the resolution should be passed.[45] Approval was given soon after the Montana Senator had concluded his speech.

A very important exchange of views between the President and the members of the Senate Committee on Foreign Relations took place at the White House on August 19, 1919. The meeting was at Wilson's invitation.[46] After some remarks relative to the Treaty of Peace and the purposes of the League Covenant, the group questioned the President concerning the special treaty with France. Senator Borah wanted to know if there were any underlying reasons (comparable to a *quid pro quo*), or secret agreements of a legal or moral nature, for making the assistance pact. He meant in addition to the reason publicly given that Articles X and XI needed support.[47] The President said there were none. Whereupon Borah then observed that the treaty was simply a moral obligation entered into with France.

Wilson also was asked if he thought the treaty provision which required the approval of the Council of the League was a wise one and if it violated the constitutional provision which required the advice and consent of the Senate. Such was not the belief in the mind of the President. Brandegee made the inquiry, "Do you think it is wise for us to adopt the Franco-American treaty, which in substance provides that we cannot denounce it until the Council . . . gives us permission to do so or agrees to denounce it?"[48] Wilson answered, "I do, Senator. I have a very strong feeling with regard to . . . France and also a very keen appreciation of her own sense of danger, and I think it would be one of the handsomest acts of history to enter into that."[49]

Brandegee was not convinced. He thought it unwise for this nation to tie itself to any foreign nation. A very important point was then raised. Wilson was asked by the Connecticut Senator that if it were true that the treaty to aid France had been designed to be a temporary one, would it not have been prudent to include a time limit in the terms. Such a limit as ten years for example. The League of Nations should certainly be effective enough to preserve the territorial integrity and the political independence of its members by that time. The only objection to that, as Wilson saw it, was the psychological effect on the two countries. He admitted that there was no other alternative, if the time limit were not included, than to guarantee the aid indefinitely or until the Council released the signers from their obligations.[50] Senator McCumber wanted the President to explain why there was need for the special aid treaty when the same object was to be attained through the operation of Article X of the Covenant. As Wilson construed it, there might be delay on the part of the Council, and by the respective governments in executing the League's decisions. The aid treaty was intended to bridge that delay. After a short discussion of the question of keeping American troops in Europe, the meeting was adjourned.[51] More than three and one-half hours had been spent in canvassing the situation. Judging from their actions later, most of the members who participated in the conference were unaffected by Wilson's arguments and explanations.

There was an indication on August 20, 1919, in a speech by Senator Albert B. Fall (New Mexico), that the idea of defending France was not unacceptable to some members of the Senate. He defended making such a move if first, all references to the League were removed from the aid treaty. He believed that no constitutional objections could be raised against such a proposal.[52] The question of constitutionality was disposed of by a report made on September 22, 1919, by the Judiciary Committee.[53] Senator Thomas J. Walsh (Montana) submitted the opinion of the group that the treaty with France was clearly within the power of the United States to make, and that it was in accordance with international law and custom.[54] On September 24, 1919, Senator Joseph S. Frelinghuysen (New Jersey) spoke scornfully of the idea of helping Europe to keep the peace and of the projected commitments to "police the Rhine."[55] Harry S. New of Indiana informed the Senate the next day that America would be unable to withdraw from the treaty with France because the latter was a member of the League Council. He did not want any pledges of "guarantees in perpetuity."[56] Senator John W. Smith (Maryland) touched briefly on the value of the pledges of aid in retarding Germany from future warlike acts. He said, "The oceans are avenues of access, possibly, for attack, and not insuperable and protecting barriers . . . ."[57] On September 27, Senator Fall advanced the argument that the separate treaty with France was a violation of the spirit, the words, and the letter of the Versailles Treaty. He was not able to clarify that stand to many of the other members.[58] Only four days later, October 1, another Senator, Joseph O. Wolcott (Delaware) advocated the approval of the special aid pact as suitable for an extraordinary emergency.[59] Appeals to the memory of Washington were made in the Senate on October 6, by Joseph I. France (Maryland) who opinioned that Washington would not advocate a policy of narrow isolation, and would not oppose the plans for international cooperation.[60]

Furthermore, on October 14, Chairman Lodge made the assertion that Wilson had not cooperated with the Senate in supplying the necessary documents[61] and other information on the French treaty. Francis E. Warren of Wyoming, on October 17, excoriated the separate treaties as examples of a lack of faith in the League's guarantee against unprovoked external aggression.[62] He was followed on October 21,[63] by Seldon P. Spencer (Missouri) who read into the official record an article by a Thomas F. Millard on the "Anglo-French-American Entente or Alliance," in which it was stated that the treaties were in effect a tripartite defensive alliance. Nothing but confusion, according to the Senator, could result from such a pledge of support.[64] A short time before the vote on the approval or rejection of the Versailles Treaty on November 19, 1919, Senator Brandegee had urged the Senate to accept instead of the aid treaty, section 5 of

Senate Joint Resolution 76.[65] "France will be satisfied with that
. . . . All they want to know is that they will be secure. I think
we ought to do something for France."[66] Brandegee made the
charge that the United States had prevented France from protecting herself when she could have had the means to do so. The
French had wanted the Rhine as a boundary between themselves
and Germany. The Senator was sure that the League and its
guarantees meant little to the leaders in Paris. He accused Wilson
of having made' the French "back down" from their stand and
take as a substitute, the treaties with Britain and the United
States. "Maybe they will not get either now. I do not know. I
hope they will . . . ."[67] This was striking evidence that some
support existed among the Republican leaders in the Senate for
the defense of France whether that aid should be given by a
treaty or otherwise.[68]

In March, 1920, Senator James A. Reed of Missouri made
a vitriolic attack on President Wilson's motives for offering
France the Guarantee Treaty in 1919. In a speech of March 2,
Reed charged Wilson with telling the conference at Paris that
the world's peace would be lost without a League. Wilson had
threatened to withdraw from the conference unless his terms
were met and unless France and Britain would yield to him on
several matters. Then, according to Reed, France was told by
the President:

> I agree that, in addition to the League of Nations' protection,
> you ought to have for some years of time an absolute guar-
> anty of the assistance of Great Britain and of America in
> case you are unjustly attacked by Germany. Therefore, I
> propose to recommend to the Senate, and do recommend,
> that it shall pledge the last drop of blood of our boys and.
> the last dollar of our treasure to defend you against unjust
> attack by Germany.[69]

No comment is required to determine the attitude of the speaker
toward Wilson and the assistance pact. Although a member of
the Democratic Party, Reed was bitter in his assaults on the
party's titular head. Eleven days before the final vote on the

motion for the Senate to advise and consent to the ratification of the Versailles Treaty (March 19, 1919), the chairman of the Foreign Relations Committee, Senator Lodge, made a final reference to the Guarantee Treaty. He said, in part, "I think she (France) desires to have protection against the repetition of such sufferings as she had endured, and I think that is a feeling which we all must share . . . ."[70] But Lodge's Committee allowed the aid pact to remain dormant.[71] The document was returned to the State Department in 1935 by the Senate. A niche in the filing cases of the archives was the final resting place of the treaty. Mementos of other lost causes were there too.

Expressions of opinion on the aid pact are as varied as the individuals who made them. One of the most interesting was that of ex-President William H. Taft. Taft was working in the Republican Party for not only the acceptance of the League of Nations' idea but also for the assumption of responsibility for peace through the making of other commitments. He remarked that if the United States withdrew from its responsibilities there would be a return to the concept of alliances, balance of power, and a jockeying for positions of advantage.[72] William C. Bullitt had participated in much of the discussion at Paris during the peace conference. His disagreement over the policies to be followed and with the terms of the final settlements made, prompted his resignation on May 17, 1919, as an assistant in the State Department. The letter resigning that post was sent to Robert Lansing, the Secretary of State. In part, it follows:

> . . . I respectfully submit . . . my resignation as an assistant in the Department of State, Attaché to the American Commission to Negotiate Peace . . . . It is my conviction that . . . the United States will be drawn into them [wars] by the obligations undertaken . . . in the special understanding with France. I believe that the welfare of the American people and mankind would be promoted by the refusal of the United States to sign or ratify . . . the understanding with France.[73]

Senator Lodge was aware of Bullitt's opposition to the Versailles Treaty and also to the supplementary treaty. The public hearings of the Senate were enlivened on September 12, 1919, by the revelation of some confidential conversations with Lansing by Bullitt who had been called as a witness. The witness stated that he and Lansing were opposed to the work done at Paris and that the Secretary of State had told him, "I believe that if the Senate could only understand what this Treaty means . . . it would unquestionably be defeated, but I wonder if they will ever understand what it lets them in for."[74] Of course such testimony was heavily damaging to the prospects for an impartial consideration of the two treaties by the Senate. Whether true or not, the appearance of dissension among the Presidential advisers was a serious blow to the friends of the work done at Paris. Lansing had told Wilson of his opposition to the French aid treaty. This was in Paris in March and April of 1919. Although he admitted there were strong arguments in favor of such a step as that contemplated by the treaty with France, Lansing was against it. He said that he considered the policy of doing so very bad when viewed from the standpoint of national interests. Also it was of doubtful value because of the almost certain rejection of it by the United States Senate.[75] This strong isolationist view is in vivid contrast with Lansing's more internationalist outlook in 1915. Perhaps he had become more conservative and paid more attention in 1919 to what he thought of as actions for saving the interests of America.

In addition, Lansing believed the treaty was a mistake as it discredited Article X of the Covenant.[76] Such a pledge might lead to a demand for a similar guarantee by any nation which was disposed to demand such pledges. The narrowness of such a legalistic mind was never so clear as in the continued insistence by Lansing that American rights were being jeopardized. The majority of the members of the American Commission to Negotiate Peace had been in agreement with Lansing that the principle of a special guarantee to France was dangerous to the League of Nations and might wreck the whole peace structure as well. Henry White,[77] in a vigorous and straightforward manner, had opposed the agreement with France by saying that he believed a separate peace should be signed with Germany if some amicable settlement could not be made with France.[78]

Another member, General Tasker H. Bliss, stated later (in 1920) that he agreed with the French point of view that in the event of another war France would have little chance for success unless she had an alliance. He believed, further, that if a war did come — whether there was an alliance or not — it was his hope that the United States would go more promptly than in 1914 to the aid of France. The General predicted that it would be better to minimize the possibility of such a future war by the modification of the policy of his nation's aloofness from European affairs.[79]

The attitude of Colonel House on the assistance treaty seems to have varied from time to time. He declared in June after the treaties were signed that, "The United States could not afford to leave the peace settlement to Europe, thus risking another war in the future."[80] The offer of House to go before the Senate and testify in favor of the agreements signed at Paris was made in spite of the fact that he was quite ill at the time and had just returned from Europe (October 12, 1919). Generally speaking, the Colonel was in favor of the commitments to aid France. On October 13, 1919, he sent a letter to Senator Lodge pointing out that illness had confined him to his bed since leaving Paris, and stating that, "I am asking Commander McLean . . . to explain to you my condition and when I would . . . be able to come to Washington in the event your Committee think I may give any information which may be useful."[81] House was not called to testify. Later in November 1919, he sent a letter to Wilson asking him to advise Senator Hitchcock to save the treaty (even with reservations) to avoid losing all the agreements reached at Paris. To do so, House said, ". . . would be a disaster not less to civilization than to you."[82] Charles Homer Haskins, a noted historian who served as an adviser at the Paris meeting, believed there was justification for the treaty of assistance because it would prevent another war. He said the world should have learned that the Franco-German frontier was an international matter upon which world peace depended. The Anglo-American guarantee would prove superfluous if Germany refrained from unprovoked aggression. There was a useful purpose such a pact could serve.[83]

Furthermore, the general uncertainty which prevailed in the United States in 1919 and 1920 regarding the aid pact was heightened still more. This resulted from the part played by the magazines and newspapers of the nation. One writer, H. N. Brailsford, an English liberal, stated in the *New Republic* that he was opposed to the assistance treaty because it gave France too much leeway in her political action. If immoderate circumstances should force France into war, she would have the pledged help of the United States (and also of Great Britain).[84] According to another popular magazine of the day, Elihu Root had written to Senator Lodge that the United States should agree to go to the aid of France, if attacked, and that we should make this very plain.[85]

At the same time but in an entirely different manner and from another point of view George Harvey was attacking the pledge of aid to France because it was linked with the League Covenant. He asserted that if the treaty were to apply to France it would in time separate us from our traditional policy of abstaining from alliances of a permanent nature.[86] Thus in that respect, Lodge and Harvey were in complete agreement. If Wilson had separated the main treaty from the supplementary one and had placed a time limit for the enforcement of the obligations assumed, there might not have been such severe opposition in the Senate. The *Literary Digest* quoted Senator Borah as declaring that all of Wilson's work at Paris had been undone by his making by means of the Anglo-French-American Treaty an alliance for war.[87] The *New Republic* accused the President of an unwarranted twisting of words to achieve an alliance with France which could be reconciled with Article X of the Covenant.[88] The real purpose of the alliance was, in the words of the magazine editors:

> . . . to create a Franco-British-American bloc for diplomatic purposes. For the *Quai d'Orsay* knows, though Mr. Wilson may not, that the *words* of an alliance mean nothing, that the *fact* of the alliance is all-important.[89]

A cross-section of newspaper attitudes on the subject was presented by a nationally circulated magazine which made a survey of the question. According to that source, the Kansas City *Times* favored the guarantees, while the New York *Times* accepted such an agreement but desired that some leeway be left to the United States to interpret her course of action in any future troubles (how this was to be done was not explained). It was all very puzzling to the Boston *Transcript*. That paper wanted to know a suitable explanation which could be made for having a tripartite alliance outside the League to protect France, a member of the league. The New York *Sun* opined that it would be impossible to pledge American assistance to France in one treaty and accomplish disarmament in another document. That popular confidence in the League and the Versailles Treaty would be shaken by a special pact with France was the attitude of *The Republican* in Springfield, Massachusetts. A New York paper, the *Courrier des États-Unis,* expressed only the highest of praise for the assistance pact with France.[90] But the Philadelphia *Public Ledger* showed its disapproval by an editorial entitled "Americans do not love European Alliances."

The St. Louis *Globe Democrat* was skeptical as to whether the American people wanted to enter such a far-reaching compact as the assistance treaty. In New York, the *Brooklyn Citizen* declared that the proposed aid pact was an offensive as well as a defensive treaty against Germany, but the Seattle (Washington) *Times* stated there was no need for the treaty if the League was practical. If the League did not work, America should not be tied by an "entangling alliance." The New York *World* insisted there was absolutely no relation between the idea of the balance of power and the French Guarantee Treaty, and that such a step did not involve a departure from American traditions, to which the New York *Evening Post* added its stamp of approbation. The New York *Herald* thought the French aid pact was a confession of the "impotence of the League of Nation's guarantee," but the New York *Tribune* asserted American security would be enhanced by the measure. The Chicago *Daily News* believed that American interests would be served along with those of France by adopting the treaty, and pointed out that since we had made powerful enemies in Europe, we would need friends.[91] An interesting and somewhat unusual suggestion was made by the Chicago *Tribune* which objected to the aid agreement because America had failed to secure anything that was a recognized and particular obligation in reciprocity. Such a suitable 'obligation,' said the editor, might be for England to guarantee to bar trouble from our shores with her fleet in case necessity arose.[92] The *Literary Digest* quoted an un-named Michigan editor (listed as an independent in politics) as having expressed the idea that the proposed Treaty of Great Britain, the United States and France was merely a pledge that we would do again what we had found it essential to do before.[93]

The division of opinion in 1919 in the American press was about evenly divided over the advisability of accepting the guarantee treaty. It was to be expected that certain papers would oppose such a move. Likewise, those sections of the press which were published in Democratic strongholds, such as the South, could be counted on to uphold the President's action. There were exceptions, but they were not important. During the period from May 10, 1919,[94] to September, 1919, apparently, there was more approval of the assistance pact than there was opposition to it. The exact amounts of each cannot be ascertained. There was an increasing acceptance, too, at that time of the idea expressed in an article in the *New Independent* magazine, which referred to the League Covenant and the aid pact in stating that we might lose the war which had been won, by neglecting to assume our position of world responsibility to help maintain peace.[95] Recent events have shown the almost uncanny wisdom of that statement. But in 1919-1921, a large proportion of the American people evidently did not devote very much time to questions of diplomacy and their related problems. Anyhow it seemed to be much easier to let others think about those things or, what was better, one could forget the entire matter.

The Guarantee Treaty was lost by default in the Senate of the United States. Inasmuch as there was no motion to have the Senate give its advice and consent to the ratification of the document, no vote was taken. There was no formal adverse vote. There was no rejection because of a failure to receive the required constitutional majority of approving votes. The effect, however, was the same as though a formal vote had been taken. Perhaps

nothing could have been more deadly (except an outright overwhelming vote against it) to the proposed aid treaty than the
inattention and the inaction it received.

It is difficult to explain satisfactorily the lack of action in
the Senate. Senator Lodge was, at one time, favorably disposed
to aiding France against a resurgent Germany. Likewise, Senators Brandegee, Fall, and McCumber, to name but a few, were
willing to concede the need for assuring French security against
Germany. The Republicans just named were active members on
the Senate Foreign Relations Committee to which the Aid Treaty
was referred. Perhaps there would have been enough votes to
approve a treaty of similar purpose which was not directly de-
pendent upon or connected with the League of Nations. Perhaps
not. No one knows. But had a formal vote been taken on the form
in which Wilson submitted the aid treaty, there seems little doubt
that approval by the necessary majority would not have been
forthcoming. Again, this statement cannot be substantiated. It is
a matter of conjecture. The point to be made here is that many
members of the Senate, Democrats and Republicans, were in
agreement with Wilson that France deserved assistance against
Germany. They differed *as to how* that aid could and should be
supplied.

Professor J. Eugene Harley writing of this period, has made
the statement that Wilson's plans for guaranteeing the peace were
not accepted by the Senate because there were political dissen-
sions of an overwhelming nature, a tradition of isolationism, together with a lack of education concerning the relative merits of
collective efforts for peace as opposed to isolationism.[96] Moreover, Dr. Harley went on to observe that not only had the
isolationists failed to bring peace, but the balance of power
system had similarly failed.[97] Thus he implies that Wilson's
proposals conceivably *could not have done less than fail* and
they might have succeeded. The plans for guaranteeing the peace
— it should be recalled that hardly any peace outlasts the force
which imposes it — had within themselves possibilities of potential success.

Unfortunately, the Guarantee Treaty was never fairly considered *on its own merits*. It was condemned and it was praised

largely because of its close connection with the Covenant of the
League. Few, if any of those who considered it, gave it reasonable consideration. Minds were inflamed by propaganda and
half-truths. So many other factors were injected into the discussion that prejudice had a field day. Consequently, there was
never a clear indication of what the final reaction would have
been in the Senate had calm reasoning prevailed.

Therefore the death knell for the Treaties of Guarantee was
sounded in the halls of the Senate. Mishandling, apathy, ignorance, misguided judgments, prejudice, personal animosities, and
honest doubts had done their work well. The Assistance Pact
passed into archival oblivion, "unwept, unhonored" and unaccepted.

> ". . . fundamentally . . . French security . . . had
> been endangered by the loss of the American and
> British guarantees. It is not too much to say that the
> failure of the United States and England to imple-
> ment their guarantees was one of the chief causes
> of the failure of the peace settlement with all its
> disastrous consequences, including the present war
> (1939). The guarantees would have preserved the
> peace of Europe."
>
> Dr. Robert Dell, British author, in *The Geneva
> Racket, 1920-1939*

> "The failure of the United States to ratify the Treaty
> has hampered the whole conclusion of peace . . . .
> More fatal than all, however, has been the American
> failure to ratify the Guarantee Treaty, promising
> to protect France . . . . For the British guarantee
> depended on the American being taken up, and
> lapsed when American ratification was refused.
> That guarantee was a separate instrument and not
> part of the Peace Treaties as such. Yet its failure to
> materialize has most painfully affected France and
> for that failure the United States is responsible . . . ."
>
> Harold W. V. Temperley, British historian, in
> *A History of the Peace Conference*

NOTES

1. Varied points of view on the work of the Versailles Conference will be found in these works: D. F. Fleming, *The United States and the League of Nations*, 1918-1920 (New York and London, 1932); Richard W. Van Alstyne, *American Diplomacy in Action* (Stanford University, Calif., 1947, revised edition), Chapter 23, pp. 290-323, "The Paris Peace Conference and the League of Nations"; and W. Stull Holt, *Treaties Defeated by the Senate* (Baltimore, Md., 1935).

2. The state of war between Germany and the United States officially was terminated as of July 2, 1921. The treaty was signed at Berlin on August 25, 1921. For a very brief statement of the terms of that treaty, see Appendix I, pp. 219-220.

3. State Dept., *Papers of the Paris Peace Conference*, XIII, 759.

4. Richard W. Van Alstyne, *American Diplomacy in Action*, 298.

5. Philip C. Jessup, *International Security* (New York, 1935), 99.

6. Thompson, *The Peace Conference Day by Day*, 410.

7. *Congressional Record*, 66th Congr., 1st sess., Vol. 38, part 3, 2336-2339. The italics have been added.

8. Woodrow Wilson, *Constitutional Government in the United States* (New York, 1908), 139-140. In part it was as follows: "The Senate has shown itself particularly stiff and jealous in insisting upon exercising an independent judgment upon foreign affairs. A wise president may act in the true spirit of the Constitution and establish intimate relations of confidence with the Senate on his own initiative, not carrying his plans to completion and then laying them in final form before the Senate to be accepted or rejected, but keeping himself in . . . communication with the leaders of the Senate . . . when their advice will be of service to him and his information of the greatest service to them, in order that there may be veritable counsel and a real accommodation of views instead of a final challenge and contest."

9. James Brown Scott (ed.), *President Wilson's Foreign Policy, Messages, Addresses, Papers* (New York, 1918), 200-201.

10. Quoted in Noble, *Opinions at Paris*, 42.

11. Hamilton Foley (compiler), *Woodrow Wilson's Case for the League of Nations* (Princeton, N. J., 1923), 149-150.

12. Denna F. Fleming, *The United States and the League of Nations, 1918-1920*, 47-48.

13. For the complete text of the United States Aid Treaty and the British Aid Treaty see Appendix H, pp. 214-218.

14. *Congressional Record*, 66th Congr., 1st sess., Vol. 58, part 4, 3310-3311. The full text of the message will be found on those pages. Wilson seemed to desire delaying the submission of the supplemental treaty until after the Senate had given two or three weeks' study to the Versailles Treaty. The President apparently did not consider it opportune to make a simultaneous submission of the two documents even though he was under a legal as well as a moral obligation to do so.

15. Quoted by Tardieu in *The Treaty*, 470. Tardieu stated that Roosevelt told him in 1908, that, "What the United States lacks most is an understanding of the fact that we have interests all over the world . . . Some of us are aware of this. But the American people as a whole must be accustomed to the idea, they must learn to understand the meaning of our world interests."

16. Lansing, *Peace Negotiations*, 180.

17. *Ibid.*, 124-125.

18. *Congressional Record*, 66th Congr., 1st sess., Vol. 58, part 4, 3310.

19. *Ibid.*, 3312.

20. Wilson had called the 66th Congress to meet in a special session beginning May 19, 1919. The Republicans were in control of both houses of Congress.

21. *Congressional Record*, 66th Congr., 1st sess., Vol. 58, part 1, 330-331. Among other things, Senator Moses maintained that, "France has suffered and is anxious. Let us not refuse her plea discourteously or offensively decline to hear her cause. Are we justified in foreclosing the case against her before hearing it?"

22. *Ibid.*, 66th Congr., 1st sess., Vol. 58, part 1, 508.

23. *Ibid.*, 509.

24. *Ibid.*, part 3, 2592-2593.

25. *Ibid.*, part 3, 2600.

26. *Ibid.*, 66th Congr., 1st sess., Vol. 58, part 3, 2932.

27. *Ibid.*, 66th Congr., 1st sess., Vol. 58, part 3, 2986-2987.

28. Brandegee was a brilliant lawyer, a good speaker, and quick in repartee. He ended his career by taking his own life, despondent and disillusioned. There seems to be little evidence that he was not sincere in his opposition to the League of Nations and the agreements to assist France.

29. *Congressional Record*, 66th Congr., 1st sess., Vol. 58, part 3, 3075.

30. *Ibid.*, 66th Congr., 1st sess., Vol. 58, part 3, 3076.

31. *Ibid.*, 3077-3080.

32. *Ibid.*, 3081.

33. *Ibid.*, 66th Congr., 1st sess., Vol. 58, part 3, 3083.

34. *Ibid.*, 66th Congr., 1st sess., Vol. 58, part 3, 3144.

35. The Nebraska Senator also observed that he did not believe the people of the United States thought the pact was necessary in view of the protection to be afforded by the League of Nations to France.

36. *Congressional Record*, 66th Congr., 1st sess., Vol. 58, part 3, 3144.

37. *Ibid.*, 3143.

38. *Ibid.*, 66th Congr., 1st sess., Vol. 58, part 4, 3407.

39. *Ibid.*, 3230-3235. Among other things, Williams declared that the New York *Times* had sent him a telegram (he was, at the time, July 3, on his plantation in Mississippi) asking if he thought the Senate would ratify

the Franco-American Treaty. The reply, sent by telegram was, "God alone knows what the Senate of the United States will do, but I know what it ought to do; it ought to ratify it." Another item of interest disclosed by Williams in his speech that day was the letter sent from the Republican National Committee headquarters on July 22, 1919. It was signed by Will H. Hays, the chairman. "You will of course hear of and no doubt will see in full the editorial by Colonel George Harvey published this week in *Harvey's Weekly*, relative to the proposed Franco-American treaty. I want to be sure that you see this, with its remarkable subject matter; hence this letter calling your attention to it." In a vein of irony the Senator asked his colleagues if the Republican National Committee was working for Harvey or if they were both trying to increase the sales of the weekly magazine. Harvey was characterized in this manner, "Poor George Harvey. If he ever had been a sure-enough colonel, he would have had a hard time keeping up with his regiment; would have been twenty days behind all rumors of its whereabouts." His final parting shot was, "a man could go through the Lord's Prayer and find fault with it here and there provided he put his own interpretation upon it." The work of Brandegee was made to appear ludicrous by the witty characterization presented by Williams. No lasting effects except a heightening of tension were discernible.

40. *Congressional Record*, 66th Congr., 1st sess., Vol. 58, part 4, 3236.

41. *Ibid.*, 3314-3315.

42. *Ibid.*, 66th Congr., 1st sess., Vol. 58, part 4, 3316. With prophetic insight, Senator Gay gave an idea of the dangers to come unless war were destroyed: "The application of modern science . . . in the art of destruction is in its infancy . . . it will soon come into vigorous manhood, and then humanity will perish. When the sky is black with airplanes; the ocean thick with submarines; when poisonous gases and liquid fires are projected from enormous distances . . . when means of destruction far more powerful than the biggest guns command vast areas of land and sea and are guided by foes hidden in far distant shelters . . . when distinction between combatant and non-combatant has vanished; and there is no security on earth, air, or sea, then humanity will perish from the earth."

43. *Ibid.*, 3318-3320.

44. *Ibid.*, 3632. The resolution, in part, stated, ". . . That the Committee on Judiciary be, and it hereby is, requested to inquire and advise the Senate whether there are any constitutional obstacles to the making of the said treaty."

45. *Ibid.*, 66th Congr., 1st sess., Vol. 58, part 4, 3680-3697.

46. *Senate Document No. 76*, Report of the Conference between Members of the Senate Committee on Foreign Relations and the President of the United States, Tuesday, August 19, 1919, 66th Congress, 1st session, 1919), the members in attendance were: Lodge, McCumber (North Dakota), Borah, Brandegee, Knox (Penn.), Fall (New Mexico), Harding (Ohio), Hiram Johnson (Calif.), New (Indiana), Moses (New Hampshire), Hitchcock, Williams (Mississippi), Swanson (Virginia), Pomerene (Ohio),

Smith (Arizona), Pittman (Nevada), and President Wilson. Hereafter, citations from this reference will be as *Senate Document No. 76.*

47. See Appendix G, for League of Nations Covenant, pages 203-214.

48. *Senate Document No. 76,* 47-48.

49. *Ibid.,* 49.

50. *Ibid.,* 49-50.

51. *Ibid.,* 62-56.

52. *Congressional Record,* 66th Congr., 1st sess., Vol. 58, part 4, 4052-4053.

53. *Ibid.,* part 6, 5678-5679. The report (*Senate Report No. 215,* 66th Congr., 1st sess.) stated, among other things: "The material covenant of the treaty is found in the following words, 'The United States of America shall be bound to come immediately to her (France) assistance in the event of any unprovoked movement of aggression against her (France) being made by Germany.' It will be seen that this covenant only aims at protection against Germany and that it is of a temporary character, to be merged in and substituted by the authority of the league of nations when that is established and put into operation. As the Armistice covers the ground between the end of the war and the ratification of the treaty of peace, so the treaty in question aims to cover the ground from the time of the adoption of the treaty until the league of nations, provided for in the treaty, can take its place. In other words, the treaty in question is of a temporary character, to be merged in the final treaty of peace. Such a treaty is clearly warranted by international law and usage, and is therefore within the scope of the treaty-making power of the United States . . . No attempt is made in the treaty, it will be noted, to invest the Council with power to add to or subtract from its provisions or to modify them in any way. The treaty under consideration is clearly warranted by international law, and as such is within the scope of the treaty-making power; and there is nothing in the Constitution which can be construed to prohibit it."

54. *Ibid.,* 66th Congr., 1st sess., Vol. 58, part 6, 5679.

55. *Ibid.,* 5849.

56. *Ibid.,* 5901.

57. *Ibid.,* 66th Congr., 1st sess., Vol. 58, part 6, 5903.

58. *Ibid.,* 6030.

59. *Ibid.,* 6199.

60. *Ibid.,* 6598-6599.

61. *Ibid.,* part 7, 6876.

62. *Ibid.,* 66th Congr., 1st sess., Vol. 58, part 7, 7065.

63. On October 24, 1919, Senator Hitchcock read to the Senate several telegrams which he had received from the Los Angeles (California) constituents of Senator Hiram Johnson. The messages had protested Johnson's action in opposing Wilson's efforts for peace as embodied in the Covenant and in the accompanying treaties. Among the groups which had joined forces in the messages were church organizations, the League

to Enforce Peace (Roy Malcolm was secretary of the local branch), the faculty of the University of Southern California, and women's clubs, (*Congressional Record*, 66th Congr., 1st sess., Vol. 58, part 7, 7404-7405.

64. *Ibid.*, 7239.

65. The author of the Resolution was Philander C. Knox (Pennsylvania). Section 5, as quoted by Brandegee in the Senate, was as follows: "That, finally, it shall be the declared policy of our Government, in order to meet fully and fairly our obligations to ourselves and to the world, that the freedom and peace of Europe being again threatened by any power or combination of powers, the United States will regard such a situation with grave concern as a menace to its own peace and freedom, will consult with other powers affected with a view to devising means for the removal of such menace, and will, the necessity arising in the future, carry out the same complete accord and cooperation with our chief co-belligerents for the defense of civilization."

66. *Congressional Record*, 66th Congr., 1st sess., Vol. 58, parts 1-9, 8776.

67. *Ibid.*, 8777.

68. Claude G. Bowers in his book, *Beveridge and the Progressive Era* (Boston, 1932), states that Lodge had written a letter on August 11, 1919, to Senator Albert J. Beveridge (Indiana) to the effect that while he, Lodge, was opposed to Article X of the Covenant which would undertake to respect and preserve as against external aggression the territorial integrity and existing political independence of all members of the League, *he would support a simple proposition that, in the event of an attack by Germany, we should go to the rescue of France.* This attitude by Lodge was a recognition of the international policy of collective security by cooperative assistance. It was also the same principle which Lodge materially aided in defeating in his fight on the Versailles Treaty in 1919 and 1920. Italics added.

69. *Congressional Record*, 66th Congr., 1st sess., Vol. 59, part 4, 3746.

70. *Ibid.*, 66th Congr., 1st sess., Vol. 59, part 4, 4051.

71. Senator Lodge stated in his book, *The Senate and the League of Nations* (New York and London, 1925), "This treaty (of guarantee) was meant to satisfy France for the refusal [of Wilson] . . . to give France, under the Treaty of Versailles, the Rhine boundary. The treaty . . . duly referred to the Committee on Foreign Relations . . . was never taken up and never reported out. It would have been quite useless to do so, even if the Committee had favored it, for I do not think there was the slightest chance that the Senate would ever have voted to accept it. *There was no desire on the part of senators of either Party at that stage to bind the United States irrevocably with agreements to go to war again under certain prescribed conditions.*" Pages 154-156. The italics were added. Lodge was also emphatic in stating that Wilson had broken the pledge in the treaty which bound him to submit it to the Senate at the same time as he did the Versailles Treaty. In this the Senator was undoubtedly in accord with the facts of the case.

Just why Lodge completely changed his attitude on an alliance to protect France against a renascent Germany is difficult to determine. He had wanted White to inform the European leaders that such a plan for controlling Germany was very desirable. But White refused to be a party to such a plan. And when Wilson bound the aid treaty so close to the Covenant that one could hardly separate them, Lodge was furious. He probably would have voted for an alliance with France against Germany if the question had been solely that and nothing else. But there were so many ramifications to the question before the Senate, insofar as the aid treaty was concerned, that Lodge resolved to oppose all efforts to do what he had proposed doing in 1918.

72. Theodore Marburg and Horace E. Flack, (eds.), *Taft Papers on League of Nations* (New York, 1920), 279-280. The date of the speech was March 4, 1919.

73. State Dept., *op. cit.*, XI, 74.

74. *Senate Document No. 106* (Treaty of Peace with Germany, Hearings before the Committee on Foreign Relations . . .), 66th Congr., 1st sess., 1919, p. 1276.

75. Lansing, *op. cit.*, 183.

76. *Ibid.*, 182.

77. The only Republican member of the Commission to Negotiate Peace was Henry White, a career diplomat. He was a friend of Theodore Roosevelt, of Elihu Root, and of Senator Henry Cabot Lodge. During the peace conference White sent numerous letters to Roosevelt and Lodge.

78. State Dept., *op. cit.*, XI, 125-126. White was of the opinion that the suggestion by the United States that it might sign a separate peace with Germany would be enough to persuade the French to be more reasonable and thereby permit an agreement to be reached.

79. House and Seymour (eds.), *What Really Happened at Paris*, 376-377.

80. Seymour (ed.), *House Papers*, IV, 150.

81. *Ibid.*, 503-504.

82. *Ibid.*, 509.

83. House and Seymour (eds.), *op. cit.*, 54-55.

84. "The Alliance and the League," *New Republic*, XX, No. 256, October 1, 1919, 255.

85. *Literary Digest*, LXII, No. 1, July 5, 1919, 26-27.

86. George Harvey, "America and Humanity," *North American Review*, Vol. 210, July 1919, 5.

87. "How the Press Answers the President's Plea," *Literary Digest*, LXII, No. 3, July 19, 1919, 10.

88. "Unprovoked Aggression," *New Republic*, XIX, No. 245, July 16, 1919, 340.

89. *Ibid.*, 341.

90. "Our Pledge to Aid France," *Literary Digest*, LXI, No. 5, May 3, 1919, 20.

91. "That 'Entangling Alliance' with France and England," *Literary Digest*, LXII, No. 3, July 19, 1919, 12.

92. "The Ado about the French Treaty," *Literary Digest*, LXII, No. 6, August 9, 1919, 10.

93. *Ibid.*, 10.

94. On May 10, 1919, a cable was sent by Wilson to his secretary, Joseph Tumulty, at the White House, with general details of the pledge to France.

95. "The Airplane and the Covenant," Vol. 99, September 20, 1919, 396.

96. Harley, *Woodrow Wilson still Lives — His World Ideals Triumphant* (Los Angeles, California, 1944), 42-43.

97. *Ibid.*, 44.

CHAPTER SEVEN

Some Observations and Conclusions on the Importance of the Treaties of Guarantee

When Professor D. F. Fleming observed that final judgments of history and of God cannot be known, perhaps he was nearer to the truth than he realized. It may be that conclusions are defined and shaped by the perspective of the times in which they are reached. Often it is true that additional information which was not available at the time the conclusions were reached may alter them at a later date. So many are the variables and the imponderables involved in arriving at a conclusion that one almost is tempted to state, "This is my conclusion now. Perhaps twenty or thirty or fifty years from now it might be a different one."

Since the Peace Conference of 1919 has passed into history, many appraisals and reappraisals have been made of its work. One result of these works has been to give added meaning to the role played by the supplemental treaties of guarantee. The relative importance of the treaties has been increasing because of changes in perspective as well as the development of a deeper understanding of the more important problems faced at that conference. Many events which were seemingly unimportant and practically meaningless have assumed great importance when placed in their proper frame of reference and positions of rela-

146

tionship. Thus in one era society accepts conclusions which, to it, in another era under different circumstances would be totally unacceptable. Even though in the historical sense judgments and conclusions obviously rest upon interpretations placed upon the materials available at that particular time, there is no degree of ultimate finality in them. It is assumed that certain factors which are primarily subjective and personal in nature have entered into the making of every conclusion. Among these factors are: judgment, interpretation, the selection or the rejection of facts and ideas as well as the ability to draw inferential observations, and the reliability of the materials used. Likewise it is assumed that no observation should be drawn unless there is reliable supporting and substantiating evidence. Often too, a decisive role is played in the shaping of conclusive observations by the so-called "imponderables of life." Among these are such things as psychological traits, personal peculiarities, untoward events — floods, fires, coincidences, acts of God, and eccentric behaviorisms. In the most exhaustive studies the most exacting and difficult part is to synthesize the results. Sometimes there are no logical definitive conclusions. Again, an investigation may disclose no final answer to the subject under inquiry. In other cases there are "obvious conclusions" which fail in their validity under closer scrutiny. These, however, are all inescapable factors which one may expect to encounter if he is engaged in research. Perhaps above all else there should be something at least potentially useful in what has been learned during the special study. While it is not always possible to give immediate shape to such a goal, nevertheless such an objective should be kept in mind. Whether there be a positive value or a negative value in the results of a study does not seem to make too much difference. Mankind may be given a guide as to *what to avoid* as well as *what to do* under given situations.

The conclusions in this study are three in number. They are: (1) the extreme significance of the parts played by the offers of assistance to France which enabled a series of compromise agreements to be reached in 1919 at Versailles. In the opinion of the author, the fact that the offers of aid to France (later eventuated into the guarantee treaties) were the levers with which the deadlock was broken, lends to them an importance transcending the fact that they were not implemented later in the future. (2) The very substantial, and little short of revolutionary, changes in the field of foreign policy of the United States. The herald of that change was shown in President Wilson's pledge — made in conjunction with that of Great Britain — to give immediate aid to France in case of unprovoked German aggression. It is true there were factors which would control the kind and the amount of aid, but the important thing was the pledge itself. Furthermore, it is recognized that the signing by the United States of the Versailles Treaty with its Covenant for a world league was an additional example of the change in diplomacy as contemplated by Wilson. It is also true that there was a very close relationship between the Versailles Treaty and the Guarantee Pacts which made the latter in reality little less than a supplementary provision of the larger agreement. (3) There were disastrous effects upon the world's efforts to achieve collective security. In large measure these effects stemmed from the failure of the United States to ratify the Versailles Settlement and, of course, the non-ratification of the aid pact. This failure to implement the latter treaty carried in its train the obvious corollary to the above conclusion, namely, that the United States undermined its own prestige and self-respect by refusing to participate in efforts to solve the world's problems in a collective manner.

When one considers the fact that *agreements were made* in Paris after the deadlocked conference had been in grave danger of breaking up, the first point which has been mentioned takes on added meaning and becomes more important. The offers of Britain and of the United States to assist France under certain conditions were apparently the catalyst which brought the series of compromises into being. The analogy is not quite true, in a chemical way, for there the catalyst merely enables the reactions to take place and does not enter into the final results in any other way. In the present instance, however, the offer was embodied in the final compromise settlement. That other factors of great importance were present and were given consideration cannot be denied. But the terrible possibilities of what was involved in a potential breakdown in the conference adds unusually grave import to this conclusion relating to the great importance of the Treaties of Guarantee in influencing the final peace.

The second point implies an acceptance of the revolutionary changes in diplomatic concepts involving the United States and the rest of the world with particular regard to France. Wilson personified the forces of Internationalism when he made the proposals which would have been of much greater importance to American diplomacy if the Senate had adopted them. President Wilson was convinced that it was the duty and the destiny of the United States to assume responsibility for world leadership for the preservation of peace by collective action. He declared that the United States could stabilize world conditions by participating in a league of nations. Such an advance pledge of co-operation by the United States as exemplified in the aid pact would be, in effect, a concerted effort to control the course of future events. Admittedly it was the need and the desire to avoid the experiences of past wars — which had so often placed nations at the mercy of events over which no control could be exercised — which dictated this change in policy. To assume that peace automatically selected its own sustaining factors was sheer stupidity. Not only did such reckless and irresponsible thinking endanger the security of the United States, but it likewise seriously compromised that of the rest of the world as well. Every nation which had taken a leading part in the Peace Conference thereby incurred an inescapable responsibility — implicit as well as explicit — for the maintenance of a relatively secure and peaceful world. There can be little doubt that Wilson's pledge of aid to France represented a much sharper break with the traditional foreign policies of the United States than otherwise would have been the case, if for example, he had given assurances for acting only in concert with a league of nations or some association to keep the peace. The dogma of insularity, of nationalism, of isolationism — it matters not what term denotes that concept or policy — was unquestionably renounced by the guarantee treaty. The former policy of remaining aloof, or not interfering in an official, diplomatic manner in the political and economic life of Europe was unceremoniously shattered by the explicit terms of the aid pact.

The President had spoken of this wider scope of action when, in 1917, he had asked for the declaration of war against Germany. He reaffirmed and extended the idea in his message to the Senate in July, 1919, when the guarantee treaty was submitted for the formal consideration of that body. An extremely tenuous line separates national from international interests — at least in many cases. That line was crossed by Wilson in Paris when he undertook to commit the United States to a new foreign policy of aiding in the preservation of the security of another nation — France. Actually as well as inferentially, it was a momentous decision. The guarantee to France was a pledge of support by the United States for collective international security. The fact that the advice and the consent of the United States Senate was not given to the proposals cannot and does not alter that statement.

The effects upon world security which were the consequences of the failure of the United States to accept the responsibilities as pledged by the agreement with France, and in the Versailles Treaty, were as serious as they were far reaching in scope. From today's perspective the results are clearly etched against a somber and a critical background of world affairs. Without quibbling over the technicalities of cause and effect, the evidence which has been presented in this study seems to show unmistakably that the United States should assume much of the responsibility for two things. The first is that a system of collective security predicated upon the assumption of part of the burden by the United States could not and did not effectively function when deprived of that support. The second point is that the United States' action in signing a separate peace with Germany in 1921 merely gave impetus to those forces tending toward the disintegration of world stability and peace at the time when they were in need of encouragement and support. This failure of the United States to ally itself alongside the French and the British, who were working in conjunction with many smaller powers for security and stability, played its part in vitiating the guarantees which had been made at Versailles. The defection of the United States left unguarded the key tower in the ramparts for collective action by the world to preserve peace and to make wars of aggression more difficult, if not impossible. As a result, there was a close relationship between the spasmodic and irritating moves made by France against Germany and the growing realization that the United States did not intend to implement either the Versailles Treaty or the Guarantee Treaty. In the resulting chaos and instability World War II was spawned.

The United States and the rest of the world should not have forgotten that a serious danger spot was that of the Franco-German border and its related issues. The aid pact was to have acted as a quarantine against the repetition of the 1914 invasion of France. By the terms of the larger treaty there was a recognition that unprovoked aggression against France was not only a hostile action against the signers of the peace treaty, but that it was also a threat to the peace of the world. Any potential aggression by Germany was to be controlled by the arrangements of France with Great Britain and the United States. But when the opportunity for leadership in peace and security on the part of the United States was declined in 1920-21 by the Senate, one of the strongest supports for preventive action to discourage a would-be aggressor was removed. As a consequence the future security of the United States was jeopardized by this indirect invitation to the forces of aggression. Part of the blame for this debacle must be placed on the shoulders of Woodrow Wilson for it was his inept handling of the entire matter, especially his tardy, almost apologetic submission of the guarantee pact to the Senate, which lost some much-needed support for the document. By his uncompromising attitude Wilson played into the hands of the bitter opponents of the entire peace settlement. When the Senate rejected directly the Versailles Treaty and the Covenant, there was no good reason for further consideration of the lesser agreement. It is perhaps not an unreasonable interpretation of the events from 1919 to 1939 to state that participation by the United States in efforts for international collective security might have given a totally different direction to world events.

Finally, the author believes that this study has shown the desirability for re-examining the whole case of international cooperation to achieve collective security during the period from 1921 to 1939. This should be done to ascertain more fully, if possible, other underlying reasons for the breakdown of the efforts for world peace. If the statesmen of the future are to avoid such pitfalls as those from 1921-1939, then certainly there is a need to have the pitfalls pointed out. The North Atlantic Pact which was signed in April, 1949, by the United States, Canada, and the nations of Western Europe is an example of the grouping together of nations with parallel or similar interests to protect themselves against a potential aggressor. There seems to be a close analogy between the Guarantee Pacts and the North Atlantic Pact. Some of the lessons presented by World War I had to be reinforced by those of World War II before their implications were made clear to the people of many nations including those in the United States.

Universal peace — as of now — still remains one of the unachieved hopes of mankind. However, the lessons of the thus far futile struggles to reach that goal by warfare are written very clearly in blood and destruction. What the final outcome will be of man's additional efforts to achieve peace remains locked in the mysteries of time, or perhaps one should say of the Atom.

APPENDICES

Appendices

APPENDIX A. OUTLINE OF THE CONTENTS OF THE TREATY OF VERSAILLES[1]

Preamble

Part I

The Covenant of the League of Nations
    Articles 1 — 26 and
    Annex

Part II

Boundaries of Germany
    Articles 27 — 30

Part III

Political Clauses for Europe
    Section I — Belgium — articles 31 — 39
    Section II — Luxemburg — articles 40 — 41
    Section III — Left bank of the Rhine — articles 42 — 44
    Section IV — Saar Basin — articles 45 — 50
        Annex
        Chapter I — Cession and exploitation of mining property — 1 — 15
        Chapter II — Government of the territory of the Saar Basin — 16 — 33
        Chapter III — Plebiscite — 34 — 40
    Section V — Alsace-Lorraine (articles 51 — 79)
        Annex (1 — 4)
    Section VI — Austria (article 80)
    Section VII — Czecho-Slovak State (articles 81 — 86)

---

  1. *British Command Papers* (*153*), Treaty Series No. 4 (1919), pp. II — VII. Only the chapter and sectional headings are indicated with the actual textual materials being omitted. In the source these provisions are given in full.

Part XI

Part XII

Part XIII

Part XIV

Part XV

APPENDIX B. MEMORANDUM OF MARSHAL FOCH[2]

G.Q.G.A. 10th January 1919

C-in-C. Allied Armies

The Marshal.

The following memorandum, laid by the Marshal Commanding-in-Chief of the Allied Armies before the Plenipotentiaries, states, from the point of view of the military security of the Allied and Associated Powers, the problem of the German Western Frontiers.

The question of the frontiers, special to France and Belgium, is not examined, but only the European collective and international guarantees necessary for the whole mass of States, which after having fought for right, freedom, and justice, intend to prepare, on new bases, inspired by these three ideas, the relations between Nations.

Memorandum

Without any doubt we may rely, in an uncertain future, on a development of civilization and of the moral sense of nations, such that it will be possible to find in a Society or League of Nations, strongly organized, an efficient barrier to wars of conquest. But, in order that this rising society should acquire an authority so strong, that it may be by itself a guarantee of the preservation of peace, it is necessary that this society should receive, at once, a sufficiently secure basis and an especial strength that will ensure its development. Therefore, we must know the past situation of today, and also take into account the peace securities, which a costly victory has put in the hands of the Allied nations, thanks to their perfect cooperation, and which could not be given up, without endangering in the future the preservation of peace.

I

Germany of 1914 is the result of a steady work of 150 years long, begun by Frederick II, methodically continued by his successors, and which had lead to the prussification of Germany.

---

2. Ministère des Affaires Étrangéres. *Documents Diplomatiques: Documents Relatifs aux négociations concernant Les Garanties de Sécurité Contre une Agression de L' Allemagne,* (10 janvier 1919 — 7 décembre 1923), (Paris, 1924), pp. 7-14.

From the very outset the Hohenzollern have based the Prussian power upon an exaggerated militarism, for instance, the keeping up of an army, whose strength was much larger than would be consistent with the total of population. Thanks to this inflated military organization Prussia played an important part in the wars of the eighteenth century, realized important territorial expansion, and took an important part in the wars of 1813, 1814, and 1815. In the same way, she soon secured, among European powers, a rank very superior to the one which should have been alloted to her on account of her natural means, population, trade, industry . . . .

In fact, the investment of its resources in a strong army, produced by personal and compulsory service and the practice of war as an industry of national conquests have given to Prussia serious profits. She was going to apply them to a triumph of her policy.

Thus, in 1866, by the victory of Sadowa, she expelled Austria from the German territory, upset the German Confederation, and took control of reorganized Germany, so as to militarize it, according to the Prussian model and under Prussian hands.

Thus, in 1871, in the days which followed a victorious campaign, she created the Empire, in view of making of Germany a stronger unity, more in Prussian hands, always on the same basis of compulsory service, and of Hohenzollern command.

But, at the same time, Prussian activity exercised itself far beyond purely military ground. All classes, all resources of action or production, all associations as well as all individuals were drilled, centralized, and militarized. An ingenious State monopoly system, applied by a covetous and despotic monarchy, was always backed by a strong aristocracy and making use of an undenied military superiority and of profitable wars, that is, the supremacy of might. Public education was soon imbued with the same principles, and compulsory schools, a fairly old institution in this country, found, thanks to an acute management, the means of spreading these principles, and of creating a German state of mind, "Kultur," with its own morals. The rule is that might is above right. Might creates right, for its benefit. Lastly Germany more and more believed in a superior nature, in a special fate and mission, which justified the most unjust doings, the most cruel methods, provided that they led to German victory. Morals are summed up in a word: "Deutschland Uber Alles." The German ideal and the driving power, which justifies its existence, are to dominate the world for the Germans' benefit.

Besides, the centralized authority of the King of Prussia, who has concentrated in his hands all the forces thus created, so as to apply them, at the time he chooses, to the development of Germany by war, has given by the "Rights of the Native," a privilege situation to each of his subjects. The Bavarian, the Saxon, the Wurttemberger, the inhabitant of Baden is above all a German subject. He is protected and claimed by the Empire, interested therefore in the preservation and greatness of the Empire. Once more, on the physical and moral power of Germany the King of Prussia laid his hand and used it as a buttress for his system.

All this explains the irresistible, unanimous and blind rising of 1914, called by William II.

After having, at the highest degree, exaggerated the military organization so as to make of it a war machine ready for conquests, after having strained the morale of his people, and roused, in appealing to his interest, the devotion of the individual to the Prussian Emperor's cause, it is on the whole an army of scientific and convinced hooligans, which prussified Germany has turned out, against all treaties, on the peaceful populations, and even on the countries of Europe vowed to neutrality, and lastly, on the seas of the world.

It is against this whole fabric of forces, result of a hundred years' continuous drilling, that the Entente had taken up the struggle, without being prepared, in the name of the principles of Right, and Liberty of Peoples, and soon followed in the fight by a mass of nations, urged by the same principles, the United States in the first rank.

Thanks to the effort of all, and at the price of a victory, which has been costly, especially for the first nations engaged in the fight the crisis is now at an end, but it may start again.

II

So as to prevent it from being renewed, it shall not be enough, without any doubt, to change the form of the German Government. Now that the Hohenzollerns have left, under conditions which are of specially disqualifying character for this dynasty, and for all military monarchies, the reestablishment of the Imperial regime appears to be improbable at least for some time. But a Republic, built on the same principles of centralized authority and militarism, taking in hand the whole of Germany, will be as dangerous, and remain as threatening for the peace. It might be perhaps easily realized[3] in a country, imbued with the Prussian spirit, Prussian methods, militarists' theories, and where, as much on account of the natural characters as of historical traditions, there is revealed in a supreme way, the principle of authority and of centralisation. Moreover, a German republic, freed from the hindrance due without any doubt to the existing small principalities, has a chance of finding a surplus of forces in her unity thus completely achieved, and also in the vitality and activity, specially on economic grounds, of a country now more in touch with its government.

It is only in so straightening minds, brought back by defeat and free discussion to a more correct conception of right and justice, and by the sharing in a large proportion of the control of executive power, that may be brought about a democratic working of institutions, in appearance republican, which should have otherwise all the strength of a despotic authority. We shall not see the coming out of such an evolution without some time, a long time, without any doubt, as we are decided not to quicken the work of persuasion by using force, not to interfere in the internal working of German affairs. But then, full of respect for German tenure, can we be so over-confident as to endanger our principles of Liberty and Justice, even our existence, by a shifting opinion and by a reactionary force which may take place on the other side of the Rhine, and can immediately throw into a new war regimental staffs and numerous classes of well-drilled soldiers, that is, a very strong Army?

Thus Germany remains, for yet a long time, until the achievement of its political and philosophical change, a dangerous menace for civilization. Therefore, the Entente, embryo of a Society

---

3. Pour former l'Empire en 1871, il a suffi de faire rentrer dans la Confédération de Nord les États de Sud et de remplacer dans la Constitution le mot 'Bund' par 'Reids' et celui de 'Praesidium' par 'Kaiser' Une manoeuvre en sens inverse, qui remplacerait, dans la Constitution impériale, le mot de 'Reich' par 'Bund' et celui de 'Kaiser' par 'Praesidium' aboutirait á maintenis, sons une forme d' apparence républicaine, toute la force que représentait l' Empire.

of Nations, is absolutely compelled by mere prudence to take towards Germany systematic measures of a purely defensive character, first emergency precautions. At the same time, these will be enough, so as to show that the Allies have well made up their mind to reach the goal, peace, and make it impossible for Germany to start again a war of conquest, to take up once more her plan for armed domination.

In view of this lasting German threat, what forces can we call out?

III

During a great part of the war, which is ending, Russia, with her large armies, has detained a fair number of the German forces. Thus, in 1915, 1916, and even during the greater part of 1917, the Allied powers have been superior in numbers on the Western front.

Today, the future of Russia is uncertain, probably for many years. Therefore, Western Europe, cradle of and necessary guarantee of the future organization of nations, can rely only on her own strength for studying, preparing and ensuring her prospects towards Germany, and in case of a possible German attack.

To play this part, Western Europe cannot have a superiority of numbers. In fact, whichever type of political organization should be agreed to in the near future by the people on the other side of the Rhine, there will always remain, on the eastern bank of the river, a German population of 64 to 75 millions of inhabitants[4] naturally bound together by common language, and therefore by common ideas, as by common interest.

To these German forces, Belgium, Luxembourg, Alsace-Lorraine and France can oppose a total of only 49 millions of inhabitants. Only with the cooperation of the countries on the other side of the sea, can they reach the level of the enemy's figures,

---

4. Empire Allemand (1914)		68,000,000
Provinces Allemandes d' Autriche		7,000,000
Posnanie	2,100,000	
Alsace-Lorraine	1,900,000	
Pays rhenans de la rine gauche du Rhin	5,400,000	
Slesing-Holstein	1,600,000	
	11,000,000	75,000,000
Différence		64,000,000

as they did in 1914-1918. But this help must be waited for, and for how long, especially from the United States?

Now then, what has been the cause of the present calamity? Above all the fact that Germany was tempted by the possibility of striking, with one blow, only in stretching the fist, our vital parts. Without this conviction, she certainly would have hesitated. Impressed with that conviction, she did not even look for pretexts. "We can't wait," said Bethmann-Hollweg.

Therefore, to put an end to the encroachments on the West of Germany, which has always been warlike and covetous of others' property, which lately had been prepared and trained for conquering by force, against all right, and with methods the most inconsistent with law, which can start without delay a terrific war — if we want at least to postpone the decisive battle — we must first of all appeal to the help of nature. Nature has provided a barrier on the road to invasion, but only one: the Rhine. The Rhine must be used and defended, and therefore occupied and organized in peace time. Without this fundamental precaution, Western Europe remains deprived of her natural frontier and open, as in the past, to the danger of an invasion, which may be stronger. Without this precaution, the industrial and peaceful countries of N. W. Europe are immediately drowned under the flow of barbarous wars, which no dike checks.

The Rhine, in itself a serious obstacle, renders especially difficult the crossing at a time when the machine guns of the defense compel the assailant to resort to the use of tanks.

From Switzerland to Holland, on a front of more than six hundred kilometers, this continuous obstacle covers the allied countries, without possibility of being outflanked.

Further, on account of fortified towns, by which it is reinforced, the means of communication (roads and railroads) which converge on it, or run laterally along it, it is a magnificent basis of manoeuvre for a counter-offensive.

Mayence, Coblenz, Cologne are only at three days' march from each other. Any attempt by the enemy to effect a crossing between these towns would be threatened in flank and in the rear, on both banks of the river, as each bridgehead, which we are in possession of, on the Rhine, flanks its neighbors and allows such an offensive to be dealt with in the flank or from behind.

Marshal von Moltke, considered the Rhine to be the German

military frontier, and concluded certain studies of his by writing: *"The extraordinary strength of our centre of operations on the Rhine cannot be ignored. It could only be compromised, should we undertake a premature offensive on the left bank, with insufficient forces."* And further: *"The defensive front of Prussia against France is made up by the Rhine with its fortresses. This line is so strong that it would be far from requiring all the forces of the Monarchy."* The situation is today reversed for the benefit of the coalition.

She can't give up the advantage thus secured and abandon the defensive shield in this area — the Rhine — without seriously endangering its future. "Wacht am Rhein" must be its rallying word.

Henceforward, the Rhine ought to be the western military frontier of the German peoples. Germany ought to be deprived of all entrance and assembling ground, that is, of all territorial sovereignty on the left bank of the river, that is, of all facilities for invading quickly, as in 1914, Belgium, Luxembourg, for reaching the coast of the North Sea and threatening England, for outflanking the natural defences of France, the Rhine, the Meuse, and conquering the northern provinces and entering upon the Parisian area.

This is for the time being, in the near future, an *indispensable guarantee of peace,* on account of:

1. The material and moral situation of Germany.
2. Her numerical superiority over the democratic nations of Western Europe.

IV

The Rhine, military frontier, without which cannot be maintained the peace aimed at by the coalition, is not a territorial benefit for any country. It is not a question, in fact, of annexing the left bank of the Rhine, of increasing France or Belgium's territory, or of the protection against German revindication, but to hold securely on the Rhine, the *common* barrier of security necessary to the League of Democratic Nations. It is not a question of confiding to a single power the guarding of this common barrier, but to ensure by the cooperation, either moral or material, of all the democratic powers, the defence of their existence and of their future, by forbidding Germany once for all from carrying war and its influence of domination across the river.

It must be understood that it will be for the treaty of peace to lay down the status of the populations of the left bank of the Rhine, not included within French or Belgian frontiers.

But this organization, whatever form it may take, must take, into account the essential military factor stated above, as follows:

1. The total prevention of German Military access to and political propaganda in the territories on the left bank of the Rhine; perhaps even the covering of these territories by military neutral zones on the right bank.
2. The ensuring of the military occupation of the territories of the left bank of the Rhine by Allied forces.
3. The guaranteeing to the territories on the left bank of the Rhine the outlets necessary for their economic activities, in uniting them with the other Western States by a common system of customs.

Under these conditions, and in conformity with the principles, admitted by all, of the liberty of peoples, it is possible to conceive the constitution on the left bank of the Rhine of new autonomous States, administering themselves under the reservations stated above, a constitution which, with the aid of the Rhine as a strong natural frontier, will be the only means capable of securing peace to Western Europe.

V

To sum up, the Powers of the Coalition, France, in spite of her legitimate claims and her imprescriptible rights; Belgium controlled by neutrality, Great Britain in her insular position, never prepared an offensive against Germany, but in 1914 were brutally assailed by this State. For a certain time, the situation may again arise. If in 1914, 1915, 1916, and 1917, these Powers were able to resist Germany, to give time to Great Britain to develop fully her Armies, notably by her compulsory service and other improvised measures, and to enable the United States to arrive with her decisive support, it was because Russia was fighting on their side, and on this account they were able to maintain during a certain period numerical superiority on the Western front. Russia is no longer of assistance, for a time which it is impossible to foresee. It becomes necessary, therefore, that the Western barrier against German invasion should be more strongly constituted than in the past, and that the Powers of the Entente, which are geographically in the front row of the defenders of civilization, be organized henceforth on a military basis to render possible the timely intervention of the other States which are the defenders of civilization.

The organization defensively of the Coalition is therefore necessary.

This defensive organization involves, before all, a natural frontier; the first barrier placed to withstand a Germanic invasion. There exists only the Rhine. It must be held by the forces of the Coalition until further orders.

VI

The object of this decision, which is purely defensive and to be adopted at once, is to withstand an attack by Germany and to answer the first needs created thereby. It is an essential organization, for war, as soon as it breaks, lives only on realities, on material forces brought into play under definite conditions of time: natural lines of defence or defensive organization, numbers, armament. These are the conditions laid down above as necessary. They could be carried out, as has been seen here, under supervision and patronage of the Nations founding the League of Nations of Right: France, England, Belgium, the United States.

Under the protection of these defensive measures, and to provide them with a moral support, the League of Nations, securely established, would be strengthened by those Nations which have come to defend the same principles of Right and Justice, and it would establish definite statutes, henceforward practicable of enforcing.

The League once thus founded, with its statutes and powers of coercion, could progressively develop into the League of Nations, by the successive adhesion of other nations; neutral Nations first, enemy nations afterward. The results aimed at, once achieved, would be of such a nature as to diminish by degrees the military burdens of the nations of which the League will be composed.

That is an ideal to be realized in a future, which is necessarily indefinite.

It will be possible of achievement under the protection of the defensive measures explained above, without which civilization will be placed in danger by a new German attack, which this time it would not be possible to stop in time.

The fortune of war has placed the line of the Rhine in our hands, thanks to a combination of circumstances and a cooperation of Allied Forces, which cannot for a long time be reproduced. The abandonment today of this solid natural barrier, without other guarantee than institutions of a moral character and of distant and unknown difficulty, would mean, from the military point of view, the incurring of the greatest of risks.

The Armies, moreover, know how much blood it has cost them.

(signed) F. Foch

APPENDIX C. SOME CONSIDERATIONS FOR THE PEACE CONFERENCE BEFORE THEY DRAFT THEIR TERMS[5]

. . . When nations are exhausted by wars in which they have put forth all their strength and which leave them tired, bleeding and broken, it is not difficult to patch up a peace that may last until the generation which experienced the horrors of the war has passed away. Pictures of heroism and triumph only tempt those who know nothing of the suffering and terrors of war. It is therefore comparatively easy to patch up a peace which will last thirty years.

What is difficult, however, is to draw up a peace which will not provoke a fresh struggle when those who have had practical experience of what war means have passed away. History has proved that a peace, which has been hailed by a victorious nation as a triumph of diplomatic skill and statesmanship, even of moderation in the long run, has proved itself to be shortsighted and charged with danger to the victor. The peace of

---

5. *Parliamentary (Command) Papers*: Cmd. 1614, *Memorandum Circulated by the Prime Minister on 25th March, 1919*, (1922). Lloyd George expressed his views on these phases of peace terms in this letter which he sent to the French Government.

1871 was believed by Germany to ensure not only her security but her permanent supremacy. The facts have shown exactly the contrary. France itself has demonstrated that those who say you can make Germany so feeble that she will never be able to hit back are utterly wrong. Year by year France became numerically weaker in comparison with her victorious neighbor, but in reality she became ever more powerful. She kept watch on Europe; she made alliance with those whom Germany had wronged or menaced; she never ceased to warn the world of its danger and ultimately she was able to secure the overthrow of the far mightier power which had trampled so brutally upon her. You may strip Germany of her colonies, reduce her armaments to a mere police force and her navy to that of a fifth-rate power; all the same in the end if she feels that she has been unjustly treated in the peace of 1919 she will find means of exacting retribution from her conquerors. The impression, the deep impression, made upon the human heart by four years of unexampled slaughter will disappear with the hearts upon which it has been marked by the terrible sword of the great war. The maintenance of peace will then depend upon there being no causes of exasperation constantly stirring up the spirit of patriotism, of justice or of fair play. To achieve redress our terms may be severe, they may be stern and even ruthless, but at the same time they can be so just that the country on which they are imposed will feel in its heart that it has no right to complain. But injustice, arrogance, displayed in the hour of triumph, will never be forgotten or forgiven.

For these reasons I am, therefore, strongly averse to transferring more Germans from German rule to the rule of some other nation than can possibly be helped. I cannot conceive any greater cause of future war than that the German people, who have certainly proved themselves one of the most vigorous and powerful races in the world, should be surrounded by a number of small States, many of them consisting of people who have never previously set up a stable government for themselves, but each of them containing large masses of Germans clamouring for reunion with their native land. The proposal of the Polish Commissioner that we should place 2,100,000 Germans under the control of a people which is of a different religion and which has never proved its capacity for stable self-government throughout history must, in my judgment, lead sooner or later to a new war in the East of Europe . . . . Secondly, I would say that the duration for the payments of reparation ought to disappear if possible with the generation which made the war.

But there is a consideration in favour of a long-sighted peace which influences me even more than the desire to leave no causes justifying a fresh outbreak thirty years hence. There is one element in the present condition of nations which differentiates it from the situation as it was in 1815. In the Napoleonic war the countries were equally exhausted, but the revolutionary spirit had spent its force in the country of its birth, and Germany had satisfied the legitimate popular demands for the time being . . . .

If we are wise, we shall offer to Germany a peace, which, while just, will be preferable for all sensible men to the alternative of Bolshevism. I would therefore, put it in the forefront of the peace that once she accepts our terms, especially reparation, we will open to her the raw materials and markets of the world on equal terms with ourselves, and will do everything possible to enable the German people to get upon their legs again. We cannot both cripple her and expect her to pay.

Finally, we must offer terms which a responsible Government in Germany can expect to be able to carry out . . . .

From every point of view, therefore, it seems to me that we ought to endeavor to draw up a peace settlement as if we were impartial arbiters, forgetful of the passions of the war . . . .

II

It is not, however, enough to draw up a just and farsighted peace with Germany. If we are to offer Europe an alternative to Bolshevism we must make the League of Nations into something which will be both a safeguard to those nations who are prepared for fair dealing with their neighbours and a menace to those who would trespass on the rights of their neighbours, whether they are imperialist empires or imperialist Bolshevists. An essential element, therefore, in the peace settlement is the constitution of the League of Nations as the effective guardian of international right and international liberty throughout the world. If this is to happen the first thing to do is that the leading members of the League of Nations should arrive at an understanding between themselves in regard to armaments . . . . The first condition of success for the League of Nations is, therefore, a firm understanding between the British Empire and the United States of America and France and Italy that there will be no competitive building up of fleets or armies between them. Unless this is arrived at before the Covenant is signed the League of Nations will be a sham and a mockery . . . .

I should like to ask why Germany, if she accepts the terms we consider just and fair, should not be admitted to the League of Nations, at any rate as soon as she has established a stable and democratic Government. Would it not be an inducement to her both to sign the terms and to resist Bolshevism? Might it not be safer that she should be inside the League than that she should be outside it?

Finally, I believe that until the authority and effectiveness of the League of Nations has been demonstrated, the British Empire and the United States ought to give to France a guarantee against the possibility of a new German aggression. France has special reason for asking for such a guarantee. She has twice been attacked and twice invaded by Germany in half a century. She has been so attacked because she has been the principal guardian of liberal and democratic civilization against Central European autocracy on the Continent of Europe. It is right that the other great Western democracies should enter into an undertaking which will ensure that they stand by her side in time to protect her against invasion, should Germany ever threaten her again or until the League of Nations has proved its capacity to preserve the peace and liberty of the world.

III

If, however, the Peace Conference is really to secure peace and prove to the world a complete plan of settlement which all reasonable men will recognize as an alternative preferable to anarchy, it must deal with the Russian situation . . . . It threatens the whole of Asia and is as near to America as it is to France . . . .

OUTLINE OF PEACE TERMS

Part I

Termination of State of War

War, i.e., the state of belligerency, cannot be brought to an end more than once. If the forthcoming treaty is to enable the transition of the Allied countries to a peace footing to be carried through, and demobilization to be completed, it should put an end to the state of war.

Part II

The League of Nations

(1) All high contracting parties, as part of the Treaty of Peace to become members of the League of Nations . . . .

Part III

Political

A. Cession of territory by Germany and the consequential arrangements.

Eastern Boundaries of Germany

(1) Poland to be given a corridor to Danzig . . . .

Western Boundaries of Germany

(3) No attempt is made to separate the Rhenish Provinces from the rest of Germany. These provinces to be demilitarized; that is to say, the inhabitants of this territory will not be permitted to bear arms or receive any military training, or to be incorporated in any military organization either on a voluntary or compulsory basis, and no fortifications, depots, establishments, railway construction, or works of any kind adapted to military purposes will be permitted to exist within the area. No troops to be sent into this area for any purpose whatsoever without previous notification to the League of Nations. As France is naturally anxious about a neighbour who has twice within living memory invaded and devastated her land with surprising rapidity, the British Empire and the United States of America undertake to come to the assistance of France with their whole strength in the event of Germany moving her troops across the Rhine without the consent of the Council of the League of Nations. This guarantee to last until the League of Nations has proved itself to be an adequate security.

(4) Germany to cede Alsace-Lorraine to France.

(5) Germany to cede to France the 1814 frontier, or in the alternative, . . . compensate France for . . . coal-fields . . . .

(6) . . .

(7) . . .

(8) . . .

Northern Boundaries of Germany

(9) . . .

German Oversea Possessions and Rights

(10) . . .

B. Recognition of New States which receive no German territory

C. Russian Section

    (1) . . .
    (2) . . .
    (3) . . .

D. Turkish Section

    (1) . . .

E. Miscellaneous

    (1) Acceptance by Germany of Arms Convention.
    (2) . . .
    (3) . . .
    (4) . . .
    (5) . . .
    (6) . . .
    (7) . . .
    (8) . . .
    (9) . . .
  (10) . . .
  (11) . . .

Part IV

Reduction of Armaments

Preamble explaining that the disarmament of Germany is the first step in the limitation of the armaments of all nations . . . .

Part V

Reparation

(1) Germany to undertake to pay full reparation to the Allies. It is difficult to assess the amount chargeable against Germany under this head . . . .

Part VI

Breaches of the Laws of War

(1) . . .

Part VII

Economic

Germany to be given full access to raw materials and markets of the world . . . .

(1) . . .
(2) . . .
(3) . . .
(4) Revival of Economic Treaties.
(5) . . .
(6) . . .
(7) . . .
(8) . . .
(9) . . .
(10) . . .

Paris.

March 25, 1919.

APPENDIX D.   THE FOURTEEN POINTS[6]

. . . We entered this war because violations of right had occurred which touched us to the quick and made the life of our people impossible unless they were corrected and the world secured once for all against their recurrence. What we demand in this war, therefore, is nothing peculiar to ourselves. It is that the world be made fit and safe to live in; and particularly that it be made safe for every peace-loving nation which, like our own, wishes to live its own life, determine its own institutions, be assured of justice and fair dealing by the other peoples of the world . . . . The programme of the world's peace, therefore, is our programme; and that programme, the only possible programme, as we see it, is this:

I.   Open convenants of peace, openly arrived at, after which there shall be no private international, understandings of any

---

6. *Congressional Record,* 65th Congress, 2nd session, Vol. 56, Part 1, 680-681. This is part of an address delivered to the Congress of the United States, January 8, 1918, by President Wilson. The enunciation of fourteen principles necessary, as he thought, for peace, were soon known as the "Fourteen Points." These principles formed a major part of the basis for the negotiations leading to the Armistice of November 11, 1918.

kind but diplomacy shall proceed always frankly and in the public view.

II. Absolute freedom of navigation upon the seas, outside territorial waters, alike in peace and in war, except as the seas may be closed in whole or in part by international action for the enforcement of international covenants.

III. The removal, so far as possible, of all economic barriers and the establishment of an equality of trade conditions among all the nations consenting to the peace and associating themselves for its maintenance.

IV. Adequate guarantees given and taken that national armaments will be reduced to the lowest point consistent with domestic safety.

V. A free, open-minded, and absolutely impartial adjustment of all colonial claims, based upon a strict observance of the principle that in determining all such questions of sovereignty the interests of the populations concerned must have equal weight with the equitable claims of the government whose title is to be determined.

VI. The evacuation of all Russian territory and such a settlement of all questions affecting Russia as will secure the best and freest co-operation of the other nations of the world in obtaining for her an unhampered and unembarrassed opportunity for the independent determination of her own political development and national policy and assure her of a sincere welcome into the society of free nations under institutions of her own choosing; and, more than a welcome, assistance also of every kind that she may need and may herself desire. The treatment accorded Russia by her sister nations in the months to come will be the acid test of their good will, of their comprehension of her needs as distinguished from their own interests, and of their intelligent and unselfish sympathy.

VII. Belgium, the whole world will agree, must be evacuated and restored, without any attempt to limit the sovereignty which she enjoys in common with all other free nations. No other single act will serve as this will to restore confidence among the nations in the laws which they have themselves set and determined for the government of their relations with one another. Without this healing act the whole structure and validity of international law is forever impaired.

VIII. All French territory should be freed and the invaded portions restored, and the wrong done to France by Prussia in 1871 in the matter of Alsace-Lorraine, which has unsettled the peace of the world for nearly fifty years, should be righted, in order that peace may once more be made secure in the interest of all.

IX. A readjustment of the frontiers of Italy should be effected along clearly recognizable lines of nationality.

X. The peoples of Austria-Hungary, whose place among the nations we wish to see safeguarded and assured, should be accorded the freest opportunity of autonomous development.

XI. Rumania, Serbia, and Montenegro should be evacuated; occupied territories restored; Serbia accorded free and secure access to the sea; and the relations of the several Balkan states to one another determined by friendly counsel along historically established lines of allegiance and nationality; and international guarantees of the political and economic independence and territorial integrity of the several Balkan states should be entered into.

XII. The Turkish portions of the present Ottoman Empire should be assured a secure sovereignty, but the other nationalities which are now under Turkish rule should be assured an undoubted security of life and an absolutely unmolested opportunity of autonomous development, and the Dardanelles should be permanently opened as a free passage to the ships and commerce of all nations under international guarantees.

XIII. An independent Polish state should be erected which should include the territories inhabited by indisputably Polish populations, which should be assured a free and secure access to the sea, and whose political and economic independence and territorial integrity should be guaranteed by international covenant.

XIV. A general association of nations must be formed under specific covenants for the purpose of affording mutual guarantees of political independence and territorial integrity to great and small states alike.

In regard to these . . . we feel ourselves to be intimate partners of all the governments and peoples . . . . We cannot be separated in interest or divided in purpose. We stand together until the end . . . .

APPENDIX E. THE FRENCH MEMORANDUM
ON THE RHINELAND QUESTION[7]

February 26, 1919

MEMORANDUM OF THE FRENCH GOVERNMENT on the
FIXATION at the RHINE of the WESTERN FRONTIER
OF GERMANY and on INTER-ALLIED OCCUPATION
of the RHINE BRIDGES

I

THE OBJECTS TO BE ATTAINED

The considerations which the French Government submits
to the Conference on the subject of the left bank of the Rhine
have no selfish character.

They do not tend towards annexations of territories. They
aim at the suppression of a common danger and the creation
of a common protection.

It is a problem of general interest, a problem which France,
the first exposed to the danger it is sought to avert, has the
right and duty to place before the Conference, but which directly
affects all the Allied and Associated Nations and can be solved
only by them conjointly.

The essential aim which the Conference seeks to attain is to
prevent by all just means that which has been from ever occurring
again.

Now, what happened in 1914 was possible only for one
reason: Germany because of her mastery over offensive preparations made by her on the left bank of the river thought herself
capable of crushing the democracies, France and Belgium, be-

7. Ministère des Affaires Étrangéres, *Documents Diplomatiques: Documents Relatifs aux négociations concernant Les Garanties de Sécurité
contre une Agression de L'Allemagne,* (*10 janvier 1919-7 décembre 1923*),
(Paris, 1924), 15-31. M. Tardieu prepared the memorandum.

fore the latter could receive the aid of the Overseas Democracies, Great Britain, the Dominions, and the United States.

It was because this was possible that Germany determined to attack.

It is therefore this possibility which must be done away with, by depriving Germany of the means which permitted her to believe in the success of her plan.

In a word there is no question of the aggrandizement of any of the Allied Nations; it is merely a question of placing Germany in a position where she can do no harm by imposing upon her conditions indispensable to the common security of the Western Democracies and of their overseas Allies and associates, as well as to the very existence of France.

There is no question of annexing an inch of German soil; only of depriving Germany of her weapons of offense.

II

THE NECESSITY OF INTER-ALLIED OCCUPATION OF THE RHINE BRIDGES

It is necessary first to examine the nature of the danger to be averted; to show whom it threatens, in what it consists; by what means it can be suppressed.

1. *The danger is common to all the Allies.*

(a) If, in 1914, the Germans, throwing back the Belgians, the French and the few British divisions then in line, had taken the Channel ports, the aid also brought by Great Britain in 1915 to the common cause would have been greatly delayed if not entirely prevented.

If, in 1918, the Germans had taken Paris, the concentration of the French Armies south of the Loire and the forcing back of our war industries would certainly have delayed the landing and movement by rail of the American Army, then just beginning to arrive, and this delay would have had consequences of the utmost gravity.

Thus, there is no doubt, on two occasions — and it would be easy to furnish other instances — the military assistance of the two great overseas Powers came very near being hampered, if not prevented entirely, before actually taking shape.

(b) In order that this may never be so, that is to say, in order that the maritime Powers may play a useful part on the Continent in a defensive war against an aggression coming from the East, they must have the assurance that French territory will not be overrun in a few days.

In other words, should there not remain enough French ports for the Overseas Armies to debark their troops and war supplies, should there not remain enough French territory for them to concentrate and operate from their bases, the Overseas Democracies would be debarred from waging a continental war against any Power seeking to dominate the Continent. They would be deprived of their nearest and most natural battleground. Nothing would be left to them but Naval and Economic warfare.

So, the lesson made plain by the last war is that a strong natural protection on the East is a matter of common concern to the Western and Overseas Democracies. And this lesson is emphasized by the fact that Russia to-day no longer exists.

To decide upon this protection, let us first see whence the danger comes.

2. *The danger comes from the possession by Germany of the left bank and the Rhine bridges.*

If Germany was able to plan and execute the sudden attack which nearly settled the outcome of the war in five weeks, it was because she held the left bank of the Rhine and had made of it against her neighbors an offensive military base constantly and quickly supplied, thanks to the capacity of the Rhine bridges.

All military history since 1815 demonstrates this and the plan is written out in full in the publications as well as in the acts of the German General Staff.

(a) History first, that of 1870, as of 1914.

In 1870, despite the then shortcomings of the Prussian system of railways, it was on the left bank that the concentration of the Prussian troops was carried out.

This fact is all the more significant because the Prussian General Staff was still under the impression of the reputation of the French Army in attack and consequently, very cautious. Despite this, but on the hypothesis that France would have taken the initiative, Prussia had confined itself to the preparation of a plan of concentration farther east but always on the left bank.

In other words, she had no thought of using the river as a protection; and, in any contingency, she looked upon it as the offensive base indispensable to the execution of a plan of attack. It is known that in fact, thanks to its concentration on the left bank, the Prussian Army invaded France in less than three weeks.

In 1914, the same situation produced the same results. But things moved faster, thanks to the enormous developments of facilities. Germany, massed once more on the left bank of the Rhine (and much nearer to the French frontier than in 1870, because of the perfection of her railway system) was in a few hours able to carry the war to Belgium and to France, and in a few weeks to the very heart of France.

Before even the declaration of war Germany invaded a region from which France drew 90 per cent of her iron ore, 86 per cent of her pig iron, 75 per cent of her steel, while 95 out of the 127 blast furnaces fell into the hands of the enemy.

This situation permitted Germany to multiply her war resources, while depriving France of her most necessary means of defense. It nearly resulted in the taking of Paris in 1914, of Dunkirk, Calais and Boulogne six weeks later.

All this was possible only because, at our very gates, at a few days' march from our capital, Germany had the most formidable offensive military base known to history.

(b) This military base she has had for a century and in pursuit of a policy of aggression which has never varied — and which had as its objective the bridgeheads of the Sarre in 1815, of the Rhine and of the Moselle in 1870, and of the Meuse in 1914 — has constantly reinforced it, openly asserting that the left bank of the Rhine was indispensable to her for that purpose.

During the negotiations at the Conference of Vienna, Gneisenau and Grolman already indicated that the "main concentration of the Prussian Army must take place between the Rhine and the Moselle."

Won over by their insistence, Castlereagh wrote to Wellington on October 1, 1815: "Mr. Pitt was altogether right when, as early as 1805, he wanted to give Prussia more territory on the left bank of the Rhine, and thus put her in closer military contact with France."

In 1832, Boyan repeated that the point of concentration must be Treves.

In 1840, Grolman, reiterating the same idea, declared the first objective of German concentration to be an offensive in Lorraine and in Champagne.

The same idea prompted Moltke's plan of operations against France in 1870. It is this same plan that Germany carried out in 1914 on an unprecedented scale and with unprecedented violence.

Finally, need we recall that in November, 1917, Admiral von Tirpitz declared in an address to the German Fatherland League, that "without the possession of the left bank, Germany would have been unable to pass her Armies through a neutral Belgium"?

(c) Such being the doctrine Germany translated into action by organizing for military purposes the left bank of the Rhine and the bridges which are the key to that organization.

With this in view she built fortresses, concentration camps, finally and above all, a railway system powerfully equipped for attack and linked by the Rhine bridges with the whole railway system on the right bank, which also was laid out for the same purposes of attack. The fortifications of the Rhine and of its left bank comprised in addition to the fortified districts of Metz-Thionville and Strassburg-Molsheim (whose role will disappear with the return of Alsace-Lorraine to France) the Rhine fortresses — Cologne, Coblenz and Mayence — crossing points for the strategic railways, and vast entrenched camps (supplies, equipment, barracks, and factories and workshops, etc.).

The training camps, like that of Malmedy, were suitable for transformation into concentration camps — an easy way of concentrating troops under pretense of training in the neighborhood of a peaceful or even neutral state (France, Belgium, Luxemburg).

The railway system is of still wider significance. A glance at the map of German railways on the right bank of the Rhine, will show that nine great independent transportation highways converge towards the bridges and continue across them to the left bank.

Eight of these nine highways run between Duisburg and Rastatt, flooding the French frontier with troops and preparing the way for aggression.

It is, therefore, obvious that the plan of aggression, conceived and prepared as early as 1815, and twice executed — in 1870 and

1914 — was based *upon the transportation capacity of the Rhine bridges*. Without the left bank, and above all, without the bridges — the second feeding the first — aggression would not have been possible.

(d) And this is so true, that, as early as 1909, General von Falkenhausen, in his book *Der Grosse Krieg der Jetztzeit,* showed that by her mastery of the bridges, Germany could wage war in enemy territory even supposing that the French, British and Italian Armies had utilized before the opening of hostilities the territories of Holland, Belgium, Luxemburg and the Rhine, and had carried out their concentration in front of the Schlestadt-Sarreburg-Saint-Avold-Luxemburg-Bastogne line.

Even in such a contingency, according to the General, if Germany concentrated on the Rhine and controlled the bridges, the transportation capacity of these bridges would enable her, in three days to transport half of her forces — more than twenty Army Corps — to the line Juliers-Duren-Kochem-Birkenfeld-Kaiserslautern-Haguenau, without her adversaries having time to prevent it.

It will be seen that the hypothetical conditions stated by General von Falkenhausen correspond exactly to the situation which would arise if peace were to leave Germany in possession of the Rhine bridges. This possession of these bridges, according to the General's own demonstration, would suffice, no matter what happened, to assure to Germany the advantages of an offensive war.

This hypothesis proves, in other words, that the danger arises from the possession by Germany not only of the left bank but also and, above all, of the Rhine bridges.

Thus, geography, history and the doctrine of the German General Staff all go to prove that the aggressive power of Germany depends upon the strategic railway system she has built on the left bank of the Rhine, taken in combination with the river fortresses, that is to say, in the last analysis, that *her power of aggression is measured by the transportation capacity of the Rhine bridges.*

If that power of aggression is to be abolished, it is essential to take from Germany not only the left bank, but the Rhine bridges, which amounts to the fixation of her Western frontier at the Rhine.

That is an absolutely essential condition. Is it a sufficient safeguard?

3. *The safety of the Western and Overseas Democracies makes it imperative, in present circumstances, for them to guard the bridges of the Rhine.*

Would the non-occupation by Germany of the left bank and the bridges suffice to prevent the renewal of her sudden attacks of 1870 and 1914? Certainly not.

(a) If indeed the bridges are not guarded against Germany, she can easily seize them by reason of her railways system on the right bank. The railway map shows this.

Can it be said that in this case it be enough to destroy the system of strategic railways on the left bank? It would either be impossible or useless.

Impossible, because a total destruction cannot be conceived; for the railways respond to economic as well as to strategic demands.

Useless, because a partial destruction, involving only the military equipment, would be ineffective, for the military and the commercial stations are often the same.

It would always, therefore, be possible for Germany either to build new stations on commercial pretexts or to supplement those already existing with debarcation sidings along the tracks.

(b) On the other hand, even dismantled, the Rhine towns, with their bridges, railway stations, commercial equipment could always constitute splendid points for the detraining and concentration of troops.

In other words, the only positive guarantee against a German aggression is inter-allied occupation of the bridges, for, if once this occupation is effected and Germany were again to plan an aggression, it would first be necessary for her to modify her railway system on the right bank. This would quickly become known.

Therefore, the occupation of the bridges is the minimum protection essential to the Western and Overseas Democracies.

(c) It is also an indispensable protection for the new States which the Allies have called into being to the east and south of Germany.

Let us suppose that Germany, controlling the Rhine, should decide to attack the Republic of Poland, or the Republic of Bohemia.

Established defensively on the Rhine, she would hold in check for how long nobody knows the Western nations coming to the rescue of the young Republics, and the latter would be crushed before they could receive aid.

4. *Conclusion.*

To sum up:

(a) The common safety of the Western and Overseas Democracies makes it essential that Germany should be unable to renew her sudden attack of 1870 and 1914.

(b) To prevent Germany from renewing that attack, it is essential to forbid her access to the left bank of the Rhine, and to fix her western border at the river.

(c) To forbid her this access, it is essential that the bridges be occupied.

This is the one and only way:

(a) To deprive Germany of her offensive base.

(b) To provide the Western Democracies with a proper and reliable defense; first, by the width of the Rhine (preventing any sudden attack by means of gases, tanks, etc. . . .); second, by its straight course (preventing any flanking movement).

The history of a whole century shows the necessity of this defense! The common safety of the Allies demands that the Rhine should become, in President Wilson's words "the frontier of freedom."

III

INADEQUACY OF PRESENT GUARANTEES FURNISHED BY THE LIMITATIONS OF THE MILITARY FORCES OF GERMANY OR BY THE LEAGUE OF NATIONS

Everybody, we believe, will be agreed on the object to be attained. But it may be asked whether there is only one way to attain it.

In other words, is the guarantee — Germany and her military forces thrust back across the Rhine and the Rhine bridges occupied by the Allies — which the French Government deems absolutely indispensable, the only one which can possibly attain the object sought?

Would not sufficient protection be afforded, on the contrary, either by limitation of Germany's military forces or by the terms of the first draft of the League of Nations?

To this question, the French Government for the following reasons makes a negative reply.

1. *The limitation of the military forces of Germany is not at present an adequate guarantee.*

(a) Germany's military strength rests upon three basic factors.

Man Power (seventy million inhabitants, furnishing 650,000 men a year); war supplies (existing stocks and potential production); General Staff (which constitutes a veritable State within the State).

Measures for limiting Germany's military forces are under consideration. They must rest upon the three foregoing factors, and more especially restrict:

— the number and composition of divisions, the annual contingent, etc.

— the equipment and supplies.

— the old military organization (war college, manoeuvres, etc.).

Suppose Germany accepts these restrictions. Will this be a complete safeguard? No.

(b) First history — though not wishing to lay undue stress upon its lessons — teaches the value of skepticism.

Just one instance; in September, 1808, Napoleon imposed upon Prussia the undertaking that for ten years she would not keep an Army of more than 42,000 men or resort to any extraordinary levy of militia or national guards or to any other device which might give her a military force exceeding this total of 42,000 men. But what actually happened?

In spite of Napoleon's unceasing diplomatic and military supervision, Prussia managed to elude or nullify all the clauses. Knowing that with a population of five millions, she could maintain an Army of 150,000 men, she passed all her male population fit for service through the Army in the shortest time possible, by reducing the term of active service, and she also organized preliminary military instruction in her schools.

Despite her conqueror's threats and his power to bring pressure to bear upon Prussia, this military reorganization proceeded uninterruptedly and resulted in the creation of the great

National Army of several hundred thousand men which was mobilized in 1813.

(c) So much the past. Will it be said that we shall have in the future more effective means of supervision than Napoleon had? Perhaps. But we answer that the difficulties attending this supervision will increase far more than the efficacy of our means of supervision.

Instead of a small country of five million inhabitants, we shall have to deal with a country of seventy millions.

Instead of a country without industries, we shall have to deal with a country possessing huge industrial resources.

For our supervision to be real, it should extend over:
— the war budget
— the industrial budget
— the organization of the General Staff and of the Army
— the size of the Army and the recruiting laws
— the supplies of war material
— the manufacturing capacity of the whole German territory
— the moral influence including schools and education.

Does anyone believe that this supervision can be established in a day? Does anyone believe that we shall know, for many years to come, whether or not it is effective? Assuredly not.

Can it fail to be recognized, on the other hand, that during the next few years Germany will retain through forces of circumstances a military force, certain elements of which cannot be reduced — viz.:

— highly trained staffs
— an enormous corps of trained officers (110,500 in August, 1918, excluding the Bavarian Army)
— millions of soldiers broken to war
— a manpower of military age which will grow for many years in direct ratio to the steady increase in the German birth rate.
— war supplies and manufacturing potentialities, part of which Germany can conceal, since we, ourselves — the Allies — have not yet been able to make an accurate estimate of our own existing war material.

And can one on the other hand rely upon Germany for an honest fulfillment of her undertaking, when the so-called German

Democracy shows in every direction a total lack of morality and has placed at its head men who were the most active agents of militarism and imperialism: Ebert, Scheidemann, David, Erzberger and Brockdorff-Rantzau, not to mention Hindenburg?

Besides as regards their intentions, we have their own statements. The Ebert Government has declared its intention of adopting the Swiss military system. Translated into figures, what does this mean?

It means that Germany could on the basis of Swiss military law mobilize 193 divisions with the corresponding army troops — the exact force which she hurled against the Western front in her spring offensive of 1918.

Again in the *Munchner Neueste Nachrichten* of January 25, 1919, was published a statement by the Bavarian war minister, estimating at 7,700,000 men the war strength of the future German Army, 3,200,000 of them being fighting troops.

(d) From all this we may draw a conclusion, which all will admit to be just and conservative, that, at least for the present and for years to come, no limitation of Germany's forces is possible, no supervision of this limitation can assure complete safety, either to the victims of the German aggression in 1914, or to the new states now in process of formation.

On the seas the total surrender of the German Navy has, to a large extent, afforded such a safeguard. *On land nothing of the kind is possible.*

The result is that whatever improvement the future may bring to the general world situation, the limitation of Germany's military power can at present only hold out troops to the Western Democracies, but in no wise constitute a certain safeguard!

But hopes — without certainty — cannot suffice to those who suffered the aggression of 1914.

Hopes — without certainty — cannot suffice Belgium, victim of her loyalty to her pledged word, punished for her loyalty by invasion, fire, pillage, rape and ruin.

Hopes — without certainty — cannot suffice France, invaded before any declaration of war, deprived in a few hours (because she had drawn her troops back from the border to avoid incidents) of 90 per cent of her iron ore and 86 per cent of her pig iron. Hopes — without certainty — cannot suffice France whose losses were 1,364,000 killed, 790,000 crippled and 3,000,000 wounded, not to mention 438,000 prisoners who suffered physical martyrdom in German prison camps. Hopes — without certainty — cannot suffice France who lost 16 per cent of her mobilized manpower and 57 per cent of her soldiers under 31 years of age — the most productive part of the nation. Hopes — without certainty — cannot suffice France who saw a fourth of her productive capital blotted out by the systematic destruction of her industrial districts in the North and in the East, who saw taken into captivity — and what captivity — her children, her women and her girls.

To these two countries — Belgium and France — certain safeguards are essential — not only the certainty of never again being exposed to what they suffered five years ago, but also the certainty that, failing physical guarantees, they will not have to bear overwhelming military burdens. But these certain safeguards cannot be furnished France and Belgium by the limitation of German military power.

2. *Nor can the League of Nations, at present, provide an adequate guarantee.*

Can this complete security, which is indispensable and which cannot now be given either by limiting German military power, or by supervising this limitation, be found in the Covenant of the League of Nations, as now submitted to the Conference?

(a) Eight articles of the draft Covenant (Articles X to XVIII) define the guarantees against aggression assured to the members of the League. These guarantees may be said to consist in a double interval of time, viz.:

(1) The longest possible time between the threat of war and the act of war (to increase the chances of reaching agreement).

(2) The shortest possible time between the act of war and the concerted action of the League members in aid of the country attacked.

Under such conditions, we believe that this guarantee is inadequate to prevent the recurrence of what took place in 1914, i.e., a sudden attack by Germany against France and Belgium and the immediate invasion of their territory.

The reasons for our belief are numerous, principally the following:

(b) First: the measures which determine the interval of time between the threat of aggression and the act of aggression (ordinary diplomatic methods, arbitration, inquiry by the Executive Committee, undertakings of the parties not to resort to force before arbitration and inquiry, and only three months after a judicial decision has been rendered) are applicable only if the dispute arises between nations having subscribed to the Covenant of the League.

Now Germany is not and cannot be a member of the League.

The Covenant provides, it is true, a complete procedure applicable to States not members. But there is no guarantee whatever that this procedure would be accepted by Germany, should she again plan a sudden attack.

On the contrary, we have every reason to believe that she would act with the utmost speed.

In such an hypothesis, it is clear that the Germany of to-day — the Germany that is evading the question of responsibilities — the Germany of Scheidemann, Erzberger, Brockdorff-Rantzau — will be halted in her plans for aggression, neither by an invitation to join the League, nor by the threat of a financial and commercial blockade. It is clear that Germany — knowing the penalty she would have to pay if she gave international forces time to come into play — will fall upon France and Belgium with the idea, even more firmly implanted than in 1870 or 1914, that time is for her the essential factor of success.

We believe therefore that the provisions of the Covenant which enjoin legal steps between the threat of war and the act of war will not suffice to stop Germany, should she decide to attack. That is our first reason.

(c) Second: Germany's method is sudden attack. What immediate guarantee does the Covenant furnish? Remember that proposals made by the French delegation with a view to the creation of a permanent international force have been rejected.

If one of the members is attacked, what happens? The Executive Committee of the League takes action and specifies the strength of the military or naval contingents to be furnished by every member of the League.

Suppose that the Committe takes this action with the utmost speed. Only one thing is lacking, the decisions of the Committee are not of themselves executory.

Take, in order to make this clear, the case of America, for instance. What happens?

The naval and military forces of the United States cannot be used without the assent of the Congress. Suppose Congress is not in session. Between a German aggression and the moment when American aid could become effective, the following steps would have to be taken:

- a decision by the Executive Committee of the League.
- a meeting of Congress, with the necessary quorum, which might take four or five days.
- a message from the President of the United States.
- a discussion of the matter before Congress.
- the mobilization of an American Expeditionary Force and its transportation to Europe.

We have cited the case of America but it is not the only one.

Consider anew the necessary steps outlined above and apply them to the German attack of 1914.

Suppose that invaded France and invaded Belgium had had to set this complicated machinery in motion before obtaining British aid and that Great Britain, instead of beginning to ship troops within a week, had been obliged (after a meeting of and action by the Executive Committee of the League of Nations, communication of its decision, discussion of the case by the British Government, meeting of Parliament, debate, etc.) to delay her actual intervention till all these various things had been done, the left of the French Army would have been turned at Charleroi, and the war lost on August 24, 1914.

In other words, suppose that instead of the defensive military understanding — very limited indeed — which was given effect to between Great Britain and France in 1914 there had been no other bond between the two countries than the general agreements contained in the Covenant of the League, the British intervention would have been less prompt and Germany's victory thereby assured.

So we believe that, under present conditions, the aid provided for by the Covenant of the League would arrive too late. That is our second reason.

(d) Our third reason, and it is final, is that because of the geographical position of France we have two aims equally imperative:

- the one is Victory
- the other the protection of our soil.

It may be accepted as certain that, thanks to the principle of solidarity embodied in the Covenant of the League, final victory would rest with us in the case of a new German aggression.

But this is not enough. We are determined that invasion, the systematic destruction of our soil and the suffering of our fellow citizens in the North and East, shall not again be endured from the time of the aggression to that of final victory.

It is against this second danger, quite as much as against the danger of defeat, that a certain safeguard is necessary. This guarantee the League does not provide, but it is provided by the proposals put forward by the French Government.

(e) Summing up here our argument touching the guarantee provided by the League, our contention is that:

On the one hand, Germany will remain outside of the League of Nations for an indefinite length of time.

On the other hand, the decisions of the Executive Committee, instead of automatically setting in motion an international force ready for action, will have to be submitted to the approval of the various Parliaments, which will decide whether or not their national forces may join the military forces of the nation attacked.

So we obtain neither of the two guarantees on which the peace-enforcing action of the League is supposedly based, namely:

— a very long interval between the idea of war and the act of war.
— a very brief interval between the act of war and the joining together of all the military forces of the League members.

In default of these two guarantees, we ask against a Germany whose population is twice that of France, and whose word cannot be trusted for a long time to come, another kind of guarantee: *a physical guarantee.*

This physical guarantee in our mind is not intended to take the place of the other, provided by the League, but to give the latter time to operate before it is too late.

This physical guarantee — We have shown that *there is such guarantee, and only one such*: the guard of the Rhine bridges by an inter-allied force.

Let us add that, for the time being, it is to the interest of the League of Nations itself that this supplementary guarantee should insure the normal and effective working of the dual machinery conceived by the League for the maintenance of peace.

IV

SUPPRESSION BY INTER-ALLIED OCCUPATION OF THE RHINE BRIDGES OF SEVERAL CAUSES OF WAR

We have established:

(1) That a common guarantee against the recurrence of any sudden attack from Germany is necessary.

(2) That this guarantee cannot be completely assured either by the limitation or the suppression of Germany's military power, or by the proposed clauses of the Covenant of the League of Nations.

(3) That this guarantee can be found only in the fixation at the Rhine of the Western frontier of Germany, and in the occupation of the bridges by an inter-allied force.

It is easy to show, moreover, that the common guarantee assured by the occupation of the Rhine bridges accords with the common interests of the League and with its pacific ideals; it does away with a certain number of permanent causes of war which it is at once the interest and the duty of the League to eliminate.

1. *Elimination of a dangerous disproportion in strength.*

Germany (even without Poznan, Schleswig, Alsace-Lorraine and the Rhine provinces on the left bank) still has more than fifty-nine million inhabitants, to which would probably be added in case of war seven million German-Austrians, making a total of sixty-six million men. France, Belgium and Luxemburg, on the other hand, have not more than forty-nine million.

Russia no longer exists as a counter-weight and the States recently created do not yet count.. This was strongly emphasized by Mr. Winston Churchill, at a meeting of the Supreme Council of the Allies on February 15, 1919: "There are twice as many Germans as French and by reason of the high German birth rate, Germany has annually three times as many young men of military age as France. That is a tremendous fact." This "tremendous fact" is a war factor. If it cannot be eliminated, it is at least useful to try to reduce it.

2. *Elimination of one of the economic causes of German aggressions.*

It is generally admitted that it is essential that industrial zones vital to each nation should be protected.

For rapid occupation of these vital zones gives a decisive advantage to the aggressor, who thus adds to his own means of production those which he wrests from his adversary. It is thus certain that the possibility of securing such an advantage is a cause of war.

History demonstrates this. In 1815, Germany aimed at the coal of the Sarre; in 1870 at the ores of Lorraine; in 1914 at the ores of Briey.

Germany herself has explicitly admitted that, if she was able to carry on the last war it was because she was able by sudden attack to seize the French ores "without which she could never by any possibility have waged this war successfully." (Memorandum of the German iron and steel manufacturers, December, 1917).

If the Rhine had separated the two Powers, no such action would have been possible. And it is strengthening the peace to remove from Germany — in separating her from her historical objective — one of the main motives of her past aggressions.

3. *Protection for the smaller states whose safety the League of Nations seeks to secure.*

First to Belgium by removing from her a dangerous neighbor. Admiral von Tirpitz, quoted above, made this statement to the German Fatherland League (*Munchner Neueste Nachrichten,* November 11, 1917):

"Realize clearly what would happen if our existing front — now resting on the sea, — should be on the eastern border of the Rhine country, we could never again succeed in throwing our armies through a neutral Belgium."

Then to Poland, to Czecho-Slovakia, to Jugo Slavia which, should Germany take advantage of their initial difficulties and seek to throttle them, must not see the Rhine, held by Germany, cut off the aid awaited by them from the Western Democracies.

4. *Closing the great historic road of invasion.*

The left bank of the Rhine has been for centuries the road of invasions. Its natural situation on the one hand, the direction of its railway lines on the other, have made of it one of the battle grounds of history, where the peoples of the right bank (whenever they also controlled the left bank) found potentialities of aggression which the interests of peace demand should be done away with.

5. *Creation of a natural frontier equal for all.*

The Rhine, both on account of its width and of the straightness of its course, offers to the peoples of both banks the same natural guarantee against aggression.

6. *Conclusion.*

From the foregoing it is permissible to conclude that the common guarantee created by the fixation at the Rhine of the Western frontier of Germany and by the occupation of the Rhine bridges by an inter-allied force, is not only necessary but in complete accord with the principles advocated by the League of Nations for the prevention of future wars.

V

FRENCH INTERESTS IDENTICAL WITH
GENERAL INTERESTS

It is now possible to obtain a bird's-eye view of the problem which can be summed up as follows:

(a) In this matter, France claims nothing for herself, neither an inch of territory, nor any right of sovereignty. She does not want to annex the left bank of the Rhine.

What she proposes is the creation in the interest of all of a common protection for all the peaceful democracies, of the League of Nations, of the cause of Liberty and of Peace.

But it is France's duty to add that her request, which accords with the general welfare and is free from any selfish design, is of vital necessity to herself and that on its principle she cannot compromise. France sees in it in fact the only immediate and complete guarantee that what she suffered in 1870 and 1914 will not occur again and she owes it to her people, to the dead who must not have died in vain, to the living who wish to rebuild their country in peace and not to stagger beneath overpowering military burdens to obtain this guarantee.

As to the manner of applying this guarantee, the French Government is ready to consult with its Allies with a view to establishing under the most favourable conditions the national, political and economical system of the regions, access to which it demands shall be forbidden to Germany. To this end, the French Government will accept any suggestions which are not inconsistent with the principle stated.

This principle may be summed up in three paragraphs.

1.   No German military force on the left bank of the Rhine, and fixation at the Rhine of the Western frontier of Germany.

2.   Occupation of the Rhine bridges by an inter-allied force.

3.   No annexation.

This is what under present circumstances France asks as a necessary guarantee of international peace, as the indispensable safeguard of her national existence.

She hopes that all her Allies and Associates will appreciate the *General Interests* of this proposal.

She counts, on the other hand, that they will acknowledge her right and her duty to present and to support this demand for her own sake.

(b) Also this is not the only time that the vital interests of a nation have accorded with the general interests of mankind.

At all times the great naval Powers have asserted — whether the issue were Philip II or Napoleon or William II — that their strength was the only force capable of offsetting imperialistic attempts to control the continent.

It is on this ground that they have justified the mantenance, for their own advantages, of powerful fleets.

Yet, at the same time, they have never concealed the fact that these fleets were a vital necessity to themselves as well.

Of vital necessity to the British Isles and the British Empire — which have made known their refusal to give up any part of that naval power which enabled them to hold the seas against Germany.

Of a vital necessity to the United States, washed by two oceans, requiring safeguards for the export of its natural and industrial resources, and which despite its peaceful policy has for the above reason created a Navy that is even now being further expanded.

For Great Britain, in fact, as well as for the United States, the Navy is a means of pushing away from beyond their coasts the frontier which they would have to defend in case of aggression, and of creating a safety-zone in front of this frontier, in front of their national soil.

For France, the question is the same with this triple difference: that, first, she is not protected from Germany by the seas; that, second, she cannot possibly secure on land the complete guarantee which Great Britain and the United States secured on the sea by the surrender of the German fleet to the Allies, and that finally, the "one to two" ratio between her population and Germany's precludes the hope that in case of war she may ever enjoy the advantage which the naval Powers have always derived from the "two power standards."

For France, as for Great Britain and the United States, it is necessary to create a zone of safety.

This zone the naval Powers create by their fleets, and by the elimination of the German fleet. This zone France, unprotected by the ocean, unable to eliminate the millions of Germans trained to war, must create by the Rhine, by an inter-allied occupation of that river.

If she did not do so, she would once more be exposed, if not to final defeat, at least to a partial destruction of her soil by an enemy invasion.

It is a danger which she never intends to run again.

Moreover, as explained above, the guarantee of peace created by the existence of the naval Powers, could not be of full effect unless the occupation of the Rhine provided a similar guarantee for the Western Democracies.

At a recent meeting of the Supreme Council of the Allies, February 11, 1919, Mr. Winston Churchill and Mr. House showed one after the other what the future has to fear from a Russo-German rapprochement.

In such an event it is not with their fleets that the naval Powers, capable only of establishing a blockade, could defend the continent against an imperialistic aggression.

The naval Powers would still need the possibility of landing on the continent and of fighting there. For that the inter-allied guard of the Rhine is indispensable.

But there is more and one may ask whether, in such case, even the blockade established by the fleets would be effective.

Of what use would it be against Germany, mistress of Russia, colonizing and exploiting Russia, if Germany were to strike a successful and decisive blow against France and Belgium, occupying their ports and dominating all the neutral powers of Europe?

This fear was expressed by Mr. House at the meeting of February 15, when he pointed out the danger of an union "of the whole world east of the Rhine." To prevent such an union, or at least to avert its consequences, there is only one way: that the Rhine, henceforth, instead of serving as in the past Germany against the Allies, should protect the Allies against the undertakings of Germany.

In commending this viewpoint to the attention of our Allies and Associates, and more especially of the two great naval Powers, the British Empire and the United States, the French Government is deeply conscious that it is working for peace, just as the naval Powers are conscious that they serve the cause of peace by maintaining or increasing their naval forces.

And just as the naval Powers, in maintaining or increasing their fleets, have no design whatsoever to conquer the seas, so the demand of France as to the guard of the Rhine involves neither gain nor sovereignty nor annexation of territory.

France does not demand for herself the left bank of the Rhine: she would not know what to do with it, and her interest equally with her ideals forbids any such claim.

France demands one thing only. It is that the necessary and only possible and certain measures to prevent the left bank of the Rhine from again becoming a base for German aggression, shall be taken by the Powers now gathered at the Peace Conference.

In other words, with no territorial ambitions *but deeply imbued with the necessity of creating a protection both national and international,* France looks to an inter-allied occupation of the Rhine for the same results that Great Britain and the United States expect from the maintenance of their naval forces; neither more, nor less.

In both cases, a national necessity coincides with an international safeguard.

In both cases, even if the second be interpreted in different ways, the first will remain for the country concerned *an obligation subject neither to restriction nor reserve.*

Such is the principle that the French Government begs the Allied and Associated Governments to confirm and sanction by adopting the following decision to be inserted in the provisions of the preliminaries of Peace:

1. *The Western frontier of Germany must be fixed at the Rhine.*

2. *The bridges of the Rhine must be occupied by an inter-allied force.*

3. *The above measures to imply no annexation of territory to the benefit of any Power.*

APPENDIX F. FRENCH NOTE OF REPLY TO THE MARCH 14, 1919, LETTER OF PRESIDENT WILSON AND PRIME MINISTER LLOYD GEORGE[8]

17 March 1919

RESUMÉ OF THE FRENCH PROPOSAL OF FEBRUARY 25, 1919

(1) The military occupation of the Rhine by an inter-allied force (with this immediate and lasting result, separation of the left bank from the German Reich and Zollverein) is, in the present state of international relations, a vital necessity for France and of common interest to the Allies. A detailed memorandum has proved this assertion.

The object is to prevent the renewal of that which we have undergone twice in fifty years and for that to deprive Germany of her essential means of attack (the left bank, the railroads and the bridges of the Rhine).

As a guarantee of this the military occupation of the Rhine border is indispensable to France, with a far smaller population

---

8. Ministére des Affaires Étrangéres, *Documents Diplomatiques: Documents Relatifs aux négociations concernant Les Garanties de Sécurité contre une Agression de L'Allemagne* (10 janvier 1919 — 7 décembre 1923), (Paris, 1924), Document No. 4, 32-35.

than Germany, deprived of Russia's alliance, and without good natural frontiers.

On the other hand the Overseas Democracies cannot fight in Europe if the French ports and railroads are not substantially protected. The last war demonstrated how serious for them is this danger which might completely deprive them of a European battlefield.

(2) The limitation of the military forces of Germany is not a sufficient guarantee against this danger until experience has proved the method efficacious, and especially so long as Germany has at her disposal more than three million men who are trained to war, because they fought in war. The total suppression of the German fleet was not sufficient reason for the naval countries to disarm their own fleets. On land, France, too, has need of physical guarantee.

The League of Nations is also not a sufficient guarantee. The present draft of its clauses makes final victory almost certain. But the League is too slow moving a mechanism to prevent territorial invasion at the beginning of a war. Here also, therefore, a physical guarantee is necessary.

This physical guarantee is the military occupation of the Rhine and the control of its bridge traffic.

(3) The objections presented do not modify this conclusion.

It is feared on the left bank that there may be a movement for union with Germany. But the left bank is different from the rest of Germany. It fears Bolshevism and war-taxes. It is conscious of its economic independence. It has no liking for Prussian officials forced upon it by the Empire. Separatist tendencies are already making themselves felt despite the strict reserve we have maintained.

A nationalist irritation in Germany is foreseen. Defeat has aroused this sentiment. The question resolves itself into protecting ourselves against its possible consequences.

It is thought that the proposed solution may be suspected of imperialism. But it is not a question of annexation, it is a question of creating under the safeguard of the League of Nations, an independent State in accordance with the interests of the inhabitants and with the aspirations of a very large number of them. This is not a Bismarckian solution.

Anxiety is expressed concerning the effect upon British and

American opinion. But the whole lesson of the war is that the Rhine is the military frontier not only of France and Belgium, but of the Overseas Democracies as well, "The Frontier of Freedom," as President Wilson expressed it. These Democracies will understand this as they understood the necessity of conscription during the war, as British democracy understands to-day the channel tunnel.

The danger is pointed out of the indefinite duration of the occupation. But as the entire organization of the left bank is to be in the hands of the League of Nations, the latter will always have the right to alter it.

Therefore, the physical guarantee which will make impossible a renewal of the 1914 situation, remains of vital necessity to France in the present state of international relations.

II

EXAMINATION OF THE SUGGESTION PRESENTED
BY OUR ALLIES

(1) The suggestion presented on March 14, that Great Britain and the United States should pledge themselves in case of aggression by Germany to bring their military forces to the aid of France without delay, is a recognition that France needs a special guarantee; but in place of the physical guarantee demanded by France it substitutes a political guarantee designed to curtail by a definite pledge the time which would elapse between the menace of war and the joint action of the Allied forces.

The French Government fully appreciates the great value of such a guarantee, which would profoundly change the international situation, but this guarantee to be effective must be supplemented and defined.

(2) In the first place there will always be, on account of distance, a period in which France attacked will have to defend herself single-handed without her overseas Allies; she must be able to do this under fairer conditions than in the past.

On the other hand, it is important there should be no doubt about the substance and scope of the pledge — that is as to the obligations imposed upon Germany, the methods of their enforcements, the nature of the act which shall constitute a menace of war, the right of France to defend herself against it, and the importance of the military aid to be furnished by Great Britain and the United States.

(3) In other words, before we can consider giving up the first guarantee (a material guarantee founded on space) it is essential that the second guarantee (founded on time, that is on the speedy aid of our Allies) lend itself to no uncertainty and that it be supplemented by some of the other safeguards contained in the first guarantee.

It is really not possible for France to give up a certain safeguard for the sake of expectations.

III

POSSIBLE BASES OF AGREEMENT

Wishing to respond to the suggestion which has been made to it, the French Government thinks it its duty to set out in detail the general bases upon which agreement might be reached, these bases being the minimum guarantees indispensable to France.

It should be agreed, in the first place, that:

In case Germany, in violation of the peace conditions imposed upon her by the Allied and Associated Governments, should commit an act of aggression against France, Great Britain and the United States would bring to France the aid of their military forces.

Therefore:

(1) The date and the conditions of evacuation of the bridge-heads on the right bank, and of the territories on the left bank of the Rhine, to be fixed by the Peace Treaty (as one of the guarantees to be taken for the execution of the financial clauses).[9]

(2) Germany to maintain neither military force nor military organization on the left bank of the Rhine nor within fifty kilometers east of the river. The German Army to be forbidden to manoeuvre there. Recruiting to be forbidden there — even appeals for volunteers. Fortifications to be demolished there. No new fortifications to be erected there. No war material to be manufactured there . . . .

(3) Great Britain, the United States and France to have the right to satisfy themselves by means of a permanent Commission of Inspection that the conditions imposed upon Germany are

---

9. In other words an occupation for thirty years.

complied with. (For without this right the preceeding clause would be worthless.)

(4) Great Britain, the United States and France to agree to consider as an act of aggression any entry or attempted entry of all or any part of the Germany Army into the zone fixed in paragraph 2.

(5) Furthermore, Great Britain and France to recognize the right of France to occupy the line of the Rhine with five bridge-heads of a radius of twenty kilometers in case Germany, in the opinion of the Commission of Inspection, should violate the terms of paragraph 2 or any one of the military, aerial, and naval clauses of the peace preliminaries. (In fact, if France gives up after thirty years' permanent occupation she must at least in case of danger of war resulting from Germany's violation of her pledges, be able to advance her troops to the only good defensive position, that is to the Rhine.)

(6) Great Britain and the United States to recognize to France her frontier of 1814 and by way of reparation the right of occupation without annexation of that part of the coal basin of the Sarre not included within this frontier.

P.S. *It goes without saying that by act of aggression against France, the French Government also means any aggression against Belgium.*

APPENDIX G. THE COVENANT OF THE LEAGUE OF NATIONS[10]

(These are the articles 1 to 26 of the Treaty of Peace between the Allied and Associated Powers and Germany, signed on June 28, 1919, at Versailles.)

The High Contracting Parties,

In order to promote international co-operation and to achieve international peace and security

by the acceptance of obligations not to resort to war,

by the prescription of open, just and honourable relations between nations,

by the firm establishment of the understandings of international law as the actual rule of conduct among Governments, and

by the maintenance of justice and a scrupulous respect for all treaty obligations in the dealings of organized peoples with one another,

Agree to this Covenant of the League of Nations.

Article 1. The original members of the League of Nations shall be those of the Signatories which are named in the Annex to this Covenant and also such of those other States named in the Annex as shall accede without reservation to this Covenant. Such accession shall be effected by a Declaration deposited with the Secretariat within two months of the coming into force of the Covenant. Notice thereof shall be sent to all other Members of the League.

Any fully self-governing State, Dominion or Colony not named in the Annex may become a Member of the League if its admission is agreed to by two-thirds of the Assembly, provided that it shall give effective guarantees of its sincere intention to observe its international obligations, and shall accept such regulations as may be prescribed by the League in regard to its military, naval and air forces and armaments.

Any Member of the League may, after two years' notice of its intention to do so, withdraw from the League, provided that all its international obligations and all its obligations under this Covenant shall have been fulfilled at the time of its withdrawal.

Article 2. The action of the League under this Covenant shall be effected through the instrumentality of an Assembly and of a Council, with a permanent Secretariat.

---

10. *Senate Executive Document* (8167) 67th Congress, 4th sess., No. 348, pp. 3336-45. Italics have been added.

Article 3. The Assembly shall consist of Representatives of the Members of the League.

The Assembly shall meet at stated intervals and from time to time as occasion may require at the Seat of the League or at such other place as may be decided upon.

The Assembly may deal at its meetings with any matter within the sphere of action of the League or affecting the peace of the world.

At meetings of the Assembly each Member of the League shall have one vote, and may have not more than three Representatives.

Article 4. The Council shall consist of Representatives of the Principal Allied and Associated Powers, together with Representatives of four other Members of the League. These four Members of the League shall be selected by the Assembly from time to time in its discretion. Until the appointment of the Representatives of the four Members of the League first selected by the Assembly, Representatives of Belgium, Brazil, Spain and Greece shall be members of the Council.

With the approval of the majority of the Assembly, the Council may name additional Members of the League whose Representatives shall always be members of the Council; the Council with like approval may increase the number of the Members of the League to be selected by the Assembly for representation on the Council.

The Council shall meet from time to time as occasion may require, and at least once a year, at the Seat of the League, or at such other place as may be decided upon.

The Council may deal at its meetings with any matter within the sphere of action of the League or affecting the peace of the world.

Any Member of the League not represented on the Council shall be invited to send a Representative to sit as a member at any meeting of the Council during the consideration of matters specially affecting the interests of that Member of the League.

At meetings of the Council, each Member of the League represented on the Council shall have one vote, and may have not more than one Representative.

Article 5. Except where otherwise expressly provided in this Covenant or by the terms of the present Treaty, decisions at any meeting of the Assembly or of the Council shall require the agreement of all of the Members of the League represented at the meeting.

All matters of procedure at meetings of the Assembly or of the Council, including the appointment of Committees to investigate particular matters, shall be regulated by the Assembly or by the Council and may be decided by a majority of the Members of the League represented at the meeting.

The first meeting of the Assembly and the first meeting of the Council shall be summoned by the President of the United States of America.

Article 6. The permanent Secretariat shall be established at the Seat of the League. The Secretariat shall comprise a Secretary General and such secretaries and staff as may be required.

The first Secretary General shall be the person named in the Annex; thereafter the Secretary General shall be appointed by the Council with the approval of the majority of the Assembly.

The secretaries and staff of the Secretariat shall be appointed by the Secretary General with the approval of the Council.

The Secretary General shall act in that capacity at all meetings of the Assembly and of the Council.

The expenses of the Secretariat shall be borne by the Members of the League in accordance with the apportionment of the expenses of the International Bureau of the Universal Postal Union.

Article 7. The Seat of the League is established at Geneva.

The Council may at any time decide that the Seat of the League shall be established elsewhere.

All positions under or in connection with the League, including the Secretariat, shall be open equally to men and women.

Representatives of the Members of the League and officials of the League when engaged on the business of the League shall enjoy diplomatic privileges and immunities.

The buildings and other property occupied by the League or its officials or by Representatives attending its meetings shall be inviolable.

Article 8. The Members of the League recognize that the maintenance of peace requires the reduction of national armaments to the lowest point consistent with national safety and the enforcement by common action of international obligations.

The Council, taking account of the geographical situation and circumstances of each State, shall formulate plans for such reduction for the consideration and action of the several Governments.

Such plans shall be subject to reconsideration and revision at least every ten years.

After these plans shall have been adopted by the several Governments, the limits of armaments therein fixed shall not be exceeded without the concurrence of the Council.

The Members of the League agree that the manufacture by private enterprise of munitions and implements of war is open to grave objections. The Council shall advise how the evil effects attendant upon such manufacture can be prevented, due regard being had to the necessities of those Members of the League which are not able to manufacture the munitions and implements of war necessary for their safety.

The Members of the League undertake to interchange full and frank information as to the scale of their armaments, their military, naval and air programmes and the condition of such of their industries as are adaptable to war-like purposes.

Article 9. A permanent Commission shall be constituted to advise the Council on the execution of the provisions of Articles 1 and 8 and on military, naval and air questions generally.

Article 10. The Members of the League undertake to respect and preserve as against external aggression the territorial integrity and existing political independence of all Members of the League. In case of any such aggression or in case of any threat or danger of such aggression the Council shall advise upon the means by which this obligation shall be fulfilled.

Article 11. Any war or threat of war, whether immediately affecting any of the Members of the League or not, *is hereby declared a matter of concern to the whole League,* and the League shall take any action that may be deemed wise and effectual to safeguard the peace of nations. *In case any such emergency should arise the Secretary General shall on the request of any Member of the League forthwith summon a meeting of the Council.*

It is also declared to be the friendly right of each Member of the League to bring to the attention of the Assembly or of the Council any circumstances whatever affecting international relations which threatens to disturb international peace or the good understanding between nations upon which peace depends.

Article 12. The Members of the League agree that if there should arise between them any dispute likely to lead to a rupture, they will submit the matter either to arbitration or to inquiry by the Council, and they agree in no case to resort to war until three months after the award by the arbitrators or the report by the Council.

In any case under this Article the award of the arbitrators shall be made within a reasonable time, and the report of the Council shall be made within six months after the submission of the dispute.

Article 13. The Members of the League agree that whenever any dispute shall arise between them which they recognize to be suitable for submission to arbitration and which cannot be satisfactorily settled by diplomacy, they will submit the whole subject-matter to arbitration.

Disputes as to the interpretation of a treaty, as to any question of international law, as to the existence of any fact which if established would constitute a breach of any international obligation, or as to the extent and nature of the reparation to be made for any such breach, are declared to be among those which are generally suitable for submission to arbitration.

For the consideration of any such dispute the court of arbitration to which the case is referred shall be the Court agreed on by the parties to the dispute or stipulated in any convention existing between them.

The Members of the League agree that they will carry out in full good faith any award that may be rendered, and that they will not resort to war against a Member of the League which complies therewith. In the event of any failure to carry out such an award, the Council shall propose what steps should be taken to give effect thereto.

Article 14. The Council shall formulate and submit to the Members of the League for adoption plans for the establishment of a Permanent Court of International Justice. The Court shall be competent to hear and determine any dispute of an international character which the parties thereto submit to it. The Court may also give an advisory opinion upon any dispute or question referred to it by the Council or by the Assembly.

Article 15. If there should arise between Members of the League any dispute likely to lead to a rupture, which is not submitted to arbitration in accordance with Article 13, the Members of the League agree that they will submit the matter to the Council. Any party to the dispute may effect such submission by giving notice of the existence of the dispute to the Secretary General, who will make all necessary arrangements for a full investigation and consideration thereof.

For this purpose the parties to the dispute will communicate to the Secretary General, as promptly as possible, statements of their case with all the relevant facts, and papers, and the Council may forthwith direct the publication thereof.

The Council shall endeavour to effect a settlement of the dispute, and if such efforts are successful, a statement shall be made public giving such facts and explanations regarding the dispute and the terms of settlement thereof as the Council may deem appropriate.

If the dispute is not settled, the Council either unanimously or by a majority vote shall make and publish a report containing a statement of the facts of the dispute and the recommendations which are deemed just and proper in regard thereto.

Any Member of the League represented on the Council may make public a statement of the facts of the dispute and of its conclusions regarding the same.

If a report by the Council is unanimously agreed to by the members thereof other than the representatives of one or more of the parties to the dispute, the Members of the League agree that they will not go to war with any party to the dispute which complies with the recommendations of the report.

If the Council fails to reach a report which is unanimously agreed to by the members thereof, other than the Representatives of one or more of the parties to the dispute, the Members of the League reserve to themselves the right to take such action as they shall consider necessary for the maintenance of right and justice.

If the dispute between the parties is claimed by one of them, and is found by the Council, to arise out of a matter which by international law is solely within the domestic jurisdiction of that party, the Council shall so report, and shall make no recommendation as to its settlement.

The Council may in any case under this Article refer the dispute to the Assembly. The dispute shall be so referred at the request of either party to the dispute, provided that such request be made within fourteen days after the submission of the dispute to the Council.

In any case referred to the Assembly, all the provisions of this Article and of Article 12 relating to the action and powers of the Council shall apply to the action and powers of the Assembly, provided that a report made by the Assembly, if concurred in by the Representatives of those Members of the League represented on the Council and of a majority of the other Members of the League, exclusive in each case of the Representatives of the parties to the dispute, shall have the same force as a report by the Council concurred in by all the members thereof other than the Representatives of one or more of the parties to the dispute.

Article 16. Should any Member of the League resort to war in disregard of its covenants under Articles 12, 13, or 15, it shall *ipso facto* be deemed to have committed an act of war against all other Members of the League, which hereby undertake immediately to subject it to the severance of all trade or financial relations, the prohibition of all intercourse between their nationals and the nationals of the covenant-breaking State, and the prevention of all financial, commercial or personal intercourse between the nationals of the covenant-breaking State and the nationals of any other State, whether a Member of the League or not.

It shall be the duty of the Council in such case to recommend to the several Governments concerned what effective military, naval or air force the Members of the League shall severally contribute to the armed forces to be used to protect the covenants of the League.

The Members of the League agree, further, that they will mutually support one another in the financial and economic measures which are taken under this Article in order to minimise the loss and inconvenience resulting from the above measures, and that they will mutually support one another in resisting any special measures aimed at one of their number by the covenant-breaking State, and that they will take the necessary steps to afford passage through their territory to the forces of any of the Members of the League which are co-operating to protect the covenants of the League.

Any Member of the League which has violated any covenant of the League may be declared to be no longer a Member of the League by a vote of the Council concurred in by the Representatives of all the other Members of the League represented thereon.

Article 17. In the event of a dispute between a Member of the League and a State which is not a Member of the League, or between States not members of the League, the State or States not Members of the League shall be invited to accept the obligations of membership in the League for the purposes of such dispute, upon such conditions as the Council may deem just. If such invitation is accepted, the provisions of Articles 12 to 16 inclusive shall be applied with such modifications as may be deemed necessary by the Council.

Upon such invitation being given the Council shall immediately institute an inquiry into the circumstances of the dispute and recommend such action as may seem best and most effectual in the circumstances.

If a State so invited shall refuse to accept the obligations of membership in the League for the purposes of such dispute, and shall resort to war against a Member of the League, the provisions of Article 16 shall be applicable as against the State taking such action.

If both parties to the dispute when so invited refuse to accept the obligations of membership in the League for the purposes of such dispute, the Council may take such measures and make such recommendations as will prevent hostilities and will result in the settlement of the dispute.

Article 18. Every treaty or international engagement entered into hereafter by any Member of the League shall be forthwith registered with the Secretariat and shall as soon as possible be published by it. No such treaty or international engagement shall be binding until so registered.

Article 19. The Assembly may from time to time advise the reconsideration by Members of the League of treaties which have become inapplicable and the consideration of international conditions whose continuance might endanger the peace of the world.

Article 20.   The Members of the League severally agree that this Covenant is accepted as abrogating all obligations or understandings *inter se* which are inconsistent with the terms thereof, and solemnly undertake that they will not hereafter enter any engagements inconsistent with the terms thereof.

In case any Member of the League shall, before becoming a Member of the League, have undertaken any obligations inconsistent with the terms of this Covenant, it shall be the duty of such Member to take immediate steps to procure its release from such obligations.

Article 21.   Nothing in this Covenant shall be deemed to affect the validity of international engagements, such as treaties of arbitration or regional understandings like the Monroe Doctrine, for securing the maintenance of peace.

Article 22.   To those colonies and territories which as a consequence of the late war have ceased to be under the sovereignty of the States which formerly governed them and which are inhabited by peoples not yet able to stand by themselves under the strenuous conditions of the modern world, there should be applied the principle that the well-being and development of such peoples form a sacred trust of civilization and that securities for the performance of this trust should be embodied in this Covenant.

The best method of giving practical effect to this principle is that the tutelage of such peoples should be entrusted to advanced nations who by reason of their resources, their experience or their geographical position can best undertake this responsibility, and who are willing to accept it, and that this tutelage should be exercised by them as Mandatories on behalf of the League.

The character of the mandate must differ according to the stage of the development of the people, the geographical situation of the territory, its economic conditions and other similar circumstances.

Certain communities formerly belonging to the Turkish Empire have reached a stage of development where their existence as independent nations can be provisionally recognised subject to the rendering of administrative advice and assistance by a Mandatory until such time as they are able to stand alone. The wishes of these communities must be a principal consideration in the selection of the Mandatory.

Other peoples, especially those of Central Africa, are at such a stage that the Mandatory must be responsible for the administration of the territory under conditions which will guarantee freedom of conscience and religion, subject only to the maintenance of public order and morals, the prohibition of abuses such as the slave trade, the arms traffic and the liquor traffic, and the prevention of the establishment of fortifications or military or naval bases and of military training of the natives for other than police purposes and the defense of territory, and will also secure equal opportunities for the trade and commerce of other Members of the League.

There are territories, such as South-West Africa and certain of the South Pacific Islands, which, owing to the sparseness of their population, or their small size, or their remoteness from the centres of civilization, or their geographical contiguity to the territory of the Mandatory, and other circumstances, can be best administered under the laws of the Mandatory as integral portions of its territory, subject to the safeguards above mentioned in the interests of the indigenous population.

In every case of mandate, the Mandatory shall render to the Council an annual report in reference to the territory committed to its charge.

The degree of authority, control, or administration to be exercised by the Mandatory shall, if not previously agreed upon by the Members of the League, be explicitly defined in each case by the Council.

A permanent Commission shall be constituted to receive and examine the annual reports of the Mandatories and to advise the Council on all matters relating to the observance of the mandates.

Article 23. Subject to and in accordance with the provisions of international conventions existing or hereafter to be agreed upon, the Members of the League:

(a) will endeavour to secure and maintain fair and humane conditions of labour for men, women, and children, both in their own countries and in all countries to which their commercial and industrial relations extend, and for that purpose will establish and maintain the necessary international organizations;

(b) undertake to secure just treatment of the native inhabitants of territories under their control;

(c) will entrust the League with the general supervision over the execution of agreements with regard to the traffic in women and children, and the traffic in opium and other dangerous drugs;

(d) will entrust the League with the general supervision of the trade in arms and ammunition with the countries in which the control of this traffic is necessary in the common interest;

(e) will make provision to secure and maintain freedom of communications and transit and equitable treatment for the commerce of all Members of the League. In this connection, the special necessities of the regions devastated during the war of 1914-1918 shall be borne in mind;

(f) will endeavour to take steps in matters of international concern for the prevention and control of disease.

Article 24. There shall be placed under the direction of the League all international bureaux already established by general treaties if the parties to such treaties consent. All such international bureaux and all commissions for the regulation of matters of international interest hereafter constituted shall be placed under the direction of the League.

In all matters of international interest which are regulated by general conventions but which are not placed under the control of international bureaux or commissions, the Secretariat of the League shall, subject to the consent of the Council and if desired by the Parties, collect and distribute all relevant information and shall render any other assistance which may be necessary or desirable.

The Council may include as part of the expenses of the Secretariat the expenses of any bureau or commission which is placed under the direction of the League.

Article 25. The Members of the League agree to encourage and promote the establishment and co-operation of duly authorized voluntary national Red Cross organizations having as purposes the improvement of health, the prevention of disease and the mitigation of suffering throughout the world.

Article 26. Amendments to this Covenant will take effect when ratified by the Members of the League whose Representatives compose the Council and by a majority of the Members of the League whose Representatives compose the Assembly.

No such amendment shall bind any Member of the League which signifies its dissent therefrom, but in that case it shall cease to be a Member of the League . . . .

APPENDIX H.   THE TREATIES OF GUARANTEE

For ease of comparison and clarification, the two treaties are presented in this manner.

FRANCO-AMERICAN TREATY[11]

Whereas the United States of America and the French Republic are equally animated by the desire to maintain the peace of the world so happily restored by the treaty of peace signed at Versailles the 28th day of June 1919, putting an end to the war begun by the aggression of the German Empire and ended by the defeat of that Power; and

ANGLO-FRENCH TREATY[12]

Whereas His Majesty the King and the President of the French Republic have, subject to the approval of their respective Parliaments, concluded the treaty set out in the schedule to this Act, and it is expedient to give such approval:

Be it enacted by the King's most Excellent Majesty therefore, by and with the advice and consent of the Lords Spiritual and Temporal, and Commons, in this present parliament assembled, and by the authority of the same as follows: —

1. The approval of Parliament is hereby given to the Treaty set out in the schedule to this Act.

2. This Act may be cited as "The Anglo-French Treaty (Defence of France) Act, 1919."

Treaty between the British Empire and France respecting assistance to France in the event of unprovoked aggression by Germany. Signed at Versailles, June 28, 1919.

---

11. *Congressional Record*, 66th Cong., 1st session, Vol. 58, part 4, July 28 to August 23, 1919, 3310-3311.

12. *British and Foreign State Papers*, 1919, CXII, 601-602.

FRANCO-AMERICAN TREATY
(Continued)

Whereas the United States of America and the French Republic are fully persuaded that an unprovoked movement of aggression by Germany against France would not only violate both the letter and the spirit of the treaty of Versailles to which the United States of America and the French Republic are parties, thus exposing France anew to the intolerable burdens of an unprovoked war, but that such aggression on the part of Germany would be and is so regarded by the treaty of Versailles as a hostile act against all the powers signatory to that treaty and as calculated to disturb the peace of the world by involving inevitably and directly, as experience has amply and unfortunately demonstrated, the world at large; and,

Whereas, the United States of America and the French Republic fear that the stipulations relating to the left bank of the Rhine contained in the said treaty of Versailles may not at first provide adequate security and protection to France on the one hand, and the United States of America as one of the signatories of the Treaty of Versailles on the other;

Therefore, the United States of America and the French Republic having decided to conclude a treaty to effect these necessary purposes, Woodrow Wilson, Presi-

ANGLO-FRENCH TREATY
(Continued)

Whereas there is a danger that the stipulations relating to the left bank of the Rhine contained in the Treaty of Peace signed this day at Versailles may not at first provide adequate security and protection to the French Republic; and

Whereas His Britannic Majesty is willing, subject to the consent of His Parliament and provided that a similar obligation is entered into by the United States of America, to undertake to support the French Government in the case of an unprovoked movement of aggression being made against France by Germany; and

Whereas His Britannic Majesty and the President of the French Republic have determined to conclude a treaty to that effect and have named as their Plenipotenti-

dent of the United States of America, and Robert Lansing, Secretary of State of the United States, specially authorized thereto by the President of the United States, and Georges Clemenceau, President of the Council, Minister of War, and Stephen Pichon, Minister of Foreign Affairs, specially authorized thereto by Raymond Poincaré, President of the French Republic, have agreed upon the following articles.

Article 1

In case the following stipulations relating to the left bank of the Rhine contained in the Treaty of Peace with Germany signed at Versailles the 28th day of June 1919, by the British Empire; the French Republic, and the United States of America among other powers:

Article 42. Germany is forbidden to maintain or construct any fortifications either on the left bank of the Rhine or on the right bank to the west of a line drawn 50 kilometers to the East of the Rhine.

Article 43. In the area defined above, the maintenance and assembly of armed forces, either permanently or temporarily, and

aries for the purpose, that is, to say: —

His Majesty the King of the United Kingdom of Great Britain and Ireland and of the British Dominions beyond the Seas, Emperor of India:

The Right Honorable David Lloyd George, M.P., 1st Lord of His Treasury and Prime Minister;

The Right Honorable Arthur J. Balfour, O.M., M.P., His Secretary of State for Foreign Affairs,

The President of the French Republic:

Mr. Georges Clemenceau, President of the Council, Minister of War;

Mr. Stephen Pichon, Minister of Foreign Affairs;

who having communicated their full powers found in due and good form, have agreed as follows:

Article 1

In case the following stipulations relating to the left bank of the Rhine contained in the Treaty of Peace with Germany signed at Versailles the 28th day of June 1919, by the British Empire; the French Republic, and the United States of America among other powers:

Article 42. Germany is forbidden to maintain or construct any fortifications either on the left bank of the Rhine or on the right bank to the west of a line drawn 50 kilometers to the East of the Rhine.

Article 43. In the area defined above, the maintenance and assembly of armed forces, either permanently or temporarily, and

FRANCO-AMERICAN TREATY
(Continued)

military manoeuvers of any kind, as well as the upkeep of all permanent works for mobilisation, are in the same way forbidden.

Article 44. In case Germany violates in any manner whatever the provisions of articles 42 and 43, she shall be regarded as committing a hostile act against the powers signatory of the present treaty and as calculated to disturb the peace of the world.

may not at first provide adequate security and protection to France, the United States of America shall be bound to come immediately to her assistance.

Article 2

The present treaty, in similar terms with the treaty of even date for the same purpose concluded between the French Republic and Great Britain, a copy of which is annexed hereto, will only come into force when the latter is ratified.

Article 3

The present treaty must be submitted to the Council of the League of Nations by the Council, acting if need be by a majority, as an engagement which is consistent with the Covenant of the League; it will continue in force until on the application of one of the Parties to it the Council, acting if need be by a majority, agrees that the League itself affords sufficient protection.

ANGLO-FRENCH TREATY
(Continued)

military manoeuvers of any kind, as well as the upkeep of all permanent works for mobilisation, are in the same way forbidden.

Article 44. In case Germany violates in any manner whatever the provisions of articles 42 and 43, she shall be regarded as committing a hostile act against the powers signatory of the present treaty and as calculated to disturb the peace of the world.

may not at first provide adequate security and protection to France, Great Britain agrees to come immediately to her assistance in the event of any unprovoked movement of aggression against her being made by Germany.

Article 2

The present treaty, in similar terms with the treaty of even date for the same purpose concluded between the French Republic and the United States of America, a copy of which is annexed hereto, will only come into force when the latter is ratified.

Article 3

The present treaty must be submitted to the Council of the League of Nations and must be recognized by the Council, acting if need be by a majority, as an engagement which is consistent with the Covenant of the League; it will continue in force until on the application of one of the Parties to it the Council, acting if need be by a majority, agrees that the League itself affords sufficient protection.

Article 4

The present treaty shall, before ratification by His Majesty be submitted to Parliament for approval.

FRANCO-AMERICAN TREATY
(Continued)

ANGLO-FRENCH TREATY
(Continued)

It shall before ratification by the President of the French Republic be submitted to the French Chambers for approval.

Article 4

The present treaty will be submitted to the Senate of the United States at the same time as the Treaty of Versailles is submitted to the Senate for its advice and consent to ratify. It will be submitted before ratification to the French Chamber of Deputies for approval. The ratification thereof will be exchanged, on the deposit of ratification of the Treaty of Versailles at Paris or as soon thereafter as shall be possible.

In faith whereof the respective plenipotentiaries, to wit, on the part of the United States of America, Woodrow Wilson, President, and Robert Lansing, Secretary of State, of the United States; and on the part of the French Republic, Georges Clemenceau, President of the Council of Ministers, Minister of War, and Stephen Pichon, Minister of Foreign Affairs, have signed the above articles, both in the English and French languages, and they have hereunto affixed their seals.

Done in duplicate at the city of Versailles on the 28th day of June, in the year of Our Lord 1919, and the one hundred and forty-third of the independence of the United States of America.

Article 5

The present treaty shall impose no obligation upon any of the Dominions of the British Empire unless and until it is approved by the Parliament of the Dominion concerned.

The present treaty shall be ratified, and shall, subject to articles 2 and 4, come into force at the same time as the Treaty of Peace with Germany of even date comes into force for the British Empire and the French Republic.

In faith whereof the above-named Plenipotentiaries have signed the present treaty, drawn up in the English and French languages.

Done in duplicate at Versailles, on the 28th day of June, 1919.

(Seal) (Signed) Woodrow Wilson. (L.S.) D. Lloyd George.
(Seal) (Signed) Robert Lansing. (L.S.) Arthur James Balfour.
(Seal) (Signed) Georges Clemenceau. (L.S.) G. Clemenceau.
(Seal) (Signed) Stephen Pichon. (L.S.) S. Pichon.

APPENDIX I. TREATY OF PEACE BETWEEN THE UNITED STATES AND GERMANY[13]

(short outline)

. . . Article I. Germany undertakes to accord to the United States, and the United States shall have and enjoy, all the right, privileges, indemnities, reparations or advantages specified in the aforesaid Joint Resolution of the Congress of the United States of July 2, 1921, including all the rights and advantages stipulated for the benefit of the United States in the Treaty of Versailles which the United States shall fully enjoy notwithstanding the fact that such Treaty has not been ratified by the United States. Article II. With a view to defining more particularly the obligations of Germany under the foregoing Article with respect to certain provisions in the Treaty of Versailles, it is understood and agreed between the High Contracting Parties:

(1) That the rights and advantages stipulated in that Treaty for the benefit of the United States, which it is intended the United States shall have and enjoy, are those defined in Section I, of Part IV, and Parts V, VI, VIII, IX, X, XI, XII, XIV, and XV.

The United States in availing itself of the rights and advantages in the provisions of that Treaty mentioned in this paragraph will do so in a manner consistent with the rights accorded to Germany under such provisions.

(2) That the United States shall not be bound by the provisions of Part I of that Treaty nor by any provisions of that Treaty including those mentioned in Paragraph (1) of this Article, which relate to the Covenant of the League of Nations, nor shall the United States be bound by any action taken by the League of Nations, or by the Council or by the Assembly thereof, unless the United States shall expressly give its assent to such action.

---

13. *The Statutes at Large of the United States,* Vol. 42, Part 2, pp. 1939-45. This treaty was signed on August 25, 1921, at Berlin, with ratifications exchanged at Berlin, on November 11, 1921. Only the pertinent articles have been given here.

(3) That the United States assumes no obligations under or with resort to the provisions of Part II, Part III, Sections 2 to 8 inclusive of Part IV, and Part XIII of that Treaty.

(4) That, while the United States is privileged to participate in the Reparation Commission, according to the terms of Part VIII of that Treaty, and in any other Commission established under the Treaty or under any agreement supplemental thereto, the United States is not bound to participate in any such commission unless it shall elect to do so . . . .

Bibliography

I. OFFICIAL DOCUMENTS

A. France

Ministère des Affaires Étrangères

Documents Diplomatiques: Documents relatifs aux Négociations concernant les Garanties de Sécurité contre une Agression de l'Allemagne (10 janvier 1919-7 décembre 1923). Paris, Imprimerie nationale, 1924.

Chambre des Députés

Journal Officiel de la République Française, Chambre des Députés, *Débats Parlementaires,* 1919, 1920, 1921.

Journal Officiel de la République Française, Chambre des Députés, *Débats Parlementaires,* 1919. Tome LXXXXIII, 1919, Session Ordinaire, *Documents Parlementaires,* Annexes Nos. 6657 and 6658, Paris, Imprimerie des Journaux Officiels, 1920.

Journal Officiel de la République Française, Chambre des Députés, *Documents Parlementaires,* 1919.

Journal Officiel de la République Française, Chambre des Députés, *Documents Parlementaires,* 1919, Session Ordinaire: Annexes Nos. 6663: Committee on the report of August 6, 1919, on the Treaty of Versailles, Victor Augagneur, rapporteur;

6664: Committee on the report of August 6, 1919, on part of the Treaty of Versailles, Charles Benoist, rapporteur; (contains a good discussion of France's historical interest in and the history of the Rhine as a frontier, a river much fought over, etc.);

6665: Committee report of August 6, 1919, on portion of the Versailles Treaty, Rene Besnard, rapporteur;

6666: Committee report on the Versailles Treaty on August 6, 1919, Maurice Long, rapporteur;

6667: Committee report on August 6, 1919, on Versailles Treaty provisions, Henry Pate, rapporteur;

6668: Committee report on August 6, 1919, on provisions of the Versailles Treaty, Gratien Candace, rapporteur;

6669: Committee report on August 6, 1919, on other provisions of the Treaty of Versailles, Louis Dubois, rapporteur;

6670: Committee report on August 6, 1919, on the treaty of Versailles, Louis Puech, rapporteur;

6671: Committee report on Versailles Treaty, August 6, 1919, Daniel Vincent (Nord), rapporteur;

6672: Committee report on other parts of Versailles Treaty, August 6, 1919, Maurice Sibille, rapporteur;

6673: Committee report on August 6, 1919, on Versailles Treaty, André Renard, rapporteur.

Sénat

Annales du Sénat, Débats Parlementaires, Documents Parlementaires, Session Ordinaire de 1919, Paris, 1920.

Journal Officiel de la République Française, Sénat, Débats Parlementaires, 1918, 1919, 1920, 1921.

Journal Officiel de la République Française, Sénat, Documents Parlementaires, Paris, 1919, 1920, 1921.

Journal Officiel de la République Française, Sénat, Documents Parlementaires, Paris, 1919, Session Ordinaire, Annexe No. 562; Foreign Affairs Committee Report of October 3, 1919, on the Treaty of Versailles, Léon Bourgeois, rapporteur; and Annexe No. 563; Foreign Affairs Committee Report of October 3, 1919, on the Treaty of Guarantee to France by the United States and Great Britain, against unprovoked Aggression, Léon Bourgeois, rapporteur.

Journal Officiel de la République Française, Sénat, Documents Parlementaires, 1920, Session Ordinaire, Annexe No. 266, Foreign Affairs Committee report of June 23, 1920, on the Treaty of Saint Germain, Imbart de la Tour, Rapporteur.

État des Projets et Propositions de Loi Soumis a L'Examen Du Sénat, Paris, Imprimerie du Sénat, 1920-1922.

Official Publication

Comité d'Études, *Travaux du Comité d'Études,* 2 vols., Paris, Imprimerie Nationale, 1918.

B. Great Britain

Foreign Office

British and Foreign State Papers, Vol. 112 (1919) — London, H. M. Stationery Office, (1922).

Parliament

Parliamentary Debates, Fifth Series, House of Commons, Vols. 117, 118 (1919), London, H. M. Stationery Office.

Parliamentary Debates, Fifth Series, House of Lords, Vol. 35, 3rd volume of Session, (1919), London, H. M. Stationery Office.

Parliamentary (Command) Papers:

Cmd. 151, *The Covenant of the League of Nations with a Commentary thereon, Miscellaneous No. 3,* (1919).

Cmd. 153, *The Treaty of Peace between the Allied and Associated Powers and Germany,* (1919), Treaty Series No. 4, pp. II-VII.

Cmd. 221, *Treaty respecting Assistance to France in the event of Unprovoked Aggression by Germany (with an appendix of the similar treaty between the United States of America and France* (1919).

Cmd. 1325, *Protocols and Correspondence between the Supreme Council and the Conference of Ambassadors and the German Government and the German Peace Delegation, between 10th January, 1920, and 7th July, 1920, respecting the execution of the Treaty of Versailles of 28th June 1919, Miscellaneous No. 15,* (1921).

Cmd. 1614, *Memorandum Circulated by the Prime Minister on 25th March, 1919,* (1922).

Cmd. 2169, No. 9 (*Memorandum of Marshal Foch, 10th January 1919*), and No. 10 (*Memorandum of the French Government, 25th February 1919*), (1924).

C. The United States of America

United States Documents

Treaties, Conventions, International Acts, Protocols, and Agreements between the United States of America and Other Powers, 1910-1923, 3 vols., Washington, D. C., 1902-1923.

Statutes at Large, vol. 42, April 1921-March 1923, Washington, D. C., 1923.

Department of State

The Lansing Papers, 2 vols., Washington, D. C., 1939-1940.

The Paris Peace Conference, 1919, Vols. I-XI, and XIII, (Other vols. in preparation as of 1955), Washington, D. C., 1942-1947.

Papers Relating to the Foreign Relations of the United States, 1918, Supplements 1 and 2, vols. 1 and 2, *The World War,* Washington, D. C., 1932-1933.

Senate Documents:

No. 49, *Text of the Versailles Treaty of Peace with Germany,* 66th Congr., 1st sess., 1919.

No. 76, *Report of the Conference between Members of the Senate Committee on Foreign Relations and the President of the United States, Tuesday, August 19, 1919,* 66th Congr., 1st sess., 1919.

No. 106, *Treaty of Peace with Germany, Hearings before the Committee on Foreign Relations . . . .,* 66th Congr., 1st sess., 1919.

No. 70, *Treaty of Peace with Germany,* 67th Congr., 1st sess., 1921.

Congressional Record:

64th Congr., 2nd sess., Vol. 54, Parts 1-6.
65th Congr., special sess., and 1st sess., Vol. 55, Parts 1-8.
65th Congr., 2nd sess., Vol. 56, Parts 1-12.
65th Congr., 3rd sess., Vol. 57, Parts 1-5.
66th Congr., 1st sess., Vol. 58, Parts 1-9.
66th Congr., 2nd sess., Vol. 59, Parts 1-9.
66th Congr., 3rd sess., Vol. 60, Parts 1-4.

II. DOCUMENTARY COLLECTIONS
AND RELATED MATERIALS

Allied and Associated Powers (Official Publications), *Reply of the Allied and Associated Powers to the Observations of the German Delegation on the Conditions of Peace*, Paris, 1919. (Hoover War Library, Stanford University, California.)

Almond, Nina and Ralph H. Lutz (compilers), *An introduction to a Bibliography of the Paris Peace Conference*, New York, 1935.

Baker, Ray Stannard and William E. Dodd, (eds.), *The Public Papers of Woodrow Wilson*, authorized edition, 6 vols., New York, 1925-27.

Barthou, Louis, *Le Traité de Paix*, Paris, 1919. (Report made in name of Commission chosen by Chamber of Deputies to investigate and examine the Peace Treaty with Germany.)

Bartlett, Ruhl J., (ed.), *The Record of American Diplomacy*, New York, 1947.

Bemis, Samuel F., and Grace Gardner Griffin (compilers), *Guide to the Diplomatic History of the United States, 1775-1921*, Washington, D. C., 1935.

Bourgeois, Léon, *Le Traité de Paix de Versailles*, Paris, 1919. (Report on the Treaty of Peace with Germany made in the name of the Senate Commission on Foreign Affairs.)

Burnett, Philip M., *Reparation at the Paris Peace Conference from the Standpoint of the American Delegation*, 2 vols., New York, 1940.

Carnegie Endowment for International Peace, *Official German Documents Relating to the World War*, 2 vols., New York, 1923.

..............., *The Paris Peace Conference, History and Documents*, New York, 1934. General Editor, James Brown Scott.

Cocks, F. Seymour, (ed.), *The Secret Treaties*, second edition, London, 1918.

Dickinson, G. L., (ed.), *Documents and Statements Relating to Peace Proposals and War Aims, December 1916 - November 1918*, New York, 1919.

Foley, Hamilton, (compiler), *Woodrow Wilson's Case for the League of Nations*, Princeton, N. J., 1923.

Harley, J. Eugene, *Documentary Textbook on International Relations*, Los Angeles, Calif., 1934.

................, *Documentary Textbook on the United Nations*, Los Angeles, Calif., 1947.

Honnorat, André, *Un des Problemes de la Paix: le desarmement de l'Allemagne; textes et documents*, Paris, 1924.

................, *Un des Problemes de la Paix: la sécurité de textes et documents*, Paris, 1924.

Klotz, Louis L., *De la Guerre à la Paix: souvenirs et documents*, Paris, 1924.

Laloy, Emile, (ed.), *Les Documents Secrets des archives du Ministère des Affaires Étrangères de Russie publies par Les Bolcheviks*, Paris, 1919.

Langsam, Walter C., (ed.), *Documents and Readings in the History of Europe Since 1918*, Chicago, Philadelphia, and New York, 1939.

Lapradelle, Albert G. de, (ed.), *La Paix de Versailles*, 12 vols., Paris, 1929-1939. (of particular interest and value in this study are vols. i, ii, xii.)

Latané, John H., (ed.), *Development of the League of Nations Idea. Documents and Correspondence of Theodore Marburg*, 2 vols., New York, 1932.

Lichtenberger, Henri, *Relations between France and Germany*, Washington, D. C., the Carnegie Endowment for International Peace, 1923.

Marburg, Theodore, and Horace E. Flack, (eds.), *Taft Papers on League of Nations*, New York, 1920.

Maurras, Charles, *Les Conditions de la Victoire*, 8 vols., Paris, 1916-1920.

Mermeix (pseudonym of Gabriel Terrail), *Le Combat des Trois; notes et documents sur la Conference de la Paix. Fragments d'histoire, 1914-1919*, vol. VI, Paris, 1922.

Munch, P., (compiler), *Les origins et L'Oeuvre de la Société des Nations*, 2 vols., Copenhagen, Denmark.

Nevins, Allan, and Louis M. Hacker, (eds.), *The United States and its Place in World Affairs, 1918-1943*, Boston, 1943.

Padover, Saul K., (ed.), *Wilson's Ideals*, Washington, D. C., American Council on Public Affairs, 1942.

Paris Peace Conference, *Minutes of the Supreme Council*, BC, A1-BC, 62, January 12 to June 17, 1919; FM 1-29, March 27 to July 2, 1919, Hoover War Library, Stanford University, California.

Richardson, James D., (compiler), *Messages and Papers of Presidents*, 11 vols. and supplement, Washington, D. C., 1912-1917.

Scott, James B., (ed.), *President Wilson's Foreign Policy, Messages, Addresses, Papers*, New York, 1918.

Shaw, Albert, (ed.), *Messages and Papers of Woodrow Wilson*, New York, 1924.

Stiene, Friedrich, (ed.), *Iswolski im Weltkriege*, Berlin, 1925. (Many of the documents relating to Franco-Russian relations during the war.)

Temperley, H. W. V., (ed.), *A History of the Peace Conference of Paris*, 6 vols., London, 1920-1924.

Verlag, Carl H., (ed.), *The German Counter Proposals to the Draft of the Versailles Peace Treaty*, Berlin, 1919.

Wilson, Woodrow, *The Triumph of Ideals*, New York and London, n.d. (Contains speeches, messages, and addresses made by the President between February 24, 1919, and July 8, 1919, which covers the active period of the Paris Peace Conference.)

III. DIARIES AND MEMOIRS

Beadon, Roger H., *Some Memories of the Peace Conference*, London, 1923.

Bonsal, Stephen, *Unfinished Business*, Garden City, N. Y., 1944.

Clemenceau, Georges, *Discours de Paix*, Paris, 1938.

..............., *In the Evening of My Thought*, 2 vols., Boston and New York, 1929. (Translated by John Head, Jr., and C. M. Thompson.)

..............., *The Grandeur and Misery of Victory*, New York, 1930.

Foch, Ferdinand, *Mémoires pour servir à L'Histoire de la Guerre de 1914-1918*, Tome Second, Paris, 1931.

..............., *The Memoirs of Marshal Foch*, New York, 1931. (This is similar to the edition above.)

Gwynn, Stephen (ed.), *The Letters and Friendships of Sir Cecil Spring-Rice*, 2 vols., Boston and New York, 1929.

Lansing, Robert, *The Big Four and others of the Peace Conference*, New York, 1921.

..............., *The Peace Negotiations: a Personal Narrative*, New York, 1921.

................, *War Memoirs*, Indianapolis, Ind., 1935.

Lloyd George, David, *The Truth about the Peace Treaties*, 2 vols., London, 1938. (This was published in the United States in 1939 as *Memoirs of the Peace Conference*, 2 vols., New Haven, Ct.)

................, *War Memoirs*, 4 vols., Boston, 1936.

Miller, David Hunter, *My Diary at the Conference of Paris*, 20 vols., and Index, (privately printed — 40 sets), New York, 1924-26.

Poincaré, Raymond, *Au Service de la France: neuf années de souvenirs*, 10 vols., Paris, 1926-33.

................, *Messages, Discours, Allocutions, Lettres et Telegrammes*, 3 vols., Paris, 1919-1921.

Riddell, George A., *Lord Riddell's Intimate Diary of the Peace Conference and After, 1918-1923*, New York, 1934.

Seymour, Charles, (ed.), *The Intimate Papers of Colonel House*, 4 vols., Boston and New York, 1926-28.

Thompson, Charles T., *The Peace Conference Day by Day*, New York, 1920.

Viviani, Rène, *As We See It*, New York, 1923.

Wilson, Edith Bolling, *My Memoir*, Indianapolis, Ind., 1939.

IV. BIOGRAPHIES AND SPECIAL STUDIES

Adam, G. J., *The Tiger: G. Clemenceau*, London, 1930.

Annin, Robert E., *Woodrow Wilson: a Character Study*, New York, 1924.

Bailey, Thomas A., *Woodrow Wilson and the Lost Peace*, New York, 1944.

................, *Woodrow Wilson and the Great Betrayal*, New York, 1945.

Baker, Ray Stannard, *Woodrow Wilson: Life and Letters*, 8 vols., New York, 1927-1939.

................, *Woodrow Wilson and World Settlement*, 3 vols., Garden City, N. Y., 1923.

Bell, H. C. F., *Woodrow Wilson and the People*, Garden City, N. Y., 1945.

Bowers, Claude G., *Beveridge and the Progressive Era*, Boston, 1932.

Bruun, A. Geoffrey, *Clemenceau*, Cambridge, Mass., 1943.

Bugnet, Charles, *En écoutant le maréchal Foch* (*1921-1929*), Paris, 1929. (The American Edition: *Foch Speaks,* New York, 1926.)

Daniels, Josephus, *The Life of Woodrow Wilson, 1856-1924,* Philadelphia, Pa., 1924.

Daudet, Léon A., *Raymond Poincaré,* Paris, 1930.

Dillon, Emile J., *The Inside Story of the Peace Conference,* New York, 1920.

Dodd, William E., *Woodrow Wilson and His Work,* 5th ed., Garden City, N. Y., 1922.

Grasset, Alphonse L., *Le Marechal Foch,* Paris, 1919.

Harley, J. Eugene, *Woodrow Wilson Still Lives — His World Ideals Triumphant,* Los Angeles, Calif., 1944.

Hendrick, Burton J., *The Life and Letters of Walter Hines Page,* 3 vols., Garden City, N. Y., 1927.

Herron, George D., *Woodrow Wilson and the World's Peace,* New York, 1917.

Jessup, Philip C., *Elihu Root,* 2 vols., New York, 1938.

Johnson, Willis F., *George Harvey, a Passionate Patriot,* Boston, 1929.

Kerney, James, *The Political Education of Woodrow Wilson,* New York, 1926.

Knight, L. L., *Woodrow Wilson, the Dreamer and the Dream,* Atlanta, Ga., 1924.

Lawrence, David., *The True Story of Woodrow Wilson,* New York, 1924.

Lodge, Henry Cabot, *The Senate and the League of Nations,* New York, 1925.

McAdoo, Eleanor Wilson, *The Woodrow Wilsons,* New York, 1937.

McAdoo, William G., *Crowded Years,* Boston, 1931.

MacPhail, Sir Andrew, *Three Persons,* New York, 1929. (This deals with Colonels House and Lawrence; also Sir Henry Wilson.)

Martet, Jean, *Georges Clemenceau,* London and New York, 1930. (Translated by Milton Waldeman.)

..............., *Le Tigre,* Paris, 1930. (This is similar to the English Edition listed above.)

..............., *Le Silence de M. Clemenceau,* Paris 1929.

Martin, William, *Statesmen of the War in Retrospect, 1918-1928,* New York, 1928.

Mordacq, Jean, *Le Ministère Clemenceau, Journal d'un Temoin,* 4 vols., Paris, 1930-31.

Nevins, Allan, *Henry White: Thirty Years of American Diplomacy,* New York, 1930.

Nicolson, Harold, *Peacemaking 1919,* London, 1933.

Palmer, Frederick, *Bliss, Peacemaker,* New York, 1934.

Recouly, Raymond, *Foch, My Conversations with the Marshal,* New York, 1929. (Translated by Joyce Davis.)

Seymour, Charles, *Woodrow Wilson and the World War,* New Haven, Ct., 1921.

Shotwell, James T., *At the Paris Peace Conference,* New York, 1937.

Smith, Arthur D. H., *Mr. House of Texas,* London and New York, 1940.

Spender Harold, *The Prime Minister, David Lloyd George,* New York, 1920.

Steed, Wickham, *Through Thirty Years,* 2 vols., Garden City, N. Y., 1924.

Suarez, Georges, *La Vie Orgueilleuse de Georges Clemenceau,* Paris, 1930.

Tardieu, André, *The Truth about the Treaty,* Indianapolis, Ind., 1921. (American Edition.)

................, *La Paix,* Paris, 1921. (There is material on sanctions and guarantees in this edition not available in the American edition.)

Tumulty, Joseph P., *Woodrow Wilson as I Know Him,* Garden City, N. Y., 1921.

Viereck, George S., *The Strangest Friendship in History,* New York, 1932.

White, William A., *Woodrow Wilson, The Man, his Times and his Task,* Boston, 1924.

Wilson, Woodrow, *The Case for the League of Nations,* Princeton, N. J., 1923.

V.   UNPUBLISHED MATERIALS

Binkley, Robert C., "Reactions of European Public Opinion to Woodrow Wilson's Statesmanship from the Armistice to the Peace of Versailles," (Ph.D. dissertation), typescript in Hoover War Library, Stanford University, California.

Boice, Stella M., "An Historical Study of the Idea of a League of Nations," typescript in Doheny Library of the University of Southern California, Los Angeles, 1920. (Master's thesis).

Lillywhite, Carmen, "A History of the United States Rejection of the League of Nations," typescript in Doheny Library of the University of Southern California, Los Angeles, 1932. (Master's thesis).

Mehling, Albert, "Official Diplomatic Peace Maneuvers in 1917," typescript in Doheny Library of the University of Southern California, 1941. (Master's thesis).

Mitchell, Donald W., "Woodrow Wilson at the Paris Peace Conference," typescript in Doheny Library of the University of Southern California, Los Angeles, 1935. (Master's thesis).

Monosmith, Virginia M., "The Occupation of the Ruhr," typescript in Doheny Library of the University of Southern California, Los Angeles, 1941. (Master's thesis).

VI.   HISTORIES AND OTHER BOOKS

Aulard, Albert, *Histoire Politique de la Grande Guerre*, Paris, 1924.

Bailey, Thomas A., *A Diplomatic History of the American People*, 3rd edition, New York, 1946.

Bárres, Maurice, *Les Grande Problemes du Rhin*, Paris, 1930.

Bemis, Samuel Flagg, *A Diplomatic History of the United States*, rev. edition, New York, 1942.

................, (ed.), *The American Secretaries of State and their Diplomacy*, 10 vols., New York, 1927-29.

Birdsall, Paul, *Versailles Twenty Years After*, New York, 1941.

Bourgeois, Léon, *L'Oeuvre de la Société des Nations* (*1920-1923*), Paris, 1923.

Brinon, Ferdinand de, *France-Allemagne*, 1918-1934, Paris, 1934.

Buell, Raymond L., *Contemporary French Politics*, New York, 1920.

................, *Europe — History of Ten Years*, New York, 1929.

Bullard, Arthur, *American Diplomacy in the Modern World*, Philadelphia, Pa., 1928.

Carr, Edward H., *International Relations Since the Peace Treaties*, London, 1937.

Chefils, Pierre Joseph M., *La Guerre de la Delivrance*, 3 vols., Paris, 1920-1923.

Colegrove, Kenneth, *The American Senate and World Peace*, New York, 1944.

Dahlin, Ebba, *French and German Public Opinion on Declared War Aims, 1914-1918*, Stanford University, Calfornia, 1933.

Dennison, Eleanor E., *The Senate Foreign Relations Committee*, Stanford University, Calfornia, 1942.

Doumergue, Emile, *Voici Pourquoi l'Allemagne Doit Payer*, 2 vols., Paris, 1922-1924. (Gives an excellent account of the French grievances against Germany before, during, and after the war of 1914-1918.)

Dutt, R. Palme, *World Politics, 1918-1936*, New York, 1936.

Fay, Sidney B., *The Origins of the World War*, 2 vols., New York, 1928.

Fleming, Denna F., *The Treaty Veto of the American Senate*, New York and London, 1930.

..............., *The United States and the League of Nations, 1918-1920*, New York, 1932.

..............., *The United States and World Organization, 1920-1933*, New York, 1938.

Gauvain, Auguste, *L'Europe au Jour le Jour*, 14 vols., Paris, 1921-24.

Gooch, George P., *Recent Revelations of European Diplomacy*, New York, 1940.

Haines, C. George and Ross S. J. Hoffman, *The Origins and Background of the Second World War*, New York, 1943. (A revised edition came out in 1947.)

Harley, J. Eugene, *The League of Nations and the New International Law*, London and New York, 1921.

Haynes, George H., *The Senate of the United States, Its History and Practice*, Boston, 1938.

Holt, W. Stull, *Treaties Defeated in the Senate*, Baltimore, Md., 1934.

Howard-Ellis, C., *The Origin, Structure and Working of the League of Nations*, London, 1928.

Kellor, Frances A., *Security against War*, 2 vols., New York, 1924.

Knudson, John I., *A History of the League of Nations*, Atlanta, Ga., 1938.

Langsam, Walter C., *The World Since 1914*, 5th ed., New York, 1943.

Latané, John H., and David W. Wainhouse, *A History of American Foreign Policy*, 2nd revision, New York, 1940.

Luckau, Alma, *The German Delegation at the Paris Peace Conference*, New York, 1941.

Lutz, Ralph H., (ed.), *Fall of the German Empire, 1914-1918*, vol. ii, Stanford University, California, 1932. (Translations by David G. Rempel and Gertrude Renktorff.)

McCallum, R. B., *Public Opinion and the Lost Peace*, London, 1944.

Marshall-Cornwall, Major-General J. H., *Geographic Disarmament; a Study in regional Demilitarization*, London, 1935.

Marston, Frank S., *The Peace Conference of 1919 — Organization and Procedure*, London and New York, 1944.

Miller, David Hunter, *The Drafting of the Covenant*, 2 vols., New York, 1928.

Michon, Georges, *The Franco-Russian Alliance 1891-1917*, New York, 1929.

Mowat, R. B., *A History of European Diplomacy*, 1914-1925, New York, 1927.

Noble, George B., *Policies and Opinions at Paris*, New York, 1935.

Notter, Harley, *The Origins of the Foreign Policy of Woodrow Wilson*, Baltimore, Md., 1937.

Nowak, Karl F., *Versailles*, New York, 1929. (Written in Berlin in 1927.)

Ormesson, Wladimir, Comte d', *France and Germany*, Paris, 1935. (Centre d'information documentaires.)

Perkins, Dexter, *America and Two Wars*, Boston, 1944.

Poincaré, Raymond, *Histoire Politique: chronique de quizaine*, 4 vols., Paris, 1920-1922.

Raafat, Waheed, *Le Probleme de la Sécurité Internationale*, Paris, 1930.

Robinson, Edgar E., and Victor J. West, *The Foreign Policy of Woodrow Wilson*, New York, 1917.

Rudin, Harry R., *Armistice, 1918*, New Haven, Ct., 1944.

Schmidt, Bernadotte E., *From Versailles to Munich, 1918-1938*, Public Policy Pamphlets, No. 28, Chicago, 1938.

Schücking, W., and Hans Wehberg, *Die Satzung des Volkerbundes*, new and revised edition, Berlin, 1931. (Has excellent commentaries on articles 1 to 7 and of the preamble of the Covenant of the League of Nations.)

Schuman, Frederick L., *War and Diplomacy in the French Republic*, New York, 1931.

Scott, Arthur P., *An Introduction to the Peace Treaties*, Chicago, 1920.

Seymour, Charles, *American Diplomacy during the World War*, Baltimore, Md., 1934.

Sharp, Walter R., *The Government of the French Republic*, New York, 1938.

Shaw, Albert, *International Bearings of American Policy*, Baltimore, Md., 1943.

Sontag, Raymond J., *European Diplomatic History 1871-1932*, New York, 1933.

Spykman, Nicholas J., *America's Strategy in World Politics*, New York, 1944.

Stephens, Waldo E., *Revisions of the Treaty of Versailles*, New York, 1939.

Stuart, Graham H., "The Struggle of France for Hegemony and Security," in *Contemporary World Politics*, Brown, F. J., C. Hodges, J. S. Roucek, (eds.), chapter 7, New York, 1939.

The New York Times Current History (The European War), 20 vols., New York, 1919.

Toynbee, Arnold J., *et. al.*, *The Treaty of Versailles and After*, New York and London, 1935.

Van Alstyne, Richard W., *American Diplomacy in Action*, Stanford University, California, 1944. (Revised Edition, 1947.)

Vermeil, Edmond, *L'Allemagne et les Democraties Occidentales: les conditions generales des relations franco-allemandes*, Paris, 1931.

Webster, Charles K., and Sydney Herbert, *The League of Nations in Theory and Practice*, New York, 1933.

Wild, Payson S., jr., *Sanctions and Treaty Enforcement*, Cambridge, Mass., 1934.

Williams, Benjamin H., *American Diplomacy: Policies and Practice*, New York, 1936.

Williams, Bruce S., *State Security and the League of Nations*, Baltimore, Md., 1927.

Wilson, Florence, *The Origins of the League Covenant*, London, 1928.

Wilson, Woodrow, *Constitutional Government in the United States*, New York, 1908.

Wolfers, Arnold, *Britain and France Between Two Wars*, New York, 1940.

VII.   ADDRESSES AND GENERAL WORKS

Alexander, F., *From Paris to Locarno*, London, 1928.
Bainville, Jacques, *Les Consequences Politiques de la Paix*, Paris, 1920.
Barrès, Maurice, *Le Génie du Rhin*, Paris, 1921.
..............., *La Politique Rhenane: discours parlementaires*, Paris, 1922.
Bartlett, Ruhl J., *The League to Enforce Peace*, Chapel Hill, N. C., 1944.
Bassett, John S., *The League of Nations: A Chapter in World Politics*, New York, 1928.
Benoit, Charles, *Les Nouvelles Frontières d'Allemagne, et la Nouvelle Carte d' Europe*, Paris, 1919.
Berber, Fritz, (ed.), *Das Diktat von Versailles; Entstehung, Inhalt, Zerfall, eine Darstelling in Dokumenten*, 2 vols., Essen, 1939.
Bérard, Victor, *La Paix Francaise*, Paris, 1919.
Beveridge, Sir William H., *The Price of Peace*, New York, 1945.
Briand, Aristide, *Paroles de Paix*, Paris, 1927.
Bourgeois, Léon, *Le Pacte de 1919 et la Société des Nations*, Paris, 1919.
Briggs, Mitchell P., *George D. Herron and the European Settlement*, Stanford University, Calif., 1932.
Brunet, René, *La Société des Nations et la France*, Paris, 1921.
Buell, Raymond L., *Isolated America*, New York, 1940.
Cecil, Lord Robert, *A Great Experiment*, New York, 1941.
Churchill, Winston S., *The Aftermath, 1918-1928*, New York, 1929.
Colcord, Samuel, *The Great Deception*, New York, 1921.
Cranston, Alan McG., *The Killing of the Peace*, New York, 1945.
Creel, George, *The War, the World and Wilson*, New York, 1920.
Dell, Robert, *The Geneva Racket 1920-1939*, London, 1941.
Duggan, Stephen P. H. (ed.), *The League of Nations: The Principle and the Practice*, Boston, 1919.
Ebray, Alcide, *Der Unsaubere Frieden*, Berlin, 1925. This differs in several places from the English edition given below.

..............., A *Frenchman Looks at the Peace*, London, 1927. (Translated by E. W. Dickes.)

Erzberger, M., *The League of Nations: The Way to the World's Peace*, New York, 1919. (Translated by Bernard Miall.)

Florinsky, Michael T., *The Saar Struggle*, New York, 1934.

Fox, William T. R., *The Super-Powers*, New York, 1944.

Garner, James W., *American Foreign Policies*, New York, 1928.

Gelber, Lionel, *Peace by Power*, New York, 1942.

Gonsiorowski, M., *Société des Nations et Probléme de la Paix*, 2 vols., Paris, 1927.

Grelling, Richard, *La Campagne 'Innocentiste' en Allemagne et le Traité de Versailles*, Paris, 1925.

Guyot, Yves, *Les Garanties de la Paix*, 2 vols., Paris, 1918.

Haestier, Richard E., *Guilt-Edged Insecurity*, London, 1932.

Hanotaux, Gabriel, *Le Traité de Versailles*, Paris, 1919.

Harley, J. Eugene, *The Heritage of Woodrow Wilson*, Los Angeles, 1945.

Haskins, Charles H., and Robert H. Lord, *Some Problems of the Peace Conference*, Cambridge, Mass., 1920.

Hasluck, Eugene L., *Foreign Affairs, 1919-1937*, New York, 1938.

Hérisson, Charles D., *Les Nations Anglo-Saxonnes et la Paix*, Paris, 1936.

Herron, George D., *The Defeat in the Victory*, London, 1921.

Hindmarsh, Albert E., *Force in Peace: Force short of War in International Relations*, Cambridge, Mass., 1933.

Holland, M. Tappan, *et al.*, *The Treaty of Versailles and After*, New York, 1935.

House, Edward M., and Charles Seymour, (eds.), *What Really Happened at Paris*, New York, 1921.

Huddleston, Sisley, *Europe in Zigzags*, London, 1929.

Jackh, Ernst, *Deutschland, das Herz Europas*, Berlin, 1928.

Jessop, T. E., *The Treaty of Versailles, Was it Just?* London, 1942.

Jessup, Philip C., *International Security*, New York, 1935.

Jouvenal, Robert de, *Le Journalisme en Vingt Lecons*, Paris, 1920.

Kayser, Jacques, *Les États-Unis d'Europe (de Vérsailles á Locarno)*, Paris, 1926.

Kessler, Count Harry von, *Germany and Europe*, New Haven, Conn., 1923.

Keynes, John M., *A Revision of the Treaty*, New York, 1922.

..............., *The Economic Consequences of the Peace*, New York and London, 1922.

Lerry, Raphäel-Georges, *La Juste Paix,* Paris, 1920.

Lhopital, Rene M., *Foch, l'Armistice et la Paix,* Paris, 1938.

Loth, David, *Woodrow Wilson — The Fifteenth Point,* New York, 1941.

Lugan, A., *Les Problemes internationaux et le Congrès de la Paix,* Paris, 1919.

Marin, Louis, *Le Traité de Paix,* Paris, 1920.

Martel, René, *The Eastern Frontiers of Germany,* London, 1930.

Maurras, Charles, *Devant l'Allemagne eternelle,* Paris, 1937.

Montgelas, Maximilian M. K. D., von Graf Count, *The Case for the Central Powers, an Impeachment of the Versailles Verdict,* New York, 1925. (Translated by Constance Vesey of Leitfaden sur kriegsschuldfrage.)

Ormesson, Wladimir, Comte d', *La Confiance en l'Allemagne?* Les Documents Bleus, No. 43, Paris, 1928.

Orton, William, *Twenty Years' Armistice, 1918-1938,* New York, 1938.

Paxson, Frederick L., *America at War, 1917-1918,* Boston, 1939.

Pollock, Sir Frederick, *The League of Nations,* London, 1922.

Rappard, *The Geneva Experiment,* London, 1931.

Rheinbaben, Werner, Freiherr von, *Von Versailles zur Freiheit,* Hamburg, 1927.

Riddell, Lord George, *et al., The Treaty of Versailles and After,* New York, 1935.

Rohde, Hans, Major, *Franco-German Factors of Power: Comparative Studies of the Problem of Disarmament,* Berlin, 1932.
(See this work for the excellent treatment of the potentials of war and peace.)

Scelle, G., *Le Pacte des Nations,* Paris, 1919.

Schiff, Victor, *The Germans at Versailles, 1919,* London, 1930.

Schoonmaker, E. D., *Our Genial Enemy, France,* New York, 1932.

Seeckt, Hans, Generaloberst von, *Deutschland zwischen West und Ost,* Hamburg, 1933.

Selsam, John P., *The Attempts to Form an Anglo-French Alliance, 1919-1924,* Philadelphia, Pa., 1936.

Sembat, Marcel, *Defeated Victory,* London, 1925. (Translated by Flory Henri Turot.)

Simonds, Frank H., *American Foreign Policy in the Post-War Years,* Baltimore, Md., 1935.

..............., *How Europe Made Peace Without America,* New York, 1927.

Spaight, James M., *Pseudo-Security*, New York, 1928.

Tirard, Paul, *La France sur le Rhin; souze années d' occupation rhenane*, Paris, 1930.

Toscano, Mario, *Il Patto di London*, Pavia, Italy, 1931.

Toynbee, Arnold J., *The World after the Peace Conference*, London, 1925.

Vergnet, Paul, *La France au Rhin*, Paris, 1919.

Webster, Charles K., *et al.*, *The Treaty of Versailles and After*, New York, 1935.

Wells, Herbert G., *Washington and the Hope of Peace*, London, 1922.

Wheeler-Bennett, John W., and Frederic Langermann, *Information on the Problem of Security, 1917-1926*, London, 1927.

Werth, Alexander, *The Destiny of France*, London, 1937.

Zimmern, Alfred, *The League of Nations and the Rule of Law, 1918-1935*, London, 1936.

VIII. NEWSPAPERS AND PERIODICALS

A. Newspapers

L'Homme Libre (Paris), Jan. 2, 1919 to June 30, 1919.

L'Humanité (Paris), Jan. 2, 1919 to August 31, 1919.

L'Intransigeant, (Paris), Jan. 2, 1919 to August 31, 1919.

L'Opinion (Paris), January 2, 1919 to December 31, 1919.

Le Matin, (Paris), January 1, 1919 to June 30, 1919.

Le Temps, (Paris), daily from January 2, 1918 to December 31, 1920 (for texts of resolutions, speeches, etc.).

Le Rappel (Paris), January 2, 1918 to June 30, 1919.

New York Times, October 1 – 31, 1916; October 1 – December 31, 1918; January 1, 1919 – December 31, 1919; January 1, 1920 – December 23, 1920; January 1, 1921 – November 23, 1921.

New York Tribune, April 1, 1919 – December 31, 1919.

The Times (London), January 2, 1918 – December 31, 1920. (For texts, resolutions, speeches, etc.)

B. Periodicals

Alliance Française Bulletin, January 3, 1919 – July 31, 1919.

Le Cri de Paris, 1918 and 1919 inclusive.

Le Correspondant, 1918 and 1919 inclusive.

L'Europe Nouvelle, Nov. 12, 1918 — December 1, 1919.
L'Illustration, February 14, 1920.
Revue des Deux Mondes, 1918 and 1919 inclusive.
Revue Politique et Parlementaire, 1918 and 1919 inclusive.

IX. PERIODICAL AND MAGAZINE ARTICLES

Aubert, Louis, "Security: Key to French Policy," *Foreign Affairs,* XI, October 1932, 122-136.

Berle, A. A., "Betrayal at Paris," *The Nation,* 109, August 9, 1919, 170-171.

Bess, Demaree, "Roosevelt's Shadow over Paris," *Saturday Evening Post,* 218, No. 52, June 29, 1946, 9, 10, 98, 100, 101.

Binkley, Robert C. "New Light on the Paris Peace Conference," *Political Science Quarterly,* XLVI, 1931, 335-361; 509-547.

..............., "Ten Years of Peace Conference History," *Journal of Modern History,* I, 1929, 607-629.

Birdsall, Paul, *"The Second Decade of Peace Conference History,"* *Journal of Modern History,* XI, September 1939, 362-378.

"Borah and Johnson, Disturbers of the Senatorial Peace," *Literary Digest,* LXII, No. 8, August 23, 1919, 52-55.

Brailsford, H. N., "The Alliance and the League," *New Republic,* XX, No. 256, October 1, 1919, 253-255.

"Bringing the Treaty to the Senate," *The Independent,* 99, July 19, 1919, 72.

"Breakers ahead for the League," *Literary Digest,* LIX, No. 10, December 7, 1918, 21-22.

Brooks, Sydney, "Mr. Wilson and the Treaty," *The Nineteenth Century,* DXIV, December 1919, 1180-1188.

"Can Congress Compromise?" *The Independent,* 99, August 2, 1919, 139-140.

Colcord, Lincoln, "Why Wilson was defeated at Paris," *The Nation,* CVIII, No. 2811, May 17, 1919, 782-784.

Cox, Harold, "The Anglo-French Treaty: a British View," *The Living Age,* No. 3921, August 30, 1919, 519-521.

Darling, Maurice H., "Who Kept the United States out of The League of Nations?" *Canadian Historical Review,* X, Sept. 1929, 196-211.

Dickinson, G. Lowes, "S.O.S. — Europe to America," *Atlantic Monthly,* 127, February 1921, 244-249.

Dodd, William E., "President Wilson, his Treaty and his Reward," *The World's Work*, XXXIX, No. 5, March 1920, 440-447.

"Europe Proposes," *New Republic*, XIX, No. 237, May 17, 1919, 67-71.

Finch, G. A., "The Treaty of Peace with Germany in the United States Senate," *American Journal of International Law*, XIV, 1920, 155-206.

Foch, Ferdinand, "Du Malaise Mondial," *Revue de France*, VIII, janvier 1928, 5-13.

Francois-Poncet, André, "Ce que la France attend de l'Allemagne," *Revue de Genèva*, décembre 1923, 762-777.

Fraser, John F., "What Europe thinks of Woodrow Wilson," *Current Opinion*, LXVII, July 1919, 16-18.

"French Misgivings," *Literary Digest*, LX, No. 8, February 22, 1919, 18-19.

"Future Relations with Germany," *Literary Digest*, LXII, No. 1, July 5, 1919, 21-24.

Gauvain, A., "La Conférence de la Paix," *Revue de Paris*, 26, April 15, 1919, 869-894.

"Germany's Present Game," *Current Opinion*, LXXV, April 1921, 433-438.

"Germany thinking of Revenge," *Literary Digest*, LXII, No. 2, July 12, 1919, 21.

Harvey, George, "America and Humanity," *North American Review*, 210, July 1919, 1-17.

Hazen, Charles D., "The Peace Treaty and World Politics," *The World's Work*, XXXVIII, No. 2, June 1919, i-vii.

Hendrick, Burton J., "Our Proposed Pledge to France," *The World's Work*, XXXVIII, No. 2, June 1919, viii-ix.

Herriot, Edouard, "The Program of Liberal France," *Foreign Affairs*, II, June 15, 1924, 558-570.

Holt, Hamilton, "For the Greater Security of France," *The Independent*, 99, July 19, 1919, 83-84.

..............., "The Senate Outlook for Ratification," *The Independent*, 99, August 2, 1919, 151-152.

"How Lansing and Wilson Fell Out," *Current Opinion*, LXX, April 1921, 438-440.

"How the Press answer the President's Plea," *Literary Digest*, LXII, No. 3, July 19, 1919, 10.

"Is Italy out in the Cold?" *Literary Digest*, LXII, No. 6, August 9, 1919, 19.

Lansing, Robert, "The Big Four of the Peace Conference," *Saturday Evening Post*, 193, March 19, 1921, 3-4; 117-122.

Lauzanne, Stephen, "France and the Treaty," *North American Review*, 210, November 1919, 604-613.

Lawrence, David, "Crisis in the Leadership of Wilson," *Outlook*, 120, December 4, 1918, 528-529.

..............., "The Crusade that Failed but Lives On," *New York Times Magazine*, November 14, 1943, 3; 34-35.

Lippmann, Walter, "The Rivalry of Nations," *Atlantic Monthly*, 181, No. 2, February 1948, 17-20.

..............., "The Political Scene," *New Republic*, XVIII, No. 229, Part 2, supplement to March 22, 1919, 1-14.

"Making War on our Chief Peacemaker," *Literary Digest*, LIX, No. 11, December 14, 1918, 9-12.

Martet, Jean, "M. Clemenceau and the Versailles Peace Treaty," *Journal of the Royal Institute of International Affairs*, IX, November 1930, 783-800.

"Mr. Wilson and His Promises," *New Republic*, XIX, No. 238, June 29, 1919, 104-106.

"Our Pledge to Aid France," *Literary Digest*, LXI, No. 5, May 3, 1919, 20.

"Perils of Mr. Wilson's Triple Alliance," *Current Opinion*, LXVII, August 1919, 74-76.

Poincaré, Raymond, "Since Versailles," *Foreign Affairs*, VII, July 1929, 519-531.

Swain, Joseph W., "Woodrow Wilson's Fight for Peace," *Current History*, XXXV, March 1932, 805-812.

Tardieu, Andrè, "The Policy of France," *Foreign Affairs*, I, September 1922, 11-28.

"That 'Entangling Alliance' with France and England," *Literary Digest*, LXII, No. 3, July 19, 1919, 12.

"The A.B.C. of Alliances: the French Alliance," *New Republic*, XIX, No. 238, June 1919, 106-110.

"The Ado about the French Treaty," *Literary Digest*, LXII, No. 6, August 9, 1919, 10.

"The Airplane and the Covenant," *The Independent*, 99, September 20, 1919, 396.

"The Debt of Lafayette," *New Republic*, XX, No. 249, August 13, 1919, 43-44.

"The Franco-American Treaty," *The Independent*, 99, July 19, 1919, 79-80.

"The Lesson of the Supreme Council," *The Nation*, 109, December 20, 1919, 486.

"The Madness at Versailles," *The Nation*, CVIII, No. 2811, May 17, 1919, 778-780.

"The 'Moral Obligation' to Ratify," *Literary Digest*, LXII, No. 9, August 30, 1919, 11-13.

"The Pact with France," *The Review*, I, No. 9, July 12, 1919, 179-180.

"The President as Conquering Hero," *The Independent*, 99, July 19, 1919, 71.

"The President, the Senate, and the Treaty," *Outlook*, 122, No. 12, July 23, 1919, 464-466.

"The Root Reservations," *Literary Digest*, LXII, No. 1, July 5, 1919, 26-27.

"The Treaty Killed: What to do Next," *Literary Digest*, LXV, No. 1, April 3, 1920, 17-19.

"The War Not Over," *Literary Digest*, LXII, No. 2, July 12, 1919, 11-12.

"To Help France watch the Rhine," *Literary Digest*, LXII, No. 3, July 19, 1919, 22.

Trotter, Reginald G., "Canada and World Organization," *Canadian Historical Review*, XXVI, No. 2, June 1945, 128-147.

"Unprovoked Aggression," *New Republic*, XIX, No. 245, July 16, 1919, 339-342.

"Watchful Waiting in the Senate," *The Independent*, 99, August 9, 1919, 171-174.

"What Viviani's Visit Means," *Literary Digest*, LXIX, No. 2, April 9, 1921, 9-10.

"What we will do if France is attacked Again," *Literary Digest*, LXXI, No. 14, December 31, 1921, 5-9; 39-41.

Williams, T. Alcott, " 'Reservations' cannot Rescue," *The Independent*, 99, July 26, 1919, 118-119.

"Wilson and Clemenceau," *Literary Digest*, LXI, No. 1, April 5, 1919, 25.

Wilson, Woodrow, "I have come back to Report Progress," *The Independent*, 97, March 8, 1919, 321-322.

..............., "The League of Nations," *The Independent*, 97, March 1, 1919, 288-290.

"Wilson and the Senate," *The Review*, I, No. 11, July 26, 1919, 228-229.

"Workability of the Harding Peace Plans," *Literary Digest*, LXIX, No. 4, April 23, 1921, 5-6.

Index

Index